Nippon ・

Talking

about

Japan

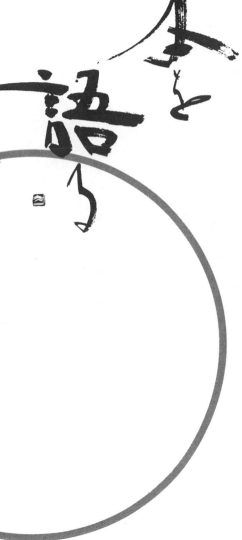

新日本製鐵株式會社
能力開発室 監修

株式会社
日鉄ヒューマンデベロプメント 著

アルク

まえがき

　日本は経済大国として、今後ますます諸外国との
関係を深め、国際的な影響力を深めていくであろう。
その過程で、外国との間に種々の誤解やトラブルが
しばしば発生する可能性がある。

　国際関係を良好・円滑に保つためには、その前提
として、各国間の相互理解が不可欠であるが、巨額
の貿易黒字国である日本は、こと情報の国際収支に
関しては、ひじょうな赤字国である。したがって、
国際社会のなかでわれわれ日本人は、今後とも諸外
国についての認識をいっそう深めていくことも大切
だが、それにもまして、あらゆる機会に日本につい
ての情報を積極的に提供し、外国人の知識や理解を
広めかつ深めていく努力が、おおいに必要であると
痛感する。

　こうした思いを込めて、さきに『日本──その
姿と心（*Nippon: the Land and its People*）』[和英
文対照、新日本製鐵㈱能力開発部（現在能力開発室）

著、学生社刊] を発刊し、幸いにもひじょうに多く
の読者にご活用いただいてきた。

　今回、㈱アルクの平本照麿社長の強いお勧めもあ
り、同書の会話編ともいえる『日本を語る（*Talking
about Japan*）』を発刊することができ、しかも、
新日本製鐵㈱から独立した新会社、㈱日鉄ヒュー
マンデベロプメントの最初の出版物として、本書の
刊行が実現したことをたいへん喜んでいる。

　本書の企画・執筆・編集は、新日本製鐵㈱能力
開発室の支援のもとに、当社の青砥安男、福沢信二、
葛　輝也、井上初美が担当した。また、㈱ミキ国際
情報企画の三木敦雄社長には、本書の企画段階から
全般にわたって、終始ご協力いただいた。

　英語表現については、長年日本に在住し、日本の
事情にもひじょうに詳しく、『日本──その姿と心』
の翻訳者でもある Richard Foster 氏、およびコミュ
ニケーションに関する学識・経験がきわめて豊富な

Howard Newmark ・ Irma Newmark ご夫妻に、全面的にご協力願った。また、これらの方々には、外国人とのコミュニケーションにおける留意点や外国人に理解しやすい説明方法などについても、貴重なご助言をいただいた。

本書の企画・製作およびカセットテープの作成などに当たってお世話になった、㈱アルク出版編集部の山口耕一局長および鈴木映子氏にも、深く感謝したい。

日本の実情や文化の理解について、外国人に積極的に働きかけていくうえで、本書および同時発刊のテープが、前述した『日本　　その姿と心』ともども、多少なりともお役に立てば幸いである。

　　昭和62年10月
　　　　㈱日鉄ヒューマンデベロプメント
　　　代表取締役社長　中村　琢磨

本書の利用にさいして

1——本書の各章は以下のように構成されています。
- 扉
- イラスト データ
- 必須語彙（Vocabulary）
- 日英対照の対話文（Dialogue）
- 会話に役立つ基本表現（Useful Expressions）

2——イラスト データ

　各章のメーン・トピックスに関するイラストを収載。会話の糸口として、またその章の内容についての事実を語るための資料として活用できます。巻末にはデータの出典と補足を併せて収録しました。

3——Vocabulary

　日本を語るための必須語彙として、ダイアローグ中の語彙およびその関連語彙を収録しました。

　〔記号の見方〕　　　；　　　　　別表現の併記
　　　　　　　　　　〔　　〕　　　いい換え
　　　　　　　　　　（　　）　　　補足

4——Dialogue

　ジョーンズ夫妻（アメリカ人）と鈴木夫妻（日本人）の対話形式で進行します。参照の便宜を考え、和文の左側に小見出しを付けるとともに、和文と英文を対比して収載しています。

　英文中、日本語(音)をローマ字つづりで表示した語句(タイトルおよび固有名詞を除く)については、それが英語化しているか否かにかかわらず、各章ごとに初出のものに限り、斜体(イタリック)を用いています。

5——Useful Expressions

　ダイアローグのなかから、覚えておくと便利な表現を抜粋。豊かな表現力を身につけるために、応用表現も併記しました。（例文のあとのカッコ内の数字は、引用した章の番号を示しています）

6——巻末に「日本を語るためのキーワード インデックス」を収載。

　伝えたいことを的確に表すための英語表現をすぐに探し出すことができます。

7——各章の内容を耳から学ぶために

　1章から40章までの Vocabulary / Dialogue / Useful Expressions を完全収録したテープセットも別売されています。

C O N T

● 目次

E   N   T   S

C O N T

E　N　T　S

C O N T

E N T S

題字 飯島太久磨
AD 篠田昌三
レイアウト P-201
イラスト アクトインワークス

C O N T

Chapter 1

地理
Geography

日本は島国だったんですね

日本がアジア大陸の一部だと
思っている外国人は意外にたくさんいます。
一方で、日本人は
自分の国の面積を、世界の国々のなかでも
ひじょうに小さいほうだと考えているようです。

〔各国の面積と人口〕

日本
面積378（千km²）
人口120,018（千人）

イギリス
244
55,624

ソ連
22,402
275,000

アメリカ
9,373
236,681

中国 9,561
1,032,751

オーストラリア
7,687
15,544

（1984年）

Vocabulary ●────────────────────────

～の眺めがよい	☐☐	to have a great view of . . .
富士山	☐☐	Mt. Fuji
山が多い	☐☐	to have a lot of mountains
五合目	☐☐	the fifth station
簡単に登れる	☐☐	to be easy to climb
山地	☐☐	mountainous area
平地	☐☐	flatland
農業用地	☐☐	land for agriculture; farmland
宅地	☐☐	land for houses; housing land
工業用地	☐☐	land for industrial purposes
リムジン	☐☐	a limousine
島国	☐☐	an island country
大陸国家	☐☐	a continent country
アジア大陸	☐☐	the Asian mainland; the Asian Continent
日本列島	☐☐	the Japanese Archipelago; the Isles of Japan
～の一部である	☐☐	to be part of . . .
～から成っている	☐☐	to be made up of . . .
面積	☐☐	area
合衆国の25分の1の大きさである	☐☐	to be one twenty-fifth the size of the U.S.
AとBの4分の3の距離	☐☐	three quarters of the distance between A and B
～と同じ緯度である	☐☐	to be at the same latitude as . . .
地球の裏側	☐☐	the other side of the world
日本アルプス	☐☐	the Japan Alps
活火山	☐☐	an active volcano
死火山	☐☐	a dead volcano
噴火する	☐☐	to erupt
～からひとり残らず避難させる	☐☐	to evacuate from . . .

日本は島国だったんですね

国土面積・国土の利用・地理上の位置

鈴木氏：5年ぶりの東京の朝はいかがでしたか。

富士山

ジョーンズ氏：快適でした。ホテルの窓から見た富士山は素晴らしい眺めでしたよ。

ジョーンズ夫人：富士山って、本当に美しいですね。

鈴木夫人：そうです。日本にはたくさん山がありますが、高さも美しさも、やはり富士山が日本一です。一年中、その時期によって、いろいろ変わった美しさがあります。

鈴木氏：富士山は比較的簡単に登れるんですよ。いまは五合目まで車で行けます。

ジョーンズ氏：今回の旅行ではちょっと無理ですが、いつか登りたいですね。日本は国全体のどのていどが山地なんですか。

国土の利用

鈴木氏：67%です。農業用地は15%、宅地は3%、工業用地はわずかに0.4%しかありません。

ジョーンズ夫人：そんなに山が多いんですか。成田空港から東京まで、リムジンのなかから見た感じでは平坦でしたけど……。子供の頃には、日本が島国だということも知らなかったんです。日本はアジア大陸の一部だと思ってましたのよ。

島国

鈴木夫人：いまでも、そう思っている欧米人は多いようですね。私も、アメリカに滞在しておりましたときにはパーティーでよく尋ねられて、日本が島国で、北から北海道、本州、四国、九州の4つの大きな島から成っていることを説明したものですわ。

C h a p t e r 1

Mr. Suzuki: So, how did it feel to wake up in Tokyo for the first time in five years?

Mr. Jones: Really good. We had a great view of Mt. Fuji from our hotel window.

Mrs. Jones: It's really a beautiful mountain!

Mrs. Suzuki: It certainly is. Japan has lots of mountains, but none can compare with Mt. Fuji in beauty or height. It's always magnificent, in different ways at different times of the year.

Mr. S: Mt. Fuji is fairly easy to climb, you know. These days you can go as far as the fifth station by car.

Mr. J: I would like to make the climb sometime, but it's going to be impossible during this trip. How much of Japan is covered with mountains?

Mr. S: Sixty-seven percent. Fifteen percent of the land is used for agriculture, three percent for houses and only 0.4 percent for industrial purposes.

Mrs. J: Is the country really that mountainous? In the limousine coming into Tokyo from Narita Airport it seemed rather flat. . . But then when I was a school girl, I didn't even know Japan was an island country. I thought it was part of the Asian mainland.

Mrs. S: A lot of Westerners still seem to think so. I remember being asked about Japan at parties while we were living in America. I often had to explain that Japan is made up mainly of four major islands: Hokkaido at the northern end, then Honshu, Shikoku and Kyushu.

ジョーンズ氏：日本の面積は、アメリカ合衆国の25分の1くらいと聞きましたが……。

面積

鈴木氏：そうです。面積は約38万km²で、モンタナ州とだいたい同じです。ですから、カリフォルニア州よりも小さいんですよ。その国に、アメリカの人口のほぼ半分の1億2000万人が生活しているわけです。

人口

ジョーンズ夫人：地図で見ますと、日本はそうとう細長い国ですが、どのくらいの延長距離があるんですの。

列島の長さ

鈴木夫人：南北に3,000kmです。アメリカ合衆国の東海岸から西海岸までの4分の3ぐらいの距離ですわ。

ジョーンズ夫人：南と北ではずいぶん気温も違うんでしょうね。

鈴木夫人：日本の北の端がアメリカとカナダとの国境と緯度がほぼ同じで、南の端がメキシコ中央部辺りになります。ですから、かなり温度差があります。

日本の位置

鈴木氏：ところで、日本の真下を真っすぐに下っていくと、地球の裏側のどのへんに出ると思いますか。

ジョーンズ夫人：さあ、ちょっと想像つきませんわ。

鈴木氏：アルゼンチンだそうです。そして、東京から真っすぐ南に行くと、オーストラリア中央を通ります。西に行きますと、ジブラルタル海峡を通ります。東に行きますと、ちょうどグランドキャニオンの上を通ることになります。

ジョーンズ氏：なるほど。さっき富士山の話が出ましたが、ほかに有名な山でどんなものがありますか。

日本アルプス

鈴木氏：本州の中央に日本アルプスという3,000m

Mr. J: I've heard that Japan is about one twenty-fifth the size of the United States . . .

Mr. S: That's right. It has an area of around 380,000 square kilometers, about the same as Montana. That makes it smaller than California. And there are 120 million people living in this area, about half the U.S. population.

Mrs. J: Japan looks quite long and narrow on a map. How long is it?

Mrs. S: Three thousand kilometers from north to south, three-quarters of the distance between the east and west coasts of the U.S.

Mrs. J: The temperature difference between the north and south must be rather large.

Mrs. S: Well, the northern tip is at about the same latitude as the U.S.-Canadian border and the southern end is on a line with central Mexico. So, yes, the difference is fairly big.

Mr. S: If you went straight down from Japan, where do you think you'd come out on the other side of the world?

Mrs. J: I really have no idea.

Mr. S: They say Argentina, and if you drew a line straight south from Tokyo, it'd pass through the middle of Australia, while one drawn west would go through the Strait of Gibraltar. Going east, the line would pass through the Grand Canyon.

Mrs. J: Hmmm . . . We talked about Mt. Fuji a moment ago. What other famous mountains are there?

Mr. S: Well, we have a range of peaks measuring over 3,000

級の山脈があります。これは北・中央・南アルプスの3つの山脈から成っています。ちょうど、本州の背骨という感じです。また、ハワイのキラウエア火山のように活動している火山もいくつかあります。なかでも、本州の浅間山、大島の三原山、九州にある阿蘇山、桜島などが有名です。

・火山

・大島

鈴木夫人：1986年の暮れには、東京から海上約100kmしか離れていない大島の三原山が噴火したんです。そのとき、島民全員、1万人以上の人が1カ月くらい東京都内に避難して、それはそれはたいへんな騒ぎでしたわ。

日本語と英語の狭間で❶

日本語の発想から脱却する

　自分の勤務している会社を名乗るのに、「わが社は○○です」という日本語的発想から、

　　"My company is ○○."

という人が意外に多い。会社の所有者ならともかく、社員としては、せいぜいいえても our company ぐらいまでであろう。「私は○○会社に勤務しています」の適切な英語表現は、

　　"I work for ○○ company." または、

　　"I'm employed by ○○ company."

などである。ところが、「私は○○会社に行っています」という日本語表現の影響から、

　　"I'm going to ○○ company."

とする間違いをおかしやすい。これでは「私は○○会社に出勤する途上です」という意味になってしまう。

　電話で呼び出した相手に対して、「ご多忙中とは存じますが、お話ししてよろしいですか」のつもりで、

　　"I know your work is busy, but may I talk with you?"

meters in central Honshu known as the Japan Alps. The Japan Alps are divided into three ranges called the North, Central and South Alps. They run down the middle of Honshu like a backbone. Then there are also a number of volcanic mountains, some nearly as active as Kilauea in Hawaii. Among the most famous are Mt. Asama on Honshu, Mt. Mihara on Oshima Island, and Mt. Aso and Mt. Sakurajima on Kyushu.

Mrs. S: Oshima Island is only about 100 kilometers from Tokyo and its Mt. Mihara erupted in late 1986. All of the island's inhabitants, more than 10,000, had to be evacuated from the island for about a month — mostly to Tokyo. You can imagine the confusion and excitement that caused!

Column

などと、ついいってしまいがちである。日本語では、「仕事が忙しい」という表現をすることから、これに惑わされてしまうためである。この場合、忙しいのは相手自身であるから、

"I know you're busy, but may I talk with you?"
とするのが正しい。

ところで、次のような例も、日本語の表現に惑わされないように注意しよう。

「夢を見る」── see a dream ではなく、正しい英語表現は、have [dream] a dream。

「計画を立てる」── set up a plan ではなく、make a plan。

「風呂に入る」── enter a bath ではなく、take [have] a bath。

「さじを投げる」── throw a spoon ではなく、give up on。

「頭を冷やす」── cool one's head ではなく、cool off。

「スープを飲む」── drink soup ではなく、eat [have] soup が正しい表現である。

Useful Expressions ——————— 1

1

Mt. Fuji is fairly _easy_ to climb.

ノート
be easy to ... で「〜するのが容易である（やさしい）」。注意したいのは、to 以下が to be climbed とはならないで、to climb と能動形になること。

例文 The story _is_ fairly _easy to_ follow.　　　　(27)

2

I would like to make the climb.

ノート
would like to ... は「もしできれば」の意を含んでいるので want to よりもやわらかな表現。

例文 1 I'_d like to_ experience that!　　　　(2)

例文 2 _Would you like me to_ open the window?
「窓を開けましょうか」

「〜しましょうか」は Shall I ...?／Shall we ...? をよく使うが、かしこまらない間柄では Do you want me to ...?／丁寧に話す場合は Would you like me to ...? も使いたい。

3

It's going to be impossible during this trip.

ノート
be going to ... は便利な句。次の 4 とおりの意味を再確認しておくこと。
（1）「〜しに行くところ」I'_m going to_ do some shopping.（2）「（まさに）〜するところだ」That's what I _was going to_ say. （3）「（人が）〜するつもりだ」I'_m going to_ go to California next month. （4）「（人・物事が）〜しそうだ」It's _going to_ rain.

Chapter

2

人口と気候
Population and Climate

東京の人口はどれくらいですか

日本に来た外国人が驚くのが
首都圏の通勤ラッシュ。
大都市への人口集中がとくに進んでいる日本では
ありふれた光景ですが、
外国人はとてもびっくりするようです。

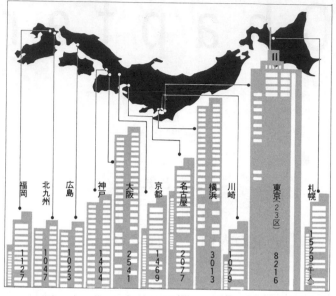

〔日本の100万都市〕

福岡 1,127
北九州 1,047
広島 1,023
神戸 1,404
大阪 2,541
京都 1,469
名古屋 2,077
横浜 3,013
川崎 1,079
東京(23区) 8,216
札幌 1,529(千人)

（1986年3月）

Vocabulary ●

ラッシュアワー	□□	rush hour
人の洪水	□□	hordes of people
（東京都の）23区	□□	the twenty-three wards
日本の人口の10分の1	□□	a tenth of Japan's population
市街地	□□	urban area
郊外で	□□	in the suburbs
人口100万以上の都市	□□	the cities with populations of over one million
3大都市圏の住人	□□	people living in and around the three major cities
紅葉	□□	red [yellow] leaves
紅葉する	□□	leaves change color
紅葉が見頃だ	□□	red and yellow leaves are at their peak
四季がはっきりしている	□□	to have four clearly defined seasons

〔日本各地の月別平均気温・降水量〕

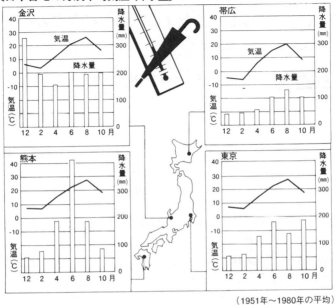

（1951年〜1980年の平均）

気候	□□	the climate
太平洋側	□□	the Pacific Sea side
日本海側	□□	the Japan Sea side
多雪地帯・豪雪地帯	□□	the heavy snow areas
湿気・湿度	□□	moist air; humidity
気温・温度	□□	temperature
空っ風	□□	a very dry wind from the north
雨量	□□	rainfall
梅雨	□□	the rainy season
豪雨	□□	a heavy rain
季節風	□□	seasonal winds
台風・台風シーズン	□□	a typhoon; the typhoon season
台風が日本に上陸する	□□	a typhoon hits Japan
台風で風水害が発生する	□□	a typhoon causes wind and water damage
水資源	□□	water resources

東京の人口はどれくらいですか

人口分布・気候・風土

・東京の人口

ジョーンズ氏：きのうの朝、東京駅に行ったら、びっくりしましたよ。ラッシュアワーにぶつかって人の洪水でした。ところで、東京の人口はどのくらいになったんですか。

鈴木氏：東京都の23区内ですと820万人ですが、郊外を入れると1,100万人くらいでしょう。ですから、日本の総人口の10分の1が、この東京に集まっているわけです。

ジョーンズ氏：東京以外で、人口の多い都市はどこですか。

・100万人
以上の都市

鈴木氏：横浜、大阪、名古屋、京都、札幌、神戸など、100万人以上の都市が10市あります。

ジョーンズ氏：大都市に人口がかなり集中しているということでしょうか。

鈴木氏：そのとおりです。東京・大阪・名古屋を中心とした三大都市圏に、日本の総人口の40％が集中していると考えれば、かなりはっきりします。

ジョーンズ氏：そうとうなものなんですね。ところ
・日光 で、あすの天気はどうでしょうね。あすは日光へ行くことになっているんです。

鈴木氏：晴れると思いますよ。いまは日光に行くには、いちばんよい時期ですよ。紅葉もいちばんの見頃でしょう。ジョーンズ夫人はきっと満足されると思いますよ。日光の中禅寺湖や華厳の滝も、なかなか素晴らしいので、ぜひ見逃さないでください。日本では同じ季節でも、本州の太平洋側と日本海側ではそうとう気候が違うのはご存じでし

C h a p t e r 2

Mr. Jones: I happened to go to Tokyo station during the rush hour yesterday morning. What hordes of people! I never saw anything like it. What is the population of Tokyo anyway?

Mr. Suzuki: There are 8.2 million people in the 23 wards that make up Tokyo proper. Including the suburbs, there must be around 11 million. A tenth of Japan's population is concentrated in Tokyo.

Mr. J: What other large cities are there?

Mr. S: There are ten cities with populations of over one million. These include Yokohama, Osaka, Nagoya, Kyoto, Sapporo and Kobe.

Mr. J: Then I guess a fair share of the country's population must live in the cities.

Mr. S: Right. It's pretty obvious if you consider that people living in and around the three major cities, Tokyo, Osaka and Nagoya, account for 40 percent of Japan's population.

Mr. J: That's impressive. Not to change the subject, but what's the weather going to be like tomorrow? We're planning to go to Nikko.

Mr. S: It's supposed to be fair. This is an ideal time to visit Nikko. The leaves will have changed color and should be at their peak. I'm sure your wife will enjoy the trip. Lake Chuzenji and Kegon Waterfall in Nikko are very beautiful and shouldn't be missed. Did you know that even during the same season the climate is quite different between the Pacific and Japan Sea sides of Honshu?

たか。

ジョーンズ氏：どんなふうにですか。

季節風

鈴木氏：アジア大陸から湿った季節風が吹きつける
ために、冬には日本海側には大量の雪が降ります。
新潟県などの多雪地帯では、ときには4、5mも積
もる所もあるんですよ。同じ時期に太平洋側は、
乾燥した晴天が多いんです。東京のある関東平野
は「空っ風」が吹くので有名です。

ジョーンズ氏：4、5mの積雪というと13～16フィー
トですか。これは驚いた。

雪国

鈴木氏：川端康成の小説『雪国』の冒頭に「トンネ
ルを抜けると、そこは雪国だった」という有名な
一節があるんです。雪のない太平洋側から、トン
ネルを抜けたとたん、一面が雪に覆われていると
いう様子が、いかにもよく表現されています。

ジョーンズ氏：こんどは冬に来て、ぜひその違いを
体験したいですね。夏はどうなるんですか。

鈴木氏：季節風は太平洋側から吹きます。そのため
全体的に高温で、湿気が多いのです。北海道を除
く地域では、6月中旬から1カ月くらい梅雨が続
きます。また、8月から10月にかけては台風シー
ズンになります。

台風

ジョーンズ氏：台風による被害もあるんでしょう。

鈴木氏：ええ、台風が上陸したり日本に近づきます
と風水害がよく起こります。しかし一方で、台風は
水資源を豊かにしてくれます。また、梅雨は稲の
生育に欠かせませんので、梅雨の季節に雨が順当
に降ることは、農家にとってひじょうに大事なん

Mr. J: In what way?

Mr. S: In winter, the Japan Sea side has extremely heavy snow-falls caused by moist air brought in by winds off the Asian continent. In the heavy snow areas like Niigata, the snow may get as deep as four or five meters. At the same time, the Pacific side will be having sunny weather and very low humidity. The wind at this time in the Kanto Plain, where Tokyo is located, is known as the Karakkaze, a very dry wind from the north.

Mr. J: Four or five meters of snow? Wow, that's 13 to 16 feet.

Mr. S: Kawabata Yasunari started his novel *Snow Country* with the sentence: "The train came out of the long tunnel into the snow country." This has become a famous quotation because it so aptly expresses the impression a person gets when he takes a train from the Pacific side, passes through the central mountains and comes out in a land of snow on the other side.

Mr. J: I'd like to experience that! Next time maybe I'll come to Japan in the winter. But what's the situation in the summer?

Mr. S: Then the winds are from the Pacific side. So it's hot and humid. For about a month, from the middle of June, the whole country, except for Hokkaido, has a rainy season. Then from August to October is the typhoon season.

Mr. J: I suppose the typhoons cause some damage.

Mr. S: Yes, the typhoons that hit or pass close to Japan often cause wind and water damage. On the other hand, these same typhoons enrich the country's water resources. The rainy season is also beneficial because the rain it brings is indispensable for growing rice. For the farmers, regular rains

2

Population and Climate

です。

気候と風土　ジョーンズ氏：気候や風土は、そこに住んでいる人
　　　　　　　を変えるといいますが、日本でもそうでしょうね。
　　　　　　鈴木氏：おそらく、そうですね。日本でも、一般的
　　　　　　　に、冬の寒い所の出身者のほうが粘り強い人が多
　　　　　　　いといわれています。また、水のきれいな所には、
　　　　　　　美人が多いといわれています。

日本語と英語の狭間で ❷

和製英語にご用心

　日本語の会話のなかで、和製英語がたくさん使われて
いるが、たとえばサラリーマンを英語だと思い込んで、
　"I'm a salaryman."
などといっても、外国人にはさっぱり通じない。英語で
は、salaried worker である。もっとも日常会話では、
office worker や factory worker のほうが多く用いられ
るようである。
　同様に、ゴルフの相手に、
　"What's your handy?"
と聞いても、外国人にはまったく意味がわからない。正
しくは、
　"What's your handicap?"
と、しなければならない。
　ご参考のために、和製英語と、それに対応する正しい
英語の例を挙げてみよう。

（和製英語）	（正しい英語）
アクセル	accelerator pedal
アフターサービス	after-sales [follow-up] service
イメージアップ	improve one's image
ガードマン	security guard

during this season are very important.

Mr. J: They say the climate and customs of a place change the people who live there. Is this also true in Japan?

Mr. S: Yes, I guess so. We often say that people from cold areas are more persevering. Then they say that the women are more beautiful where the water is good.

ガソリンスタンド	gas station
クラクション	horn
グラマー	voluptuous woman
クレーム	complaint
ゴールデンアワー	prime time
サイドブレーキ	hand brake
シーズンオフ	off-season
シャープペンシル	mechanical pencil
ジャンパー	jacket
ダンプカー	dump truck
テレビタレント	TV star [performer]
ナイター	night game
ノークラッチ	automatic transmission [drive]
バックミラー	rear-view mirror
ハンドル	steering wheel
ビジター	visiting team
ファインプレー	good [nice] play
プッシュホン	push-button phone
ベースアップ	pay raise [increase]
ボールペン	ball point pen
モラールアップ	boost [improve] morale
リビングセット	living room set
ルームクーラー	room air conditioner

Column

Useful Expressions ———— 2

1

I <u>happened to</u> go to Tokyo station.

ノート

「偶然（たまたま）〜した」といういい方はいろいろあるが、なかでも I happened to . . . はアメリカでひじょうによく使われる。「たまたま〜に会う」という場合、日本の辞書や教科書には meet . . . by accident／meet . . . by chance が出ているが、これらはイギリス用法で、アメリカではあまり使われていない。

例文1

I *happened to* be out when he called.

「彼が電話して［訪ねて］きたときは、たまたま私は外出中だった」

例文2

I just *happened to* hear someone say that the Japanese have the longest life expectancy.　　(19)

2

<u>Not to change the subject,</u> but . . .

ノート

by the way「ところで」を覚えると、やたら使いたくなるのは、多くの日本人が経験するところ。確かに便利な言葉だが、あまり多用し過ぎると、会話が分裂症的になってしまうので注意すること。

本当に話題を転換したいときには、Not to change the subject, but . . . を使いたい。

3

<u>I'm sure</u> your wife will enjoy the trip.

ノート

「〜を私は確信している、きっと〜だと思います」の基本的な使い方。なお、be sure to . . . といういい方を使って Your wife *is sure to* enjoy the trip. ということもできる。

Chapter
3

日本の歴史(1)

Japanese History (1)

日本人の祖先はどこから来たんですか

**日本人のルーツをたどると、
1万年以上前、日本が大陸の一部だった頃まで
さかのぼることができます。
同質単一民族といわれる日本人ですが、
大むかしからそうであったとは
いえないようです。**

3
日本の歴史（1）

●年代		●日本		●世界	
		[西暦年]	[史実]	[西暦年]	[史実]
紀元前	縄文・弥生	8000ごろ	縄文文化期に入る	3500ごろ	メソポタミア文明おこる
		300ごろ	弥生文化期に入る	3000ごろ	エジプトの統一
				2500ごろ	インダス文明・仰韶文化
				509	ローマ共和政の成立
				221	秦の始皇帝中国統一、万里の長城を築く
				202	漢建国
		（縄文土器）	（弥生土器）	4ごろ	イエス誕生（～30）
一世紀		57	九州地方の王、後漢に使者を送る	25	後漢建国
				67	仏教中国に伝わる
二世紀		180ごろ	邪馬台国、女王卑弥呼が立つ	117	ローマ帝国領土最大期
三世紀		239	卑弥呼魏に朝貢	220	後漢滅亡、三国時代となる（魏・呉・蜀）
四世紀	大和	350	このころ大和国家成立	356	新羅建国
				375	ゲルマン民族大移動はじまる
五世紀			このころ仁徳天皇陵築造、大陸文化(漢字・儒教・暦・技術等)伝来	449	アングロサクソンがブリタニアに移住
		478	倭王武が中国に使いを送る		

Vocabulary

東京国立博物館	☐☐	the Tokyo National Museum
考古学	☐☐	archaeology
人類学	☐☐	anthropology
民族学	☐☐	ethnology
土器	☐☐	pottery
文様	☐☐	pattern
縄文土器	☐☐	Jomon pottery
弥生土器	☐☐	Yayoi pottery
縄文時代	☐☐	the Jomon period
弥生時代	☐☐	the Yayoi period
躍動的だ	☐☐	to show a lot of life
たくましい	☐☐	to show a feeling of strength
狩猟	☐☐	hunting
漁労	☐☐	fishing
採取	☐☐	gathering
貝	☐☐	shellfish
野生植物	☐☐	wild plants
ご飯を炊く	☐☐	to cook rice
文化の原型	☐☐	a basic cultural pattern
稲作農耕社会	☐☐	a rice-growing agricultural society
石器	☐☐	a stone implement
人骨	☐☐	human bones
旧石器時代の	☐☐	paleolithic
新石器時代の	☐☐	neolithic
混血	☐☐	mixing of peoples; mixing of bloods
文字による記録・文献	☐☐	written records; (ancient) records
出土品	☐☐	excavated [unearthed] articles; things dug out
遺物	☐☐	(archaeological) remains
日本国が成立した	☐☐	the country of Japan came into being
建国記念日	☐☐	National Foundation Day
神武天皇が即位した	☐☐	the Emperor Jinmu began his reign

日本人の祖先はどこから来たんですか

縄文時代・弥生時代・日本国の起源

鈴木氏：これが東京国立博物館です。正面の建物が本館で、左側が考古学館です。

ジョーンズ氏：なるほど、本館は日本式の家の形をしていますね。考古学館のほうから見てはどうですか。

鈴木氏：そうしましょう。

ジョーンズ夫人：あら、この土器は表面に面白い文様がついていますわ。何というんでしょう。

・縄文土器

鈴木氏：これは縄文土器といわれるものです。あの文様は、土器を焼く前に縄を押しつけて作ったものなのです。この土器が作られた時期は紀元前1万年から紀元前300年ころまでです。ですから縄文土器は現在までに発見されたもののうちでは世界最古です。この時代は土器の名前をとって縄文時代と呼んでいます。

・縄文時代

ジョーンズ氏：表面は粗い作りですが、全体の形は美しいですね。なかなか躍動的ですね。

鈴木氏：ええ、色も黒みがかってたくましいでしょう。この縄文文化は日本文化の原型なのです。

**・縄文時代の
生活**

ジョーンズ夫人：この頃の人は何を食べていたんでしょう。

鈴木夫人：縄文時代の人は狩猟・漁労・採取によって生活していましたから、動物の肉や魚、貝、野生植物などを食べていたんです。

・弥生土器

ジョーンズ夫人：この土器はご飯を炊くためのものだと書いてありますわ。お米はいつごろから食べだしたのですか。

C h a p t e r 3

Mr. Suzuki: We are now at the Tokyo National Museum.
That's the main building in front of us. The one on the left is
the archaeology building.

Mr. Jones: The main building is styled after a Japanese house,
isn't it? Well, what about starting from the archaeology part?

Mr. S: OK.

Mrs. Jones: This pot has an interesting pattern. What do you
call it?

Mr. S: This is a piece of Jomon pottery. The pattern was made
by pressing a rope onto the clay before the pot was fired.
This kind of pottery was made in Japan between about
10,000 and 300 B.C. It's the oldest pottery discovered so far
any place in the world. The period when it was made is
called the Jomon period — after the pottery.

Mr. J: The texture is coarse but the shape is beautiful. It shows
a lot of life.

Mr. S: Yes, the blackish color gives it a feeling of strength.
Japanese culture has its roots in the Jomon period.

Mrs. J: What did people eat in those days?

Mrs. Suzuki: They lived by hunting, fishing and gathering so
they ate meat, fish, shellfish, wild plants and such things.

Mrs. J: It says this pot was used for cooking rice. When did
people start to eat rice?

弥生時代

稲作の開始
農耕文化

鈴木夫人：これは弥生土器です。弥生土器文化の時代は、およそ紀元前3世紀から紀元後3世紀までです。日本人が米を食べ始めたのはこの時代です。つまり稲作を始めたわけです。この時期に稲作農耕民族としての日本人の文化の原型が形づくられたのです。弥生土器は縄文土器に比べると色も明るいし、すべすべして、文様も少ないでしょ。

ジョーンズ氏：ところで、日本には何年くらい前から人が住んでいたのですか。

最古の住人

鈴木氏：考古学者によると、これまでに見つかった石器や人骨から、日本には1万年以上前に人間が住んでいたことがわかっています。

ジョーンズ氏：それで、その人々はどこから来たのでしょう。

日本人の
起源

鈴木氏：1万年くらい前は、時代によって場所は違いますが、日本はまだ大陸とつながっていたんです。ある時期は大陸の南と、またある時期は北のほうと、というふうに。ですから、最初に日本列島地域に住んでいた人々は、大陸の住人の一部であろうと思われます。日本列島がほぼいまの形になったのは1万年くらい前と考えられています。

ジョーンズ夫人：その人類が、現在の日本人の祖先なんですか。

原日本人

鈴木夫人：それがはっきり確認できないんですよ。しかし、専門家のほぼ一致した見解では、最初の日本人は、縄文土器の文化をつくった人々です。その後、中国、朝鮮、東南アジアなどからたくさんの人が日本に移住してそれぞれの文化を伝えました。これらの人がしだいに混血して現在の日本人になったのではないか、というのです。

日本国家の
成立

ジョーンズ氏：日本という国はいつできたのですか。

Mrs. S: This is Yayoi pottery. The Yayoi pottery period ran from about the third century B.C. to the third century A.D. It was during this period that the Japanese started eating rice — and raising it. The basic cultural patterns of the Japanese as a rice-growing agricultural society were formed during the Yayoi period. Yayoi pottery is brighter in color than Jomon pottery and the surface is smooth, with very little patterning.

Mr. J: What is the earliest record of people living in Japan?

Mr. S: From stone implements and human bones that they've found, archaeologists know that people have been living here for more than 10,000 years.

Mr. J: Do you know where they came from?

Mr. S: Before 10,000 years ago, Japan was still attached to the mainland, at different places during different periods. Sometimes in the north and sometimes in the south. The first people probably came from the continent. Then about 10,000 years ago Japan broke away from the continent and took its present form.

Mrs. J: And those people are the ancestors of today's Japanese?

Mrs. S: Even that's not certain. Most experts agree, though, that the people who developed the Jomon pottery were the first Japanese. Later many people came to Japan from China, Korea and Southeast Asia, bringing with them their own cultures. The modern Japanese are a result of the gradual mixing of these different peoples.

Mr. J: When did Japan emerge as a nation?

鈴木氏：それがアメリカやヨーロッパの国々のよう
　　　　にできたのではないんです。日本がいつ成立した
　　　　か正確に決めるのは難しいんですよ。

ジョーンズ氏：それはまたどうしてですか。

鈴木氏：ひとつには、日本には4世紀までは文字に
　　　　よる記録がなかったのです。大陸から文字が入っ
　　　　てきたのは4世紀ころですから。

ジョーンズ夫人：まったくわからないのですか。

鈴木氏：正確にはわかりませんが、およその年代な
　　　　らわかっています。古代中国の文献や考古学の遺
　　　　物の研究によると、紀元前1世紀ころには100以
　　　　上の小さな国があったようです。その後これらの
　　　　国々がしだいに統一され、4世紀に比較的大きな
　　　　国ができました。これが日本国だったとされてい
　　　　ますが、何年に成立したと確定するのは難しいの
　　　　です。

建国記念日　ジョーンズ氏：でも、わからないのは、日本には建
　　　　国記念日がありますね。あれはなぜですか。

鈴木氏：これは参りました。ジョーンズさんに一本
　　　　とられましたね。そう、2月11日は建国記念の日
　　　　でお休みですね。

ジョーンズ氏：いや、失礼、そういうつもりはなかっ
　　　　たんです。ちょっとつじつまが合わないと思った
　　　　ものですから。

鈴木氏：日本最古の歴史書である『古事記』と『日
　　　　本書紀』に紀元前660年に初代の天皇（神武天皇）
　　　　が即位したと記されてあり、その日がいまの暦で
　　　　2月11日に当たるからなのです。ただしこれらの
　　　　歴史書が全部真実かどうかは学者の間でもいろい
　　　　ろ意見があります。

Mr. S: It didn't happen like in America and many countries in Europe. With Japan it's hard to say exactly when the nation came into existence.

Mr. J: Why is that?

Mr. S: For one thing, we have no written records going back before the fourth century. That's when our writing system was brought in from the continent.

Mrs. J: No one has any idea at all?

Mr. S: No, not exactly. The approximate date is known. Research into ancient Chinese records and archaeological remains show that there were more than a hundred small independent countries on the islands around the first century B.C. These gradually united, becoming a fairly large country in the fourth century A.D. This was Japan, but it's hard to say exactly in which year it came into being.

Mr. J: Then I don't understand how you can have a National Foundation Day. How do you explain that?

Mr. S: I think you've led me into a trap. Yes, February 11 is National Foundation Day — a national holiday.

Mr. J: Sorry, don't get me wrong. I just felt there was a contradiction.

Mr. S: Japan's two oldest history books, the *Kojiki* and the *Nihonshoki*, say that Japan's first Emperor, Jinmu, began his reign in 660 B.C. on a day that corresponds to February 11 in the modern calendar. But there's a lot of disagreement among scholars about whether everything in these books is true.

Useful Expressions ———— 3

1

<u>What about</u> <u>starting</u> from the archaeology part?

ノート

　What about ... ?「〜するのはどうですか、〜しませんか」☞Useful Expressions 8-2

例文1
What about eating out tonight?

例文2
How about eating out tonight?
　「今晩外で食事してはどうですか」

2

It <u>says</u> this pot was used for cooking rice.

ノート

　say には大きく、3つの意味がある。(1)「いう」(2)「〜とうわさする」(3)「(新聞、書物、掲示などに)書いてある」(3)の場合、間違って write を使いがちなので注意したい。

. 例文
(○) What does the notice *say* about it?
(×) What is written in the notice about it?

3

<u>It</u> was during this period <u>that</u> the Japanese started eating rice.

ノート

　It ... that の強調構文。It と that の間の語句を強調している。It と that をとりはずしてしまうと、普通の文になる。
　この場合は、During this period the Japanese started eating rice.

例文1
It's the Prime Minister *who* does it since he's the head of the Cabinet. 　　　　　　　　(8)

例文2
It was the Japanese *who* first invented a fan which folds. 　　　　　　　　　　　　　　　(30)

Chapter
4

日本の歴史(2)

Japanese History (2)

東大寺は世界最大の木造建築です

奈良や京都は
長いあいだ、日本の文化の中心でした。
その時代に建てられた
法隆寺、東大寺、金閣寺などには
外国人観光客もたくさん訪れています。

〔年表－2〕

●年代		●日本		●世界	
		[西暦年]　[史実]		[西暦年]　[史実]	
六世紀	大和	538	仏教伝来	571	マホメット誕生
		593	聖徳太子摂政となる	589	隋、中国を統一
七世紀		607	法隆寺建立	618	唐建国
		645	大化改新	676	新羅朝鮮半島を統一
八世紀	奈良	710	奈良(平城京)遷都	712	唐文化全盛期
		712	「古事記」撰上	768	チャールズ大帝即位
		720	「日本書紀」撰上		
		752	東大寺大仏開眼		
		760ごろ　「万葉集」成立			
		794	京都(平安京)遷都		
九世紀	平安	887	藤原基経関白となる		

(東大寺大仏殿)

十世紀		905	「古今和歌集」撰進	907	唐滅亡
				962	神聖ローマ帝国成立
十一世紀		1007	紫式部「源氏物語」成る	1066	ノルマンのイングランド征服
		1017	藤原道長太政大臣となる	1096	十字軍遠征はじまる
十二世紀		1167	平清盛太政大臣となる		
		1192	源頼朝鎌倉幕府を開く		
十三世紀	鎌倉	1221	承久の変、北条政権成立	1209	チンギス・ハン、モンゴル統一
				1215	イギリス、マグナカルタ制定
				1299	マルコ・ポーロ「東方見聞録」
十四世紀	室町	1338	足利尊氏将軍となる	1338	英仏百年戦争はじまる
		1397	義満、金閣を造営	1368	明建国
				1392	李氏朝鮮王国おこる
十五世紀		1483	義政、銀閣を造営	1414	コンスタンツ宗教会議開始
				1492	コロンブスのアメリカ発見
十六世紀	桃山安土	1543	ポルトガル人、鉄砲を伝える	1517	ルター宗教改革を唱える
		1549	キリスト教伝来	1519	マゼラン世界周航に出発
		1600	関ケ原の戦い	1543	コペルニクス地動説を唱える

Vocabulary ●────────────────────────────

〜を満喫する	□□	to soak oneself in . . .
〜が印象深い	□□	to be impressed by . . .
世界一古い木造建築	□□	the world's oldest wooden structure
熱心な仏教信者	□□	a devoted Buddhist
仏教文化	□□	Buddhist culture; Buddhist civilization
政治改革	□□	political reform
法治国家	□□	a nation with a constitutional form of government
税金を収める	□□	to pay tax
国防に携わる	□□	to participate in national defense
仏像	□□	a statue of Buddha; a Buddhist statue
東大寺の大仏	□□	the statue of Buddha at Todai Temple
三重の塔	□□	a pagoda
素晴らしい	□□	great; beautiful; fascinating; fantastic; fabulous
土地と人民を支配する	□□	to take control of the land and the people
富と権力を握る	□□	to become rich and powerful
調度品	□□	home furnishings
いわゆる「日本風」	□□	what is called "Japanese style"
平安貴族文化	□□	the Heian nobility culture
雛人形	□□	*hina* dolls
禅寺	□□	a *Zen* temple
華麗な	□□	gorgeous
政治的に不安定である	□□	to be politically unstable
茶の湯	□□	tea ceremony
生け花	□□	flower arrangement
〜の基礎ができる	□□	the foundation is laid for . . .
形式が大成する	□□	to be formalized
鉄砲	□□	firearms
キリスト教	□□	Christianity
大阪城	□□	Osaka Castle

4

Japanese History (2)

東大寺は世界最大の木造建築です

古代国家・平安貴族文化・武士の登場

鈴木夫人：奈良と京都のご旅行はいかがでしたか。お楽しみいただけましたかしら。

ジョーンズ夫人：ええ、とても素晴らしかったですわ。奥様のアドバイスのおかげで、日本の歴史と文化を満喫させていただきましたわ。

法隆寺

ジョーンズ氏：私には飛鳥地方、とくに法隆寺がとても印象深かったですよ。世界一古い木造建築なんだそうですね。

鈴木氏：そうです。現在残っているものは7世紀末ごろの建築ですから、およそ、1,300年くらいむかしのものです。

聖徳太子

ジョーンズ氏：法隆寺を建てたのは聖徳太子だという説明でしたが、太子はそうとう熱心な仏教信者だったんですね。

大化改新

鈴木氏：そうなんです。それで飛鳥が仏教文化の中心になったんです。太子の死後、「大化改新」という政治改革が起こりました。それで日本に初めて法治国家ができました。一般農民は国から土地を与えられて、その代わり一定の税金を納め、国防にも携わることになったのです。

ジョーンズ氏：それはいつごろになりますか。

鈴木氏：7世紀の半ばころです。

奈良の都

ジョーンズ氏：奈良に都ができたのは、その後ですね。

鈴木氏：そのとおりです。8世紀の初めです。

東大寺

ジョーンズ夫人：奈良では、私ども東大寺の大仏を

C h a p t e r 4

Mrs. Suzuki: How was your trip to Kyoto and Nara? Did you have a good time?

Mrs. Jones: Oh, it was great. Thanks to your help and advice, we were literally able to soak ourselves in Japanese history and culture.

Mr. Jones: I was deeply impressed by the Asuka district, especially Horyu Temple. They say it's the world's oldest wooden structure.

Mr. Suzuki: That's right. The part that's still standing was built at the end of the seventh century, so it's about 1,300 years old.

Mr. J: We were told that it was built by Prince Shotoku. He must have been a very devoted Buddhist.

Mr. S: He was, and that's why Asuka became the center of a Buddhist civilization. After his death the country went through a period of political reform called the "Taikano-kaishin." A constitutional form of government was established in Japan for the first time. Also for the first time, the ordinary farmers were given plots of land of their own. In return they had to pay a fixed tax and participate in national defense.

Mr. J: When was that?

Mr. S: About the middle of the seventh century.

Mr. J: It was after that that Nara became the capital, wasn't it?

Mr. S: Yes, that happened in the early eighth century.

Mrs. J: In Nara we saw the statue of Buddha at Todai Temple.

見てきました。大きいのにはびっくりしましたわ。

鈴木夫人：完成したのは8世紀の半ばです。あれは世界最大の木造建築です。幅57.3m、奥行き50.4m、高さ48.6mあります。あれだけのものを造るというのは、当時としては大事業だったと思いますよ。

・薬師寺
唐招提寺
興福寺

ジョーンズ氏：それに奈良では薬師寺の三重塔がとくに気に入りました。唐招提寺もよかったですよ。仏像では興福寺の阿修羅像が好きになりました。

・京都

鈴木氏：京都はいかがでしたか。

ジョーンズ夫人：京都もとっても素晴らしかったですわ。京都が都になったのは、いつですか。

・平安京

鈴木夫人：8世紀の終わりなんです。その頃は「平安京」と呼ばれました。京都は、東京が都になった19世紀の半ばすぎまで、日本の都だったんです。

ジョーンズ夫人：では1,000年以上も都だったというわけですね。

鈴木氏：そうなんです。8世紀の終わりころから貴族がしだいに土地と人民を支配するようになりました。貴族は富と権力を握り、この上に新しい華やかな平安文化がつくられたんです。それまでの中国の影響から抜け出して、しだいに新しいスタイルの衣服や調度品を作り始めました。着物、障子、屏風などに見られる、こんにち「日本風」と呼ばれる様式がこの頃できたんです。

・平安貴族
文化

ジョーンズ夫人：当時の貴族はどんな衣服を着ていたのですか。

鈴木夫人：奥様、先日、雛人形をご覧になったでしょう。

ジョーンズ夫人：ええ。

It was so enormous that it took our breath away.

Mrs. S: That was completed in the middle of the eighth century. It's the world's largest wooden structure. The building's 57.3 meters wide, 50.4 meters deep and 48.6 meters high. It must have been quite a job to build something like that back in those days.

Mrs. J: I particularly liked the pagoda at Yakushi Temple in Nara, and Toshodai Temple was enjoyable. Among the Buddhist statues, the Ashura statue at Kofuku Temple was my favorite.

Mr. S: Tell us about Kyoto.

Mrs. J: Kyoto was fabulous. When did it become the capital?

Mrs. S: At the end of the eighth century. It was called "Heiankyo" at the time. It was the capital until the middle of the nineteenth century, when the Imperial Palace moved to Tokyo.

Mrs. J: So Kyoto was the center of Japan for more than 1,000 years.

Mr. S: Right. Toward the end of the eighth century, the nobility began taking control of both the land and the people. They became rich and powerful and created a new and colorful culture known as the Heian culture. They also shook off the Chinese influence and gradually developed new styles of dress and home furnishings. What we today call the "Japanese style" in clothing, doors, screens and many other things comes from this time.

Mrs. J: What kind of clothes did the upper class wear in those days?

Mrs. S: Do you remember the *hina* dolls we saw the other day?

Mrs. J: Yes . . .

鈴木夫人：当時の貴族の正装はちょうどあれに似たものだったんです。

平等院

鈴木氏：宇治の平等院をご覧になったでしょう。

ジョーンズ夫人：ええ、とても素晴らしかったですわ。

鈴木氏：あれがこの平安貴族の時代のものなのです。ほら、日本の10円銅貨に載っていますよ。そのうちに貴族の護衛や治安維持に当たっていた武士が台頭してくるんです。

武士の登場

ジョーンズ氏：それは何世紀ごろなんですか。

鈴木氏：だいたい10世紀のころです。11世紀の後半から一時期天皇家がふたたび政治の実権を握りますが、だんだん武士の力が強くなります。12世紀になって、とうとう武士が政権を握って、鎌倉に幕府ができます。でも、御所は京都に残ったままでした。

鎌倉幕府

ジョーンズ夫人：鎌倉にはこのまえ行ってきました。あそこにも大仏がありますね。

鎌倉の大仏

鈴木夫人：そうですね。あれは13世紀にできたんです。鎌倉時代も仏教はたいへん盛んで、禅寺がとくに栄えたんです。

鈴木氏：その後、武士を中心にした政権も初めは鎌倉、あとには京都へといくつか変わりました。その間、14世紀には金閣寺が京都に完成しました。

金閣寺

ジョーンズ氏：金閣寺は華麗で、素晴らしいですね。

銀閣寺
龍安寺

鈴木氏：15世紀には銀閣寺、龍安寺などの有名な寺院ができました。

ジョーンズ氏：いやあ龍安寺の石庭は印象深かったですよ。

仏教文化

鈴木氏：14世紀から16世紀の頃は、日本は政治的に不安定な時代でしたが、仏教文化は生きていたんです。茶の湯や生け花など、日本の伝統文化もこ

Mrs. S: Their formal dress was like that.

Mr. S: You also saw the Byodo-in in Uji, didn't you?

Mrs. J: Yes, it's quite beautiful.

Mr. S: It dates from the period when the Heian nobility ruled. Did you notice that it's on our ten yen coins? Look. After some time a warrior class began to emerge from among the people that the aristocrats hired as guards and police.

Mr. J: When was this?

Mr. S: Around the tenth century. Though there was a period at the end of the 11th century when the Emperor did regain power, the general trend was for the warriors to get stronger. They took over in the 12th century and set up a military government or Shogunate in Kamakura, though the Imperial Palace still remained in Kyoto.

Mrs. J: We were in Kamakura recently. There's also a large statue of Buddha there.

Mrs. S: That's the place. The statue there was made in the 13th century. Buddhism flourished during the Kamakura period and Zen temples prospered especially.

Mr. S: There were a series of military regimes, first in Kamakura, then back in Kyoto. It was during this period that Kinkaku Temple was built in Kyoto, in the 14th century.

Mr. J: That's a gorgeous temple.

Mr. S: In the 15th century several other famous temples were built in Kyoto, including Ginkaku and Ryoan Temples.

Mr. J: The stone garden at Ryoan Temple is breathtaking.

Mr. S: The 14th, 15th and 16th centuries were politically unstable but the Buddhist culture was still alive. It was during this period that the foundation was laid for such Japanese tradi-

の頃基礎ができました。そして16世紀の終わりに
形式が大成したのです。15世紀からは各地の大名
が権力を競った「戦国時代」に入ります。16世紀
の半ばには、ポルトガル人によって鉄砲とキリス
ト教が伝えられました。

●
鉄砲と
キリスト教
の伝来

ジョーンズ氏：その頃のヨーロッパは探検の時代で
　すね。

鈴木氏：そのとおりです。この頃ふたたび日本は統
　一されました。この事業は織田信長によって始め
　られ、豊臣秀吉によって16世紀の終わりに完成さ
　れました。

●
信長・秀吉
の全国統一

ジョーンズ氏：それは大阪城に行ったとき聞いた名
　前ですね。とすると、その頃大阪城ができたんで
　しょう。

鈴木氏：そうです。そして、17世紀の初めに徳川家
　康が政治の実権を握りました。こうして江戸幕府
　の時代に入るんです。

●
江戸幕府

日本語と英語の狭間で❸

「プリーズ」の神話

　英語で何かを頼みたいときに、たとえば
　　"Shut the door, please."
のように、please を添えれば丁寧ないい方になるかと
いうと、口調にもよるが、相手には命令調に聞こえてし
まうことがままある。「お願いします」という気持ちを
じゅうぶんに表すには、
　　"Will you (please) shut the door?"
のように表現したい。Would you please ...? とか
Could you please ...? を用いれば、さらに丁寧な表現
になる。

tions as the tea ceremony and flower arrangement. These were formalized toward the end of the 16th century. A period of "warring states" started from the 15th century as the feudal lords throughout the country started fighting for power. Then, in the middle of the 16th century the Portuguese arrived with Christianity and firearms.

Mr. J: That was the Age of Exploration in Europe.

Mr. S: Right. Japan was reunited about this time. The job was started by Nobunaga Oda and was finished by Hideyoshi Toyotomi toward the end of the 16th century.

Mr. J: A name I remember in connection with Osaka Castle. So this would have been about the time the castle was built.

Mr. S: Yes. Then in the early part of the 17th century, Ieyasu Tokugawa took power. That began the Edo Shogunate.

また、「～したほうがいいですよ」とか、「～したらどうですか」と、相手に助言したり忠告したりしたいときに、英語ではYou'd better ... とか、Why don't you ...? を使って、

　　"It's a good movie. You'd better see it."
　　"Why don't you take a train?"

という表現がある。しかしこれらは、話し方の調子によっては、命令調や押しつけがましい印象を相手に与えかねない。

　こういう場合には、次のようにYou should ... とか、If I were you, I'd ... を用いるほうがよい。

　　"It's a good movie. (I think) You should see it."
　　"If I were you, I'd take a train."

Useful Expressions ——— 4

1

<u>That's why</u> Asuka became the center of a Buddhist civilization.

ノート 「そういうわけで〜である」よく使う文型。

例文 *That's why* you don't use soap in the tub?　(34)

2

<u>It must have been</u> quite a job <u>to</u> build something like that.

must have been ...「〜であったに違いない」 It は to 以下の仮の主語。また、quite が「かなり、本当に、まったく」の意味で、「名詞」または「形容詞＋名詞」の前につくときは、口語では上例のように quite a ... ／quite an ... の形になる。☞ Useful Expressions 9-4

例文 He *must have been* a very devoted Buddhist.　(4)

3

<u>What kind of</u> clothes did they wear in those days?

ノート 「どんな種類の〜を〜」という質問の決まり文句。本書にも何回も登場する。

例文1 *What kind of* equipment are you talking about?

(11)

例文2 *What kind of* problems do they take up?　(17)

例文3 *What kind of* tree is that?　(31)

次のような使い分けをする場合もある。

例文4 *What kind of* car do you have?（車の種類、メーカーなどを聞く）

例文5 *What kind of a* car do you have?（車のよしあし、性能などを聞く）

Chapter 5

日本の歴史（3）

Japanese History (3)

近代化の原動力が培われた江戸300年

徳川家康が開いた江戸幕府は
約300年の長きにわたって政権を維持しました。
この平穏無事な閉鎖社会のなかで
文化や経済は独自の発展を
見せ始めます。

●年代		●日本	●世界
		[西暦年] 〔史実〕	[西暦年] 〔史実〕

十七世紀　江戸

日本	世界
1603　江戸幕府開く	1607　アメリカ、
1609　平戸オランダ商館設置	ジェームズタウンの建設
1612　キリスト教禁止令	1609　ガリレー望遠鏡を発明
1639　鎖国	1620　メイフラワー号による
歌舞伎おこる	ピューリタンの植民
1694　「奥の細道」完成	1636　清おこる
	1642　イギリスの清教徒革命
	1687　ニュートン万有引力の法則発見
	1688　名誉革命おこる

（出島）

十八世紀

日本	世界
1702　赤穂浪士事件	1742　フランクリン電気発見
1716　徳川吉宗、将軍となる	1772　イギリスに産業革命おこる
1796　エトロフ島日本領土とす	1776　アメリカ13州独立宣言
	1789　フランス革命おこる

（浮世絵、広重画）

十九世紀

日本	世界
1853　ペリー来日	1804　ナポレオン皇帝となる
1854　開国	1818　スチーブンソン蒸気機関発明
1867　大政奉還	1823　アメリカ、モンロー宣言
	1840　中国、アヘン戦争おこる
	1842　南京条約
	1859　ダーウィン「種の起源」を発表
	1861　アメリカ南北戦争はじまる
	1863　アメリカ、奴隷解放

（ペリー提督）

Vocabulary

江戸幕府	☐☐	the Edo Shogunate
皇居	☐☐	the Imperial Palace
政権を維持する	☐☐	a government survives
米がお金の代わりになる	☐☐	rice is used as money
身分制度	☐☐	a caste system
士・農・工・商	☐☐	warriors; farmers; artisans; tradesmen
武士の天下	☐☐	a paradise for the military
大名を配置する	☐☐	to deploy the feudal lords
地方行政を担当する	☐☐	to be in charge of the local government
防備する	☐☐	to build up a wall of defense
人質	☐☐	a hostage
〜と矛盾する	☐☐	to run counter to . . .
封建制度	☐☐	the feudal system
〜を防ぐ・阻止する	☐☐	to prevent from . . .
経済的に繁栄する	☐☐	to become economically powerful
禁止する	☐☐	to ban
鎖国する・鎖国政策をとる	☐☐	to shut the country off from the rest of the world; to implement an isolation policy
開国する	☐☐	to open up the country
発見する	☐☐	to make a discovery
成熟する	☐☐	to mature
近代化する	☐☐	to modernize
近代化	☐☐	modernization
儒学	☐☐	Confucianism
教育が普及する	☐☐	education becomes available to the common people
読み・書き・そろばん	☐☐	the three R's
商業	☐☐	commerce
手工業	☐☐	handicraft
航路	☐☐	a seaway
流通システム	☐☐	a distribution system

5

Japanese History (3)

57

近代化の原動力が培われた江戸300年

江戸幕府・士農工商・鎖国・文化の発展

・江戸幕府　ジョーンズ夫人：江戸幕府はどこにあったんですか。

　　　　　　鈴木夫人：現在の東京です。いまの宮城がもと江戸城だったのです。

・江戸300年　ジョーンズ夫人：江戸時代はどのくらい続いたのですか。

　　　　　　鈴木夫人：約300年くらい続きました。

　　　　　　ジョーンズ氏：よくそれだけの長い間政権を維持できましたね。

　　　　　　鈴木氏：そうなんです。そのためにはあの手この手の支配の体制をとったんです。

　　　　　　ジョーンズ氏：たとえば、どんな？

・米の生産高　鈴木氏：当時は、米がお金の代わりになっていました。幕府は米の全生産高の4分の1を産出する土地と住民を握っていました。この富によって、諸大名に対して圧倒的な軍事力を持っていたのです。それに、武士を頂点とする士農工商という社会階層を定めました。武士だけが武器を持ち、その武力によって支配階級として、絶対的な権力を持っていたのです。

・士農工商

　　　　　　ジョーンズ氏：まさに武士の天下だったんですね。

　　　　　　鈴木氏：そうです。支配体制を維持するもうひとつのカギは、幕府がとった地方の行政を担当する大名の配置の仕方だったんです。

　　　　　　ジョーンズ氏：どんな配置をしていたんですか。

・大名の配置　鈴木氏：徳川一族の大名とか徳川の家来の大名を江

Chapter 5

Mrs. Jones: Where was the Edo Shogunate located?

Mrs. Suzuki: Where Tokyo is now. Today's Imperial Palace used to be Edo Castle.

Mrs. J: How long did the Edo period last?

Mrs. S: For about 300 years.

Mr. Jones: That's a long time for a government to survive.

Mr. Suzuki: Yes. The Shogunate used various different systems to maintain its rule.

Mr. J: Such as?

Mr. S: In those days rice was used as money. The Shogunate kept control over enough land and farmers to ensure that it would have a quarter of the rice crop. With this wealth, it was able to maintain overwhelming military superiority over the feudal lords. To strengthen its authority, it also enforced a caste system that put the warriors on top and the farmers, artisans and tradesmen under them in that order. The warriors were the only class allowed to have weapons and with their military might, they had absolute power as the ruling class.

Mr. J: A paradise for the military.

Mr. S: That's right. Another key to maintaining control was the system the Shogunate used for deploying the feudal lords in charge of the local governments.

Mr. J: How did that work?

Mr. S: All important locations around Edo were put under the

戸の周辺や重要な地点に配置したんです。

ジョーンズ氏：そうして軍事的に江戸の防備をした
　　　　　　わけですね。

参勤交代

鈴木氏：そうなんです。それから、大名を1年ずつ
　　　　江戸と国もとに交互に滞在させました。大名が国
　　　　にいる間は妻子は人質として、江戸に滞在させた
　　　　のです。

ジョーンズ夫人：厳しいやり方ですわね。

ジョーンズ氏：その頃は外国との交流はどうなって
　　　　　　いたんですか。

鈴木氏：17世紀の初めには幕府は、まだ外国と交流
　　　　しようという気持ちが強かったんです。ところが、
　　　　キリスト教の自由・平等の精神は封建制度とは矛
　　　　盾するものでした。それに西南の大名が貿易に
　　　　よって経済的に繁栄するのを防ぐ必要もあったの
　　　　です。そのために、キリスト教を禁じ鎖国政策を
　　　　とったんです。

鎖国政策

ジョーンズ氏：まったくどこの国とも交易しなかっ
　　　　　　たのですか。

鈴木氏：いや、オランダ、中国、朝鮮だけとは交易
　　　　していたのです。ただ、交易の場所は長崎だけに
　　　　限られていました。

長崎

ジョーンズ氏：世界の動きから離れて、マイナス面
　　　　　　が多かったでしょうね。その頃ヨーロッパでは
　　　　　　ニュートンがいろんな発見をしたり、蒸気機関車
　　　　　　が造られたりしていた時代なんですから。

鈴木氏：確かにマイナス面もあります。しかし、プ
　　　　ラスの面も考えられます。最近では、江戸時代
　　　　300年の間に国内の文化が発展成熟して素地がで
　　　　きていたために、日本がアジアでいちばん早く近

近代化の
原動力

control of lords who were either members of the ruling Tokugawa family or the family's vassals.

Mr. J: They built up a wall of defense around the Shogunate.

Mr. S: Correct. The lords were rotated back and forth between Edo and the provinces. One year here and one year there. While a lord was in his province, his wife and children were held as hostages in Edo.

Mrs. J: Pretty severe, but pretty clever.

Mr. J: What relations did Japan have with other countries in those days?

Mr. S: In the early 17th century, the Edo Shogunate was quite positive about intercourse with other countries. However, it began to realize that the Christian concepts of freedom and equality ran counter to the feudal system. It also felt a need to prevent the lords in the southwest of Japan from becoming too economically powerful through foreign trade. It therefore banned Christianity and shut the country off from the rest of the world.

Mr. J: Did that mean that there were no relations with other countries at all?

Mr. S: No, there was still some trade with Holland, China and Korea, but only through one port — Nagasaki.

Mr. J: Those were the days when Newton was making his discoveries and the first steam locomotives were being developed in Europe. Loss of contact with the rest of the world must have had a negative effect.

Mr. S: It did, but there may have been a positive effect, too. Today there is a strong belief that the maturing of Japan occurred during the 300 years of the Edo period, and that made it possible for Japan to become the first in Asia to

代化できたのだという見方も強いんです。

ジョーンズ夫人：どのような発展があったのですか。

・**学問と教育**

鈴木夫人：学問では、儒学、歴史学の分野で、優秀な学者がたくさん出ましたし、数学、農学、薬学も独自に発展しました。和算という数学は、微分・積分に近いレベルに達していたんですよ。また、18世紀末から19世紀初めには、とくに庶民にも教育が普及しました。農民・町人を教育する寺子屋という小さな学校は2万もあり、民衆の半数近くが読み書き計算ができたようです。

・**和算**

・**寺子屋**

ジョーンズ氏：産業面でも、これと並行して発達があったんでしょう。

鈴木氏：そうです。全国の商業、手工業、農業技術が発達しました。京都・大阪・江戸などへの農産物を運ぶための街道や航路、流通機構も整備されました。

街道と航路

ジョーンズ氏：この時代は芸術家の活動も活発でしたか。

・**歌舞伎**
浮世絵

鈴木氏：文化も多彩な発展をしています。歌舞伎、浮世絵、陶磁器、漆器、文学では俳句や小説などの芸術がいっせいに花開いた時代です。

modernize.

Mrs. J: What kind of progress was there?

Mrs. S: Many brilliant Confucian scholars and historians appeared, and progress was made in mathematics, agriculture and pharmacy. A branch of mathematics called *wasan* reached a level close to differential and integral calculus. From the end of the 18th century to the beginning of the 19th, education became available to the common people on a large scale. More than 20,000 small schools called *terakoya* sprang up throughout the country for farmers and townsfolk. At this time around half the population learned the three R's.

Mr. J: Was there parallel progress in industry?

Mr. S: Yes, throughout the country — in commerce, handicraft and agricultural techniques — and roads and seaways and distribution systems were developed for transport of produce to major cities like Kyoto, Osaka and Edo.

Mr. J: Were the artists just as active during this period?

Mr. S: It was a lively period for the arts too, with *kabuki*, *ukiyoe* painting, ceramics lacquer ware and literature blooming. Some excellent *haiku* poems and novels were written during the Edo period.

Useful Expressions ——— 5

1 Today's Imperial Palace <u>used to</u> be Edo Castle.

ノート
　used to は（1）（意志を示さない動詞とともに）「以前［むかし］は～であった」（2）（意志を表す動詞とともに）「～以前［むかし］は～した」上例は（1）。

例文
The union *used to* be able to win big pay raises almost every spring. (14)

2 <u>How long</u> did the Edo period last?

ノート
　次の類例も再確認しておこう。

例文1
How long have you been in Japan?

例文2
How far into the work are you?
　「どこまで仕事は終わっているのかな」［程度］

例文3
How far are you going?　　　　　　　［距離］

例文4
How late is this store open?

例文5
How many presidents have there been before Reagan?「レーガンは何番目の大統領ですか」

3 <u>A paradise for</u> the military.

ノート
　「～にとっては天国、極楽だ」

例文
A paradise for foreign tourists!

4 At this time around half the population learned <u>the three R's.</u>

ノート
　around ＝ about。the three R's とは reading、writing、arithmetic を指す。基礎教育としての読み書き算数（そろばん）のこと。さらに「（各領域の）基本的な技術」の意味にも使われる。

Chapter
6

日本の歴史(4)

Japanese History (4)

明治政府誕生、そして激動の時代へ

開国、明治維新を契機として
近代化と富国強兵の道をひた走る日本。
そしてついに太平洋戦争に突入。
戦後、ゼロから出発した日本は
奇跡といわれる復興を遂げます。

〔年表 ― 4〕

●年代		●日本		●世界	
		[西暦年]	[史実]	[西暦年]	[史実]
一九世紀	明治	1868	明治維新		
		1889	大日本帝国憲法公布		
		1894	日清戦争はじまる		
二十世紀		1904	日露戦争はじまる	1910	韓国、日本に併合
	大正	1923	関東大震災	1912	中華民国成立
				1914	第一次世界大戦はじまる
				1917	ロシア革命おこる
	昭和	1941	太平洋戦争はじまる	1929	世界大恐慌はじまる
		1945	ポツダム宣言受諾	1933	アメリカ、
		1946	日本国憲法公布		ニューディール政策開始
		1947	労働基準法・独占禁止法・	1939	第二次世界大戦はじまる
			教育基本法公布	1945	第二次世界大戦終結
		1949	湯川秀樹ノーベル賞受賞		国際連合発足
		1951	平和条約、日米安保条約調印	1948	大韓民国、
		1956	国際連合加盟		朝鮮民主主義人民共和国成立
		1964	オリンピック東京大会	1949	中華人民共和国成立
			新幹線開通	1950	朝鮮動乱おこる
		1965	朝永振一郎ノーベル賞受賞	1953	朝鮮動乱終結
		1968	川端康成ノーベル賞受賞	1957	ソ連スプートニク1号打ち上げ
		1970	日本万国博覧会開催	1961	ベトナム戦争はじまる
		1972	沖縄復帰、日中国交正常化	1963	アメリカ、
		1973	第一次石油危機		ケネディ大統領暗殺
			江崎玲於奈ノーベル賞受賞	1966	中国、文化大革命はじまる
		1974	佐藤栄作ノーベル賞受賞	1969	アポロ11号月面着陸に成功
		1978	日中平和友好条約調印	1972	ニクソン米大統領訪中
		1979	第二次石油危機	1973	拡大EC発足
		1981	福井謙一ノーベル賞受賞	1981	アメリカ、
					レーガン大統領就任、
					有人宇宙船スペース・シャトル初飛行成功

(東京オリンピック)

Vocabulary ●

〜を基盤にする	☐☐	to be based on . . .
力が弱くなる	☐☐	the power is eroded
生活が苦しくなる	☐☐	to be faced with poverty
反幕府勢力	☐☐	the anti-Shogunate forces
近代化への道を歩み始める	☐☐	to be on the road to modernization
敷設する	☐☐	to build
５年足らずで	☐☐	only five years later; in only five years
徴兵令	☐☐	conscription; a draft (system)
兵役に服する	☐☐	to serve (in the army) ; to do military service
廃止する	☐☐	to abolish
元武士	☐☐	an ex-warrior
反乱を起こす	☐☐	to start rebellions
鎮圧する	☐☐	to put down
西欧に追いつく	☐☐	to catch up with the West
憲法を発布する	☐☐	to promulgate a constitution
日清戦争	☐☐	the Sino-Japanese War
日露戦争	☐☐	the Russo-Japancsc War
第一次産業革命	☐☐	the first phase of industrial revolution
軽工業	☐☐	light industries
重工業	☐☐	heavy industries
明治時代	☐☐	the Meiji era
大正時代	☐☐	the Taisho era
国際連盟	☐☐	the League of Nations
ワシントン会議	☐☐	the Washington Conference
金融恐慌	☐☐	a financial panic
世界恐慌	☐☐	the Great Depression
軍部	☐☐	the military
真珠湾攻撃	☐☐	the attack on Pearl Harbor
太平洋戦争	☐☐	the Pacific War
第二次世界大戦	☐☐	the Second World War

6

Japanese History (4)

明治政府誕生、そして激動の時代へ

明治新政府・産業革命・恐慌・太平洋戦争

幕府の崩壊

ジョーンズ氏：江戸幕府はなぜ崩壊したんですか。

鈴木氏：幕府の経済力は米を基盤にしていました。江戸時代の末期になりますと、貨幣経済が発達して、町人の経済力が大きくなり、逆にこうした幕府の経済力が弱まってきたんです。そして、武士や農民の生活がたいへん苦しくなってきました。

開国

また、19世紀半ばころから、各国が開国を要求してきました。1854年に幕府はペリー提督の要求を受け入れて、日米和親条約を結びました。こうして鎖国は終わったのです。

新政府誕生

鉄道の歴史

鈴木夫人：でも開国、政権をめぐって国論は分かれました。反幕府勢力が大きくなり、天皇のもとで政府が誕生し、日本は近代化の道を歩み始めたのです。イギリス人の指導を受けて、初めての鉄道が横浜と新橋の間に敷設され、完成したのが1872年です。

明治新政府

ジョーンズ氏：というと、ペリー提督が日本に来てから20年足らずで鉄道ができたのですね。

鈴木氏：そうです。新しい明治政府ができたのが1868年です。それを起点にしますと、わずか5年足らずで鉄道ができたんです。その頃の歴史を見ると、日本人は欧米から新しい思想や技術を導入するのに、日夜走っていたような印象を受けます。

ジョーンズ氏：猛烈な勢いで、世の中が変わって

C h a p t e r 6

Mr. Jones: Why did the Edo Shogunate fall?

Mr. Suzuki: The Shogunate's economic power was based on rice. Toward the end of the Edo period, this power was eroded by the development of a money-based economy that made the merchants economically strong. In contrast, the warriors and the farmers were faced with poverty. Then about the middle of the 19th century, many countries began pressing the Shogunate to open up the country. In 1854, the Shogunate gave in to Commodore Perry and signed a treaty of amity with the United States. That was the end of Japan's isolation.

Mrs. Suzuki: However, there was a lot of disagreement about whether or not the country should be opened up, and about who should rule. The anti-Shogunate forces finally prevailed and a new government was formed under the Emperor. Japan was now on the road to modernization. The first railroad was built between Yokohama and Shimbashi in Tokyo, and was completed in 1872 with the help of British engineers.

Mr. J: Let's see. That means the first railroad was built only 20 years after Perry came.

Mr. S: Yes, but the new Meiji government wasn't established until 1868. Using that as the starting point, the railroad was built in only five years. Reading the history of that period, one gets the impression that people were running about day and night trying to introduce new ideas and technology from the West.

Mr. J: Sounds like a time of turbulent change.

いった時代のようですね。

・**徴兵令**
教育制度
地租改正

鈴木氏：ええ、1873年に徴兵令が発布され、満20歳の男子に3年間の兵役が義務づけられました。学校教育制度が行われたのは72年です。また、73年には地租改正条令が出されました。

ジョーンズ氏：武士はどうなったんですか。

・**身分制度の**
廃止

鈴木氏：身分制度の廃止とともに武士の身分も廃止されました。元武士階級の一部が地方で反乱を起こしたりしましたが、政府は鎮圧することができたんです。

ジョーンズ氏：混乱した時代だったようですね。

鈴木氏：そうです。そして政府は欧米に追いつくために近代産業をつぎつぎに導入したんです。日本人の生活様式も急激に変わりました。人々は着物

・**新生活様式**

の代わりに洋服を着始め、頭髪も西洋風に変わりました。

ジョーンズ夫人：違った国になったみたいだったでしょうね。

鈴木夫人：西洋料理店も現れ、ビールも人気が出始めましたの。

・**憲法発布**

鈴木氏：1889年には憲法が発布されました。この憲法は、第二次世界大戦後の1946年まで効力を持っていたんです。

ジョーンズ氏：たしか日本とロシアとの戦争がありましたね。

・**日清戦争**
日露戦争

鈴木氏：そうです。明治時代に対外的に大きな戦争が2つありました。日清戦争と日露戦争です。ちょうど日本の産業革命の時期に当たりますね。

ジョーンズ氏：どんなようにですか。

・**第一次産業**
革命

鈴木氏：1894年の日清戦争の頃に、第一次産業革命が起こっています。これは製糸・綿紡績などの軽

Mr. S: It was. Even conscription was introduced in 1873. Men were drafted at 20 and had to serve for three years. A public educational system was established in 1872, and the land ownership and tax system was reformed in 1873.

Mr. J: What happened to the warriors?

Mr. S: Their status was abolished with the abolishment of the caste system. Some of the ex-warriors started rebellions in certain localities but the government was able to put them down.

Mr. J: Sounds like chaotic times.

Mr. S: They were. To catch up with the West, the government also started introducing all kinds of new industries. Japanese life changed dramatically. People began wearing Western-style clothing instead of *kimonos*, and Western hair styles were also adopted.

Mrs. Jones: Sounds like a whole country was being transformed.

Mrs. S: Western-style restaurants sprang up and beer became popular.

Mr. S: A constitution was promulgated in 1889. This stayed in effect until 1946.

Mr. J: Then came the war with Russia.

Mr. S: Yes. There were two important wars during the Meiji era, the Sino-Japanese War and the Russo-Japanese War. Both were fought while Japan was going through its industrial revolution.

Mr. J: How's that?

Mr. S: When the Sino-Japanese War started in 1894, Japan was in the first phase of industrial revolution centering on light

**第二次産業
革命**　工業が中心でした。1904年の日露戦争の頃に、第
　　　　二次産業革命が始まっています。中心の産業は製
　　　　鉄、造船などの重工業です。1897年に官営の八幡
　　　　製鉄所が創設されています。

　　　　ジョーンズ夫人：教育の改革ではどんなものがあり
　　　　　　　ましたか。

義務教育　鈴木夫人：1886年に義務教育が4年間と決められ、
　　　　　　　その後1907年に6年間に延長されました。

　　　　ジョーンズ夫人：明治時代って何年間でしたの。

　　　　鈴木夫人：45年間です。

　　　　ジョーンズ氏：その後は、日本では何時代っていう
　　　　　　　んですか。

大正時代　鈴木氏：大正時代です。大正は短く15年までです。

　　　　ジョーンズ氏：大正時代にはどんなことがあったん
　　　　　　　ですか。

　　　　鈴木氏：第一次世界大戦があった時代です。

国際連盟　ジョーンズ氏：すると、国際連盟が成立したり、ワ
　　　　　　　シントン会議が開かれた時代ですね。

恐慌　鈴木氏：そうなんです。その後1926年に現在の昭和
　　　　　　　時代に入ります。そして 1927年の金融恐慌に続
　　　　　　　いて、1929～31年の世界恐慌へと進んでいくわけ
　　　　　　　です。こうした社会不安を背景にして、日本では
　　　　　　　軍部の勢力がだんだん強くなります。そして1941

太平洋戦争　年の真珠湾攻撃になるんです。その後の日本の歴
　　　　　　　史はジョーンズさんもよくご存じのとおりです。

　　　　ジョーンズ氏：第二次大戦後の日本の変わり様も劇
　　　　　　　的ですが、明治もそうとう激しく変化した時代
　　　　　　　だったことが初めてわかりましたよ。

industries such as spinning and silk reeling. When the Russo-Japanese war started in 1904, Japan was in the middle of the second phase. This is when the heavy industries like steel-making and shipbuilding got into full swing. The government-run Yawata Steel Works was established in 1897.

Mrs. J: What were some of the educational reforms?

Mrs. S: Compulsory education was set at four years in 1886 and extended to six years in 1907.

Mrs. J: How long was the Meiji era?

Mrs. S: Forty-five years.

Mr. J: What was the next era called?

Mr. S: Taisho. That lasted only 15 years.

Mr. J: What happened in the Taisho era?

Mr. S: The First World War was during Taisho.

Mr. J: So that would be around the time the League of Nations was founded, and the Washington Conference was held.

Mr. S: That's right. 1926 was the beginning of the present era — Showa. The financial panic of 1927 was followed by the Great Depression between 1929 and 1931. All this time, the Japanese military preyed on the anxiety over the unstable world situation, to build up its strength. Then in 1941, the attack on Pearl Harbor. From there on, you are probably pretty familiar with Japanese history.

Mr. J: I knew about the dramatic changes in Japan after the Second World War, but I hadn't realized that there were such enormous changes during the Meiji era.

6

Japanese History (4)

Useful Expressions ———— 6

1

One <u>gets the impression that</u> people were running about day and night.

ノート　get the impression that . . . 「～という印象を抱く」

例文 1　One doesn't *get the impression that* the employees are competing very hard against each other.　(12)

例文 2　I *get the feeling that* the arrangement is supposed to represent something.　(29)

2

<u>What happened to</u> the warriors?

ノート　口語表現だから、do . . . ? の do が省略されているのだと勘違いしないこと。What などの疑問代名詞が主語の場合は、主語と述語動詞の語順は平叙文と同じで、助動詞の do は使わない。

例文 1　*Who appoints* the judges?　(8)

例文 2　*What happens* if the person runs into objections from his superiors?　(5)

例文 3　*What happens* to the ones who don't get in?　(21)

3

<u>Sounds like</u> chaotic times.

ノート　この (It) sounds . . . は「～のようだ、～のように思われる」で、(It) seems . . . と同じ意味。

例文 1　*Sounds like* a time of turbulent change.　(6)

例文 2　*Sounds like* a whole country was being transformed.　(6)

例文 3　*Sounds* reasonable.

Chapter

7

·

天皇

The Emperor

·

天皇家には姓がありません

日本の皇室は
およそ1,500年間続いています。
このような例は、
世界の王室のなかでも珍しく
不思議に思う外国人も多いようです。

[現在の皇室]

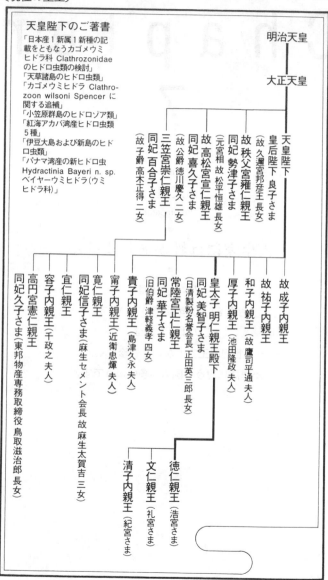

天皇陛下のご著書
「日本産1新属1新種の記
載をともなうカゴメウミ
ヒドラ科 Clathrozonidae
のヒドロ虫類の検討」
「天草諸島のヒドロ虫類」
「カゴメウミヒドラ Clathro-
zoon wilsoni Spencer に
関する追補」
「小笠原群島のヒドロゾア類」
「紅海アカバ湾産ヒドロ虫類
5種」
「伊豆大島および新島のヒド
ロ虫類」
「パナマ湾産の新ヒドロ虫
Hydractinia Bayeri n. sp.
ベイヤーウミヒドラ(ウミ
ヒドラ科)」

明治天皇

大正天皇

天皇陛下

皇后陛下 良子さま
(故久邇宮邦彦王長女)

故 成子内親王

故 祐子内親王

和子内親王(故鷹司平通夫人)

厚子内親王(池田隆政夫人)

故 秩父宮雍仁親王
同妃 勢津子さま
(元宮相 故松平恒雄 長女)

故 高松宮宣仁親王
同妃 喜久子さま
(故公爵 徳川慶久 二女)

三笠宮崇仁親王
同妃 百合子さま
(故子爵 高木正得 二女)

皇太子 明仁親王殿下
同妃 美智子さま
(日清製粉名誉会長 正田英三郎 長女)

常陸宮正仁親王
同妃 華子さま
(旧伯爵 津軽義孝 四女)

貴子内親王(島津久永夫人)

甯子内親王(近衛忠煇夫人)

寛仁親王

同妃 信子さま(麻生セメント会長 故 麻生太賀吉 三女)

宜仁親王

容子内親王(千政之夫人)

高円宮憲仁親王
同妃 久子さま(東邦物産専務取締役 鳥取滋治郎 長女)

徳仁親王(浩宮さま)

文仁親王(礼宮さま)

清子内親王(紀宮さま)

(1987年7月)

76

Vocabulary

皇位につく	☐☐	to become Emperor
在位60年になる	☐☐	to mark the sixtieth year of one's reign
生物学者	☐☐	a biologist
海洋生物の研究	☐☐	a study of the marine plants and animals
研究所	☐☐	a laboratory
立憲君主国	☐☐	a constitutional monarchy
国家元首	☐☐	the head of state
外交儀礼上	☐☐	in diplomatic and ceremonial functions
直接に政治を行う	☐☐	to take a direct part in government
国事	☐☐	state affairs
内閣の助言と承認	☐☐	the advice and approval of the cabinet
任命する	☐☐	to appoint
信任状を認証する	☐☐	to attest the credentials
外交官を接受する	☐☐	to receive foreign diplomats
国会を召集する	☐☐	to convene the Diet
衆議院を解散する	☐☐	to dissolve the House of Representatives
権力闘争から超然としている	☐☐	to remain above the power struggles
～から政治の大権を預かる	☐☐	to receive the sovereign right from . . .
人を～と呼ぶ	☐☐	to refer to someone as . . .
姓	☐☐	a family name
天皇の存命中に	☐☐	while the Emperor is alive
治世中に	☐☐	while one is in power
贈り名	☐☐	a posthumous name
元号	☐☐	an era
紀年法	☐☐	a way of reckoning years
面倒な	☐☐	troublesome
換算する	☐☐	to convert
換算表	☐☐	a conversion table

7

The Emperor

天皇家には姓がありません

天皇の地位・皇室の歴史・元号

・個人として の天皇

ジョーンズ夫人：いまの天皇のお名前は何とおっ しゃるんですか。

鈴木氏：裕仁（ひろひと）です。1926年に皇位につ かれてから1986年は在位60年目に当たります。

ジョーンズ氏：世界の王族のなかでも、そんなに長 く在位した方はいなかったと思いますね。

鈴木氏：そうです。日本の歴代天皇のなかでもいち ばん長い記録です。

ジョーンズ氏：天皇は生物学者だそうですね。

鈴木氏：そうです。長年日本近海の海洋生物の研究 をしておられます。皇居内に研究所があり、ご著 書も7冊を数えます。

ジョーンズ氏：素晴らしいですね。ところで天皇は 国政上はどんな立場にあるのですか。

・天皇の憲法 上の地位

鈴木氏：日本はイギリス、オランダなどと同じよう に立憲君主国です。天皇の立場は憲法に定められ ています。それによると、天皇は外交儀礼上は日 本の元首になっています。しかし、天皇は直接に は政治を行いません。内閣の助言と承認に基づい て、決められた国事を行います。

ジョーンズ氏：どのような国事をするのですか。

・天皇の行う 国事

鈴木氏：内閣総理大臣や最高裁判所長官を任命し、 外国大使・公使の信任状を認証します。また、外 国の元首・外交官を接受し、国会の開会・衆議院 の解散などを行います。

ジョーンズ氏：ヨーロッパ各国では、いくつか王朝

C h a p t e r 7

Mrs. Jones: What's the Emperor's name?

Mr. Suzuki: Hirohito. He became Emperor in 1926 and marked the 60th year of his reign in 1986.

Mr. Jones: I don't think there have been many monarchs who have reigned that long.

Mr. S: I know. He's set a record for Japanese Emperors.

Mr. J: I heard the Emperor's a biologist.

Mr. S: That's right. He's made a study of the marine plants and animals that live near the coast of Japan. He's got a laboratory in the Imperial Palace and has written seven books on the subject.

Mr. J: That's wonderful. I was wondering though — what is the position of the Emperor in the government?

Mr. S: Like Great Britain and the Netherlands, Japan is a constitutional monarchy. So the Emperor's role is defined in the constitution — which calls him the head of state in diplomatic and ceremonial functions. He doesn't take any direct part in government, but he does handle specific state affairs based on the advice and approval of the cabinet.

Mr. J: What kind of affairs?

Mr. S: He appoints the Prime Minister and the Chief Judge of the Supreme Court and attests the credentials of ambassadors and ministers. He also receives foreign heads of state, ambassadors and ministers, convenes the Diet and dissolves the House of Representatives.

Mr. J: Some European countries went through several dynas-

が交代していますが、日本の現在の皇室は何年ぐらい続いているのですか。

皇室の歴史

鈴木氏：歴史でわかっているところでは、1,500年くらい続いています。現在の天皇は124代目です。

ジョーンズ氏：1,500年近くも続いている王室というのも珍しいですね。どうしてそんなに長く続いたんでしょうね。

鈴木氏：それは、天皇が直接政治に携わらなかったからでしょう。つまり権力闘争から超然としていたからなんです。

ジョーンズ氏：といいますと、実際にはどのように超然としていたのですか。

鈴木氏：天皇が国の権力を握り直接政治を行った時期は、7世紀からの2世紀くらいのことです。その後、9世紀からずっと19世紀後半の明治天皇時代までは、まず貴族階級そのあと武士一族が実質的に国の権力を握っていました。しかし、こうした権力者は自らは天皇になろうとはしませんでした。彼らは、つねに政治の大権を天皇から授かるという形式をとって政治を行ったのです。

ジョーンズ氏：彼らは、なぜ自分が天皇にならなかったんでしょうね。

鈴木氏：うーん、これはなかなか難しい質問ですね。やはり、皇室の長い伝統と権威がそれほど一般に尊重されていたからではないでしょうか。

ジョーンズ氏：そして明治からはどうなったんですか。

鈴木氏：三権分立の立憲君主制国家が成立したんです。

天皇の正式名

ジョーンズ氏：日本では天皇を何と呼びますか。アメリカでは現職大統領のことを、レーガン大統領と呼んだり、ただレーガンと呼ぶこともあります

ties, with one royal family giving way to another. How long has the present Japanese Imperial Family been reigning?

Mr. S: As far as can be confirmed historically, for about 1,500 years. The present Emperor is the 124th.

Mr. J: It's unusual for a monarchy to survive that long. How was that possible?

Mr. S: It's probably because the emperors almost never became directly involved in political affairs. They remained above the power struggles.

Mr. J: As a practical matter though, how could they maintain their aloofness?

Mr. S: Well, for about two centuries beginning from the seventh century, the emperors actually did govern the country. But from the ninth century up to the time that Emperor Meiji took power, in the latter part of the 19th century, the country was ruled first by the nobility and then by the warrior class. But these rulers didn't try to become emperor themselves. They all claimed to base their governments on the sovereign right they had received from the emperor.

Mr. J: Why didn't they just take the throne for themselves?

Mr. S: That's a hard one to answer. I can only guess that it was out of respect for the long imperial tradition and imperial authority.

Mr. J: What happened after Emperor Meiji took over?

Mr. S: A constitutional monarchy with independent legislative, executive and judiciary branches was established.

Mr. J: How do you refer to your Emperor? In America when we talk about the president we call him by name — President Reagan or sometimes just Reagan.

が……。

鈴木氏：まず天皇家には姓がありません。日本では通常、存命中には天皇を名前では呼ばず、ただ天皇とお呼びします。亡くなったあとで贈り名をつけます。たとえば122代の天皇のお名前は睦仁（むつひと）でしたが、ご即位のときの元号が明治でしたので、いまは明治天皇と呼んでいます。

元号

ジョーンズ夫人：さきほどの元号というのはどんなものですか。

鈴木氏：元号というのは紀年法なんです。この発想は、東南アジア諸国から入ってきたもので、時の政治主権者は、その治世中に年号をつける特権を持っていたんです。日本の最初の元号は7世紀に定められ、いまは、法律によって定められています。現在もこの紀年法を使っているのは日本だけです。

西暦と元号暦

ジョーンズ夫人：たしか日本に来て、1987年と記したカレンダーを見ましたわ。2つのシステムを同時に使っているんですか。

鈴木氏：そのとおりです。

ジョーンズ夫人：ということは、年度を違った表し方で二重に書くということですか。

鈴木氏：いいえ。現在の元号は昭和で、1987年は昭和62年です。一般に国内では昭和を使い、国際関係では西暦を使います。

ジョーンズ夫人：混乱しませんか。

鈴木氏：慣れればそうでもありません。ただ古い年代を相互に換算するときは、やや面倒です。そうしたときには、そのための換算表を使わなければなりません。

Mr. S: First you have to understand that the Emperor has no family name and we almost never use his given name. While the Emperor is alive he's called Tenno, which simply means Emperor. After he dies, he's given a posthumous name. For example, the 122nd Emperor's name was Mutsuhito but he is now called Emperor Meiji because he ascended to the throne in the first year of the Meiji era.

Mrs. J: What do you mean by an era in this case?

Mr. S: It's a way of reckoning years. The idea came from Southeast Asia where the custom was that the political leader of the time had the right to name the years while he was in power. Japan started using the era system in the seventh century and now it's established by law. This is the only country in the world that still uses it.

Mrs. J: But I'm sure I've seen calendars here marked 1987. Are you using two systems at the same time?

Mr. S: Exactly.

Mrs. J: Do you mean you have to write every date twice, in two different ways?

Mr. S: No. The current era is called Showa and this year, 1987, is the 62nd year of Showa. Showa 62. We generally use the year of Showa for things inside the country and the Western calendar for international things.

Mrs. J: Isn't that confusing?

Mr. S: Not when you get used to it. But it's rather troublesome when we have to convert historical dates back and forth. For that we have to use a special table.

1

ノート

I don't think there have been many monarchs.

I don't think ... 「～だと思わない」

日本語では文の内容が否定なのか肯定なのかは、文尾までわからないことが多い。英語では聞き手や読み手に内容が否定なのか肯定なのか早く予期させるために、文の初めで否定・肯定の区別をはっきりさせる習慣がある。

この場合も I think there have not been many monarchs. では不自然な英語になってしまう。

think と同じような使い方をする動詞には believe、expect、feel、imagine、suppose などがある。

2

ノート

It's probably because the Emperors almost never became involved in political affairs.

相手から理由を聞かれて、自信のないときに使える表現。「たぶん～だからだろう」という意味になる。

be[become] involved in ... 「～に巻き込まれる、巻き添えになる」

例文

The minister *was involved in* the scandal.

3

What do you mean by an era in this case?

ノート

「～(by 以下)はどういうこと(意味)ですか」と問う基本的な表現。mean は「～を意味する、つまり～というわけ」という意味で使える便利な語。

例文 1　This is what I *mean by* the practice.　　　　(13)

例文 2　Is that what you *mean*?　　　　(13)

Chapter

8

政治のしくみ
Japanese Government

三権分立が日本の政治の基本です

立法・行政・司法の三権分立制は
明治憲法以来、日本の政治機構の基本となって
いますが、現在の民主的な三権分立は、
1947年に施行された日本国憲法によって
成立しました。

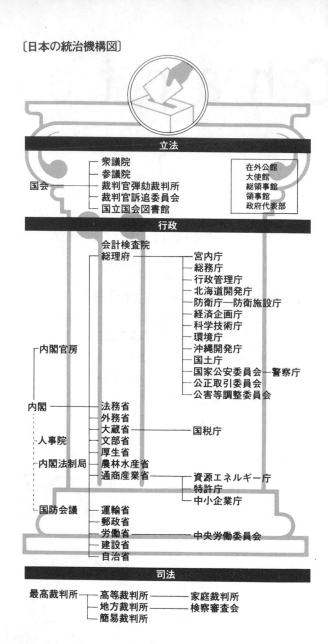

立法

国会 ─┬─ 衆議院
　　　├─ 参議院
　　　├─ 裁判官弾劾裁判所
　　　├─ 裁判官訴追委員会
　　　└─ 国立国会図書館

┌──────────┐
│ 在外公館 │
│ 大使館 │
│ 総領事館 │
│ 領事館 │
│ 政府代表部 │
└──────────┘

行政

　　　　　　　　会計検査院
　　　　　　　　総理府 ─┬─ 宮内庁
　　　　　　　　　　　　├─ 総務庁
　　　　　　　　　　　　├─ 行政管理庁
　　　　　　　　　　　　├─ 北海道開発庁
　　　　　　　　　　　　├─ 防衛庁─防衛施設庁
　　　　　　　　　　　　├─ 経済企画庁
　　　　　　　　　　　　├─ 科学技術庁
　　　　　　　　　　　　├─ 環境庁
　内閣官房　　　　　　　├─ 沖縄開発庁
　　　　　　　　　　　　├─ 国土庁
　　　　　　　　　　　　├─ 国家公安委員会─警察庁
　　　　　　　　　　　　├─ 公正取引委員会
　　　　　　　　　　　　└─ 公害等調整委員会
内閣 ─┬─ 法務省
　　　├─ 外務省
　人事院─ 大蔵省 ──── 国税庁
　　　├─ 文部省
　　　├─ 厚生省
　内閣法制局─ 農林水産省
　　　├─ 通商産業省 ─┬─ 資源エネルギー庁
　　　│　　　　　　　├─ 特許庁
　　　│　　　　　　　└─ 中小企業庁
　国防会議─ 運輸省
　　　├─ 郵政省
　　　├─ 労働省 ──── 中央労働委員会
　　　├─ 建設省
　　　└─ 自治省

司法

最高裁判所 ─┬─ 高等裁判所 ──── 家庭裁判所
　　　　　　├─ 地方裁判所 ──── 検察審査会
　　　　　　└─ 簡易裁判所

8

政治のしくみ

Vocabulary

国会議事堂	☐☐	the National Diet building
首相官邸	☐☐	the Prime Minister's official residence
国会図書館	☐☐	the Diet Library
官庁	☐☐	a government ministry; a government office
立法	☐☐	the legislative branch; legislation
行政	☐☐	the administrative branch; administration
司法	☐☐	the judiciary branch; judicature
衆議院	☐☐	the House of Representatives
参議院	☐☐	the House of Councilors
内閣総理大臣を指名する	☐☐	to choose the Prime Minister
解任する	☐☐	to dismiss
閣僚	☐☐	the Cabinet Members
最高裁判所長官	☐☐	the Chief Judge of the Supreme Court
法律の違憲審査をする	☐☐	to rule on the constitutionality of laws
被選挙権	☐☐	qualification for election
都道府県知事	☐☐	prefectural governors
政党	☐☐	a political party
与党	☐☐	the party in power
野党	☐☐	the parties out of power
自由民主党	☐☐	the Liberal Democratic Party
日本社会党	☐☐	the Japan Socialist Party
公明党	☐☐	the Komeito
民社党	☐☐	the Democratic Socialist Party
日本共産党	☐☐	the Japan Communist Party
社会民主連合	☐☐	the Social Democratic Federation
海外に派兵する	☐☐	to send troops overseas
自衛隊	☐☐	the Self-Defense Forces
徴兵制度	☐☐	conscription; a draft system
志願制度	☐☐	a volunteer system
原爆被爆国	☐☐	a country hit by nuclear bombs

8

Japanese Government

三権分立が日本の政治の基本です

統治機構・選挙権・政党・自衛隊

国会議事堂 ジョーンズ氏：先週、桜田門辺りを歩いていたら、国会議事堂が見えました。たいへん特徴のある建物ですね。

鈴木氏：そうです。あの建物は1936年に建てられたものです。あの周辺は永田町という地区です。首相官邸、国会図書館などがあります。隣接する地区は霞が関で、外務省、通産省など多くの官庁の建物が並んでいる所です。

霞が関官庁街

ジョーンズ氏：そうしますと、あの地区は日本の政治の中枢部ですね。

鈴木氏：そのとおりです。

日本の統治機構 ジョーンズ氏：日本の統治機構はどのようになっているのですか。

三権分立 鈴木氏：それは、立法・行政・司法の完全三権分立制をとっています。立法権は国会にあります。国会は衆議院と参議院の二院制です。国会議員はすべて直接選挙で選ばれます。

国会の構成

内閣総理大臣の指名 ジョーンズ氏：日本の首相は、どのようにして決めるのですか。

鈴木氏：国会が指名します。国会はまた内閣不信任案の議決によって首相と閣僚を解任できます。

ジョーンズ氏：ほかの閣僚はだれが任命するのですか。閣僚は何人くらいいるのですか。

閣僚の任免 鈴木氏：閣僚は20名くらいいます。閣僚の任免は首相が行います。

内閣の権能 ジョーンズ氏：すると国会は内閣を解散できるんで

C h a p t e r 8

Mr. Jones: Last week when we were around Sakuradamon I got a look at the National Diet building. It's an unusual looking structure.

Mr. Suzuki: Yes, it is. It was built in 1936. That part of Tokyo is the Nagatacho district. The Prime Minister's official residence and the Diet Library are also located there. The neighboring district is Kasumigaseki. That's where many government ministries are —the Foreign Ministry, the Ministry of International Trade and Industry . . .

Mr. J: Then, the two areas account for a fair part of the Japanese government, don't they?

Mr. S: They do.

Mr. J: What is the organizational structure of the Japanese government?

Mr. S: There are three independent branches, the legislative, the administrative and the judiciary. The legislative branch is the Diet. It has the House of Representatives and the House of Councilors. All Diet members are directly elected.

Mr. J: How about the Prime Minister? How is he chosen?

Mr. S: By the Diet. The Diet can also dismiss the Prime Minister and the other Cabinet members through a vote of non-confidence.

Mr. J: Who appoints the other Cabinet members? And how many are there?

Mr. S: There are about 20. The Prime Minister chooses and dismisses them.

Mr. J: So the Diet can dismiss the Cabinet. Does it work the

すね。その反対もできるのですか。

国会解散権

鈴木氏：そうです。内閣は衆議院を解散することが
できます。実際には首相が行います。内閣の代表
ですからね。首相が解散すると、総選挙が行われ、
新しい内閣が組閣されます。

**裁判官の
任命**

ジョーンズ氏：裁判官はだれが任命するのですか。

鈴木氏：最高裁判所の長官は内閣の指名に基づいて
天皇が任命します。そのほかの裁判官は内閣が任
命します。

**司法権の
独立**

ジョーンズ氏：裁判所には、どういう権限があるの
ですか。

**法令違憲
審査権**

鈴木氏：裁判所の権限のひとつは、一切の法律命令
が憲法に違反していないかどうかを審査すること
です。

ジョーンズ氏：三権分立というと、欧米自由主義諸
国のそれと基本的には同じですね。日本では選挙
権は何歳からあるんですか。

選挙権

鈴木氏：20歳以上の国民は全員選挙権を持っていま
すが、被選挙権は25歳以上の国民が持っています。
参議院議員と都道府県知事については、最低年齢
は30歳です。

政党

ジョーンズ氏：新聞で読んだんですが、日本には政
党があるんですね。

鈴木氏：ええいくつかあります。国会議員の大部分
は政党に所属しています。しかし、少数ですが、
どの政党にも属さない者もいます。

ジョーンズ氏：私は与党の自由民主党の名前しか知
らないんです。

鈴木氏：そのほかのおもな政党としては、社会党、
公明党、民社党、共産党、社会民主連合などがあ
ります。

日本の軍備

ジョーンズ氏：前々からお聞きしようと思っていた

other way around too?

Mr. S: Yes, the Cabinet can dissolve the House of Representatives. Actually it's the Prime Minister who does it since he's the head of the Cabinet. If he does, there are general elections and a new government is formed.

Mr. J: Who appoints the judges?

Mr. S: The Chief Judge of the Supreme Court is designated by the Cabinet and appointed by the Emperor. All the others are appointed by the Cabinet.

Mr. J: What powers do the courts have?

Mr. S: Well, one of their main powers is to rule on the constitutionality of laws and orders.

Mr. J: Then when you say there are three independent branches of government, it means basically what it does in the West. What is the voting age?

Mr. S: Anyone over 20 can vote. To qualify for election to public office, a person has to be a Japanese citizen and at least 25 years old. For members of the House of Councilors and prefectural governors, the minimum age is 30.

Mr. J: From reading the papers, I know you have political parties.

Mr. S: Oh, several. Most Diet members belong to a party. There are also a few independents though.

Mr. J: I only know the name of the party that's in power — the Liberal Democratic Party.

Mr. S: The other major ones are the Socialist Party, the Komeito, the Democratic Socialist Party, the Communist Party and the Social Democratic Federation.

Mr. J: There's one thing I've been meaning to ask. Japan be-

ことがあるんです。日本は国際連合に加盟しているのに、軍隊を海外に派遣したというのを聞いたことがありません。どうしてですか。

● 専守防衛
体制

鈴木氏：日本は、憲法によって、国際紛争解決のために戦争に訴えることを放棄しているからです。したがって、もっぱら自衛を目的とした行動以外には軍事力を行使できないんです。ですから「軍隊」という言葉自体も使っていないんです。自衛隊といっているんです。

ジョーンズ氏：徴兵制度はありますか。

● 志願制
軍備慎重論

鈴木氏：いいえ、すべて志願制度によっています。日本の国民は軍備に対してひじょうにデリケートなんです。日本は世界唯一の被爆国で、第二次世界大戦で苦い経験をしていますのでね。

日本語と英語の狭間で ❹	**日米なまえくらべ**

日本人の姓(名字)は、約3万まで確認されているといわれているが、学者によっては6万から12万という説もあり、正確にはつかみにくい。

日本人に多い姓のベスト3は、鈴木、佐藤、田中で、いずれも第2次大戦後の内閣総理大臣に、この姓の人がいる。

日本で多い姓の上位20は、次のようになる。

1位	鈴木	8位	中村	14位	井上
2位	佐藤	9位	伊藤	14位	木村
3位	田中	10位	斎藤	17位	清水
4位	山本	10位	加藤	17位	松本
5位	渡辺	12位	山田	17位	林
6位	高橋	13位	吉田	17位	山口
7位	小林	14位	佐々木		

8

政治のしくみ

92

longs to the UN but I've never heard of it sending any troops to join the UN forces. Why's that?

Mr. S: Our constitution says Japan can't use war as a way of settling disputes. So our military isn't allowed to do anything that's not strictly for self-defense. Even the word "military" isn't used. It's called the Self-Defense Force.

Mr. J: Do you have a draft?

Mr. S: No, it's a volunteer force. The Japanese people are very sensitive about building military power. We are the only country to have been hit by nuclear bombs and we have some pretty bitter memories of the Second World War.

ちなみに、アメリカで多い姓を挙げると次のとおりである。

1位	Smith	11位	Harris(on)
2位	Johnson	12位	Taylor
3位	Williams(on)	13位	Moore
4位	Brown	14位	Thomas
5位	Jones	15位	White
6位	Miller	16位	Thompson
7位	Davis	17位	Jackson
8位	Martin(ez),(son)	18位	Clark
9位	Anders(on)	19位	Robert(s),(son)
10位	Wilson	20位	Lewis

Column

初代 Washington から、40代 Reagan までの歴代大統領のうち、上記の姓の大統領は、Johnson と Taylor が各2名ずつ、Wilson、Harrison、Jackson が各1名ずついる。

Useful Expressions ———— 8

1

The two areas <u>account for</u> a fair part of the Japanese government.

ノート

A accounts for B は、「A は B を説明している（＝ explain）、A を見れば B がわかる、A はまさに B である」の意味。

例文

These companies *account for* less than 30% of all workers. (16)

2

<u>How about</u> the Prime Minister?

ノート

「～はいかが［どう］ですか」幅広く使える表現
☞Useful Expressions 3-1

例文 1 *How about* television? (20)

例文 2 *How about* in Japan? (21)

3

<u>There's one thing</u> I've been <u>meaning to</u> ask.

ノート

mean to ＝ have in mind as an intention or purpose「～するつもりである」

例文 *There are some things* that do not appeal to me.

4

The Japanese people <u>are</u> very <u>sensitive about</u> building military power.

ノート

be sensitive *about* ... は「～を気にする」の意味。「外からの刺激に感じやすい、～に傷つきやすい」という意味のときには be sensitive *to* ... を使う。

例文 1 He *is sensitive to* cold.「彼は寒がりだ」

例文 2 She *is sensitive about* her frizzy hair.
「ちぢれ毛を気にしている」

Chapter
9

国名と国歌
The Name of the Country and the National Anthem

日本は「日出づるところ」

「日本」のことを
「ニホン」という人もいれば
「ニッポン」という人もいます。
外国人にどちらが正しいかと聞かれたら、
どう答えますか。

〔日本の国歌〕

Vocabulary

ニッポンと呼ばれる	☐☐	to be referred to as "Nippon"
聖徳太子	☐☐	Prince Shotoku
日出づるところ	☐☐	the place from where the sun rises
マルコ・ポーロ	☐☐	Marco Polo
国旗	☐☐	the national flag
制定する	☐☐	to designate (formally)
国章	☐☐	the national emblem
16弁の菊の花	☐☐	a sixteen-petaled chrysanthemum
桐のマーク	☐☐	a mark of a paulownia leaf and flower
皇室の紋章	☐☐	the Imperial Crests; the crests of the Imperial House
日本の国歌	☐☐	the Japanese National Anthem
天皇の御世	☐☐	the reign of the Emperor

〔各国の国歌〕

アメリカ合衆国	●The Star-Spangled Banner（星条旗よ永遠に） 　1814年、米英戦争のとき、アメリカの弁護士フランシス・スコット・キーが、マックヘンリーの要塞に翻る星条旗を見て作詞。曲は当時流行していた18世紀のイギリスの乾杯歌の旋律（J·S·スミスの作曲といわれる）を流用。1931年3月、正式に国歌に選定された。
イギリス	●God Save the Queen [King]（神よ女王[王]を守りたまえ） 　詩人兼音楽家のヘンリー・ケアリーが1743年に作ったといわれるが確証はない。1745年、コベント・ガーデンなどの劇場で歌われ、以来国歌として広く親しまれている。19世紀には、約20カ国の国歌の旋律に用いられた。
フランス	●La Marseillaise（ラ・マルセイエーズ） 　1792年、フランス義勇軍の工兵大尉ド・リールが作詞・作曲した。同年7月、マルセイユの義勇兵大隊が、この歌を歌いながらパリに入ったところから、この名で呼ばれるようになった。1795年、国歌として制定された。
ドイツ連邦共和国 （西ドイツ）	●Einigkeit und Recht und Freiheit（統一と権利と自由） 　ハイドンが作曲した、かつてのオーストリア国歌の旋律が用いられている。これが1922年から『世界に冠たるドイツ』という歌詞で国歌となり、第二次世界大戦後、その第3節「統一と権利と自由」のみを正式に国歌として制定した。

9

The Name of the Country and the National Anthem

千代に八千代に	□□ for a thousand, nay, eight thousand generations
こけ	□□ moss
国花	□□ the national flower
桜	□□ *sakura*; cherry blossoms
満開の桜	□□ cherry blossoms at their peak
神話	□□ a myth
散る	□□ to lose their petals
潔さ	□□ resignation (without reluctance)
気品	□□ grace
高く評価する	□□ to rate highly
酒宴を開く	□□ to have a *sake*-drinking party
～になじみの深い花	□□ the flower close to the heart of . . .

日本は「日出づるところ」

国名の由来・国旗・国歌の意味・国花

●国名　ジョーンズ氏：鈴木さん、日本の方の話を聞いていますと、日本のことを「ニッポン」といったり「ニホン」といったりしていますね。どちらが正しいのですか。

鈴木氏：両方とも同じように使われているのですが、単独で使う場合は「ニッポン」を使うことが多いようです。たとえば、東京オリンピックでは、日本を呼ぶ場合、「ニッポン」を使いました。

●国名の由来　ジョーンズ氏：日本の国名はどこから出てきたのですか。

鈴木氏：日本という呼び方になったのは、7世紀ではないかといわれています。両方の呼び方とも「日出づるところ」という意味で、聖徳太子が中国に送った国書に、自分の国のことをそう表現しているところから、とったとされています。

●ジャパン　ジョーンズ氏：ところで、日本がどうして「ジャパン」になったんですかね。

鈴木氏：それには、2つ説があるようですよ。ひとつは、むかし、中国北部地方では、日本国のことを、Jihpênkuo と呼んでいたんですが、それをポルトガル人が Zipangu または Jipangu と聞いたというのです。

ジョーンズ氏：そういえば、マルコ・ポーロの本では Zipangu と紹介していますね。

鈴木氏：そうですね。もうひとつの説は、中国南部地方で、日本のことを Yatpun というのを、オランダ人が、Japan と聞いたという説です。

●国旗　ジョーンズ氏：日本の国旗の赤丸は太陽を表してい

C h a p t e r 9

Mr. Jones: Several times I've heard Japan referred to as both "Nippon" and "Nihon." I was wondering which is more correct.

Mr. Suzuki: They are both used the same way, but "Nippon" is more common. At the Tokyo Olympiad, for example, the name used was "Nippon."

Mr. J: Where did the names come from?

Mr. S: They say they first came into use around the seventh century. Both names mean "place from where the sun rises," which is the way Prince Shotoku referred to his country in a letter he sent to China.

Mr. J: How did the name "Japan" come into use?

Mr. S: There are two theories. One is that Japan was called "Jihpênkuo" in northern China and the Portuguese corrupted this to "Zipangu" and "Jipangu."

Mr. J: Yes, I remember. The book of Marco Polo refers to Japan as "Zipangu."

Mr. S: That's right. The other theory is that "Japan" is the Dutch way of pronouncing "Yatpun," the name for Japan used in southern China.

Mr. J: I know the red circle in your flag represents the sun.

るんですね。旗の意味と歴史をもうすこし教えていただけませんか。

鈴木氏：日本の国旗は、「日章旗」とも、「日の丸」ともいいます。両方とも「朝日の旗」という意味です。初めの頃のことはあまりはっきりしません。

国旗の起源

むかしは神社の旗として使われていました。16世紀になって、日本を表す旗として船に掲げられ、1870年に商船に掲げる国旗として制定されました。

国章

ジョーンズ氏：アメリカの国章はワシですが、日本にも国章がありますか。

鈴木氏：公式には日本には国章がないんですが、国章の代わりに2つの皇室のマークが使われることがよくあります。ひとつは16弁の菊の花、もうひとつは桐のマークです。これは、日本人でも誤解している人が多くて、菊や桐のご紋章が国章だと思っていますが、そうではないんです。あれは皇室のご紋なのです。

国歌

ジョーンズ氏：オリンピックで、日本の国歌を聞きました。なかなか落ち着いた曲ですね。

鈴木氏：曲は、100年くらい前に作曲されたものですが、歌詞は1,000年以上も前の作品です。歌詞は、『古今和歌集』という古い歌集にある歌なんですが、作者は不明です。

国歌の意味

ジョーンズ氏：歌はどんな内容なのですか。

鈴木氏：「天皇の御世は、千代に八千代も続くように。小さな小石が岩になって、それにコケが生えるほど先まで永遠に続くように」という意味です。

ジョーンズ氏：小石が岩になるという考え方は面白いですね。

鈴木氏：むかしの人は、岩は小石や砂が長年かかっ

Could you tell me anything else about the meaning and history of the flag?

Mr. S: We call it the "Nisshoki" or the "Hi no Maru." Both mean "the flag of the rising sun." The origin is not certain. In the beginning the design was used on shrine flags and banners. It was first used as a flag showing the nationality of Japanese ships in the 16th century, and was formally designated as the national flag for use on merchant ships in 1870.

Mr. J: Do you have a national emblem — like the American eagle?

Mr. S: Not officially, but two Imperial Crests are often used for this purpose. One is a 16-petaled chrysanthemum and the other a mark consisting of a paulownia leaf and flower. Quite a few Japanese think these are national emblems, but they're not. They're crests of the Imperial House.

Mr. J: I heard the Japanese National Anthem at the Olympics. It's very solemn sounding.

Mr. S: The melody was written about 100 years ago but the words are more than 1,000 years old. They come from an ancient collection of poems called the *Kokinwakashu*. The poet's name is unknown.

Mr. J: What do they say?

Mr. S: It goes: "May the reign of the Emperor continue for 1,000 nay, 8,000 generations and for the eternity that it takes for small pebbles to grow into a great rock and become covered with moss."

Mr. J: Pebbles growing into a great rock is a curious thought.

Mr. S: Back in those days, they thought that big boulders were

て固まってできると、信じていたのでしょうね。

ジョーンズ氏：アメリカ合衆国の国花はバラです。日本を代表する花はたぶん桜でしょう。

鈴木氏：そのとおりです。日本中どこにでも桜の名所があります。桜は日本の神話にも出てきます。およそ1週間で散ってしまいますので、死に赴くさいの散り方の潔さと気品の象徴として、むかしは武士階級に受けとられていたのです。この資質が武士に高く評価されたんです。いまでも満開の桜の花の下で酒宴を開いて花見を楽しみますし、現代日本人の心にも桜はいちばんなじみ深い花です。

ことわる理由

相手からの誘いを断る場合、日本人の間では、たとえば「ちょっと忙しいので」といった理由では、なかなか通用しない。このていどの理由だと、忙しさの内容を問いただされて、重ねて誘いをかけられる。

誘いをかけている人は、そうすることによって、熱心に誘っていることを相手に示そうとするし、誘われている人も、そうされることにさして抵抗を感じない。それればかりか、そうなることを予測して、最初から相手が納得するような理由を、あれこれとつける。

その反面、「残念ながら行けません」という断りの言葉をはっきりいわずに、こちらの気持ちを相手に察して

formed by little stones sticking together over the years.

Mr. J: The American national flower is the rose. I'll bet Japan's national flower is the cherry blossom.

Mr. S: Right. There are many places where the cherry blossoms are extremely beautiful throughout Japan. They appear in many Japanese myths. The blossoms lose their petals within a week and this was interpreted by the old warrior class as symbolic of resignation and grace in death. These were qualities that the warriors rated highly. Today we like to enjoy the cherry blossoms by having a *sake*-drinking party under a tree in full bloom. No flower is closer to the heart of the Japanese.

もらおうとすることが多い。

欧米人の場合には、断りの理由は、漠然とやんわりいうことも多いが、断りの言葉は、はっきりと表現する。しかし、理由についてさらに詮索するのは、プライバシーの侵害になるので慎まなければならない。

日本人は、個人的な都合を断る理由に挙げると、自分勝手で相手に対する配慮に欠けると受けとられてしまうおそれがあるので、たとえば仕事上のことなど、別の事柄を理由にする場合が多い。

しかし仕事と私生活を明確に区別する欧米人の場合には、「妻と先約があるので」とか、「毎週楽しみにしているテレビ放送を見たいから」などが、誘いを断る理由であることがよくある。こうした発想の違いを、じゅうぶんに心得ておく必要がある。

Column

1 Where did the names <u>come from</u>?

2 They <u>come from</u> an ancient collection of poems called the *Kokinwakashu*.

ノート come from ... は（1）「～の出身である、（出所・起源が）～である」（2）「～の結果である」の意味。

例文 Japanese writing *came from* China. (25)

3 <u>Could you</u> tell me anything else about the meaning and history of the flag?

ノート Can you tell me ...? だと、相手に能力があるかないか尋ねる意味合いが強く、場合によっては失礼な質問になってしまう。Could you ...? は「もしできれば」という気持ちがこもっているので、やわらかい表現になる。☞Useful Expressions 13-1

例文 *Could you* tell me a little about how you season your food? (36)

4 <u>Quite a few</u> Japanese think these are national emblems.

ノート quite a few は「かなりたくさんの」（＝fairly large number of）という意味のアメリカ口語用法。☞Useful Expressions 4-2

例文 *Quite a few* students have bicycles.

5 <u>I'll bet</u> Japan's national flower is the cherry blossom.

ノート I('ll) bet ... ＝I'm sure ... 「きっと～だ」

例文 *I'll bet* you're excited to be going home.

Chapter
10

日本経済の発展
Development of the Japanese Economy

高度経済成長を可能にした要因は……

現在、日本は
自由主義国のなかでGNP第2位の
位置を占めています。
戦後、めざましい経済成長を遂げ
経済大国となった日本は、
いろいろな意味で世界中の関心を集めています。

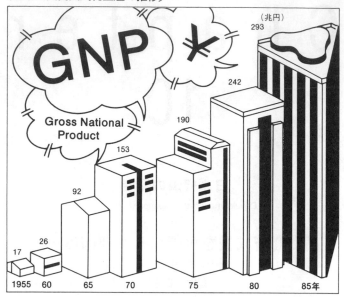

〔日本の実質国民総生産の推移〕

(兆円)

293
242
190
153
92
26
17

1955　60　65　70　75　80　85年

Vocabulary ●

自由経済社会（世界の）	□□	world's free economy
経済大国	□□	the world's strongest economic powers
復興期	□□	a recovery period
高度成長期	□□	a high-growth period
安定成長期	□□	a stable-growth period
食糧難	□□	food shortages
占領軍	□□	the occupation forces
企業家精神旺盛な　経営者	□□	a highly motivated entrepreneur
自営農	□□	an owner farmer
勤労意欲のある	□□	to have incentive to work
労働組合	□□	a labor union
合法化	□□	legalization
傾斜生産方式	□□	a priority production system
A を B に集中的に　投入する	□□	to concentrate A on B

〔輸出入額の日米比較〕

	輸出額 (100万ドル)		輸入額 (100万ドル)	
	日本	アメリカ	日本	アメリカ
1980	129,807	220,630	140,528	244,871
1982	138,831	212,193	131,931	254,885
1984	170,114	218,723	136,503	346,364
1986	209,151	216,629	126,408	382,964

10

Development of the Japanese Economy

財政引き締め(政策)	☐☐ a fiscal retrenchment policy
金融引き締め(政策)	☐☐ a tight-money policy
朝鮮動乱の特需	☐☐ the increased demand generated by the Korean War
実質成長率	☐☐ the real rate of growth
消費者物価	☐☐ consumer prices
卸売物価	☐☐ wholesale prices
公害	☐☐ pollution
輸出市場の拡大	☐☐ expanding export markets
(国民的)合言葉	☐☐ a (national) motto
「追いつき追い越せ」	☐☐ "Catch up with and overtake."
発展途上国	☐☐ a developing country
先進国	☐☐ an advanced country
第1次石油危機	☐☐ the first oil crisis
円高	☐☐ the rise in the value of the yen
貿易摩擦	☐☐ trade tension; trade friction

高度経済成長を可能にした要因は…

戦後の日本経済・高度成長・石油危機・円高

ジョーンズ氏：日本は世界の自由経済社会のなかで、現在も GNP 第2位を保っていますね。日本の戦後の発展について、すこしご説明いただけますか。日本はどうやって戦後の荒廃から経済大国へと成長してきたのですか。

- **戦後日本経済の動き**

鈴木氏：戦後の日本経済の動きは、大きく3つの時期に分けられると思います。まず、1945年から50年代前半までの復興期、ついで 50年代から60年代までの高度成長期、そして70年代後の安定成長期です。

- **終戦直後の日本経済**

ジョーンズ氏：終戦直後の日本経済はどんな状況だったのですか。

鈴木氏：鉱工業生産は、1941年の水準のわずか7分の1に低下し、厳しい食糧難とインフレーションに悩まされていました。

ジョーンズ氏：そうした経済を立て直すために、どのような経済政策がとられたのですか。

鈴木氏：占領軍は、財閥を解体し、農地制度を改革し、労働権を労働者に与えたのです。これらの3つの政策が、戦後の日本経済の発展の基盤になりました。

ジョーンズ氏：それによって、日本の経済はどのように変革したのですか。

- **財閥の解体**

- **農地制度の改革**

鈴木氏：まず、財閥の解体によって、新しい世代の企業家精神旺盛な経営者が現れ、競争も活発になりました。また、農地制度の改革によって、農民は自作農になりました。そのため農民の勤労意欲

C h a p t e r 10

Mr. Jones: Japan has the second largest GNP among the world's free economies, doesn't it? Would you mind telling me something about Japan's postwar development? How it grew out of the ashes of the war to become one of the world's strongest economic powers?

Mr. Suzuki: I think you can divide Japan's postwar economic development into three periods: the recovery period between 1945 and the early 1950s, the high-growth period from the 50s through the 60s, and the stable-growth period from the 70s on.

Mr. J: What was the economic situation just after the war?

Mr. S: Production in the mining and manufacturing industries had fallen to one-seventh of the 1941 level, and there were severe food shortages and high inflation.

Mr. J: What economic policies were implemented to get the economy moving again?

Mr. S: The occupation forces dissolved the financial cliques called the *zaibatsu*, reformed the agricultural land ownership system, and gave rights to the workers. These three policies set the framework for Japan's postwar economic development.

Mr. J: How did this change the Japanese economy?

Mr. S: Dissolution of the zaibatsu gave rise to a new generation of highly motivated entrepreneurs and stimulated competition. The agricultural land reform made the farmers their own bosses. They therefore had more incentive to work and

労働権の
確立

も高まり、農業の近代化が進みました。そして、労働権の確立については、労働組合の合法化が大きな点で、これによって労使関係安定の基盤ができました。

ジョーンズ氏：資材や資金が不足していたはずですが、どんな対応をしていたのですか。

傾斜生産

鈴木氏：1947年から、「傾斜生産方式」を実施したんです。これによって、石炭と鉄鋼の生産に資材・労働・資金を集中的に投入することになったんです。この2つのものが、経済全体が必要としている資材の2大基礎素材と考えられていたからです。その後、1949年に連合国軍は、いわゆる「ドッジライン」という厳しい財政・金融引き締めの方針を設定しました。それによって、日本の経済は深刻なデフレに落ち込みました。これから立ち直るきっかけになったのは、1950年に始まった朝鮮動乱による特需です。

朝鮮動乱の
特需

ジョーンズ氏：なるほど、そして日本経済はいよいよ高度成長期に入るわけですね。

高度成長期

鈴木氏：そのとおりです。1955年から60年代にかけて、実質平均成長率は、ほぼ10％になりました。77年には、日本のGNPは、ついに自由経済社会で世界第2位に躍進しました。一方、その代償として消費者物価はたえず上昇し、公害問題などが起こってきたのです。

高度成長の
要因

ジョーンズ氏：日本経済がそんなに高度成長した原因は何なのですか。

鈴木氏：それには意見がいろいろあります。私なりに要約しますと、

（1）各企業の積極的な新技術と設備導入

（2）教育水準の高い、豊富な労働力

（3）資源・エネルギーの大量輸入

modernize their farms. A major point in the establishment of rights for the labor force was the legalization of labor unions, and this helped lay a solid foundation for labor-management relations.

Mr. J: There must have been shortages of materials and funds. What was done about this?

Mr. S: A "priority production system" was implemented in 1947. This concentrated materials, manpower and funds on coal and steel production since these were considered to be two primary sources of material required by the economy as a whole. Then in 1949, the Allied Powers instituted a stringent fiscal retrenchment and tight-money policy that came to be known as the Dodge Line. This sent the economy into a bad deflationary spiral. What brought it out of this was the increased demand generated by the Korean War from 1950.

Mr. J: And that started the economy on its way to the period of high growth?

Mr. S: Right. The real rate of growth from 1955 into the 60s averaged around ten percent a year, and by 1977 Japan's GNP had become the second largest among the free economies. But the price for this was constantly higher consumer prices and pollution.

Mr. J: How do you explain this rapid expansion of the economy?

Mr. S: There are various opinions about that, but in my view the main factors were: one, the positive attitude companies took regarding the introduction of new technology and equipment; two, the large number of relatively well educated workers that were available; three, access to large quantities

（4）輸出市場の拡大

（5）政治や社会の安定および労使関係の安定

（6）小さな防衛費

などになります。

ジョーンズ氏：それに、日本人の勤勉さも要因になっていませんか。

鈴木氏：「先進国に追いつき追い越せ」を合言葉に国民全体が団結して努力してきたことも事実です。

• 安定成長

ジョーンズ氏：その後、日本経済が高度成長を維持できなかったのは、なぜなんですか。

鈴木氏：ひとつは、1949年以降続いた1ドル360円の固定為替レートが廃止されたことです。円は

• 変動相場制

石油危機

いったん切り上げられ、その後、変動相場制に移行しました。さらに、73年の第1次石油危機によって原油価格が40％も上がり、続いて各種輸入原材料も値上がりしました。その結果、1975年から1984年の10年間、日本経済の実質平均成長率は約4％に低下したんです。

• 円高

ジョーンズ氏：最近の円高で、私たちにも現実に日本のホテル代や物価が、ドル価に直すと、とても高く感じられます。

鈴木氏：そうでしょうね。あまりに急激な円高と最近の貿易摩擦の緊迫化によって、とくに輸出産業は、生き残るための対応に苦慮しているのが現状です。

of foreign raw materials and energy resources; four, expanding export markets; five, political and social stability, and good labor-management relations; and six, low spending on national defense.

Mr. J: Don't you think the fact that the Japanese are hard-working was also a factor?

Mr. S: Well, it is true that the people united and made it a national motto to "Catch up with and overtake the advanced countries."

Mr. J: Why couldn't Japan sustain the rapid growth?

Mr. S: One reason was the abandonment of the fixed exchange rate of 360 yen to the dollar that had been in effect since 1949. The yen was first upwardly revalued and then floated. Another was the first oil crisis in 1973, which kicked the price of crude up 40 percent and caused the price of nearly all imported materials to go up. Together, these factors pushed the average rate of real economic growth down to four percent a year for the ten-year period from 1975 to 1984.

Mr. J: With the recent rise in the value of the yen, we feel that hotel rates and other prices are very high here when we translate them into dollars.

Mr. S: I can imagine. The abrupt rise of the yen and the recent trade tensions are making many Japanese companies fight for their lives, especially those that depend a lot on exports.

Useful Expressions ———— 10

1

ノート

Japan has <u>the second largest</u> GNP among the world's free economies.

second、third などに最上級をつけて、「2番目に大きな〜、3番目に大きな〜」を表す。☞Useful Expressions 26-1

例文

Los Angeles is *the second largest* city in the United States.

2

ノート

<u>Would you mind</u> <u>telling</u> me something about Japan's postwar development?

「〜していただけませんか」という丁寧な表現。mind は「いやがる、迷惑に思う」の意なので、結構だというさいの答えは、Certainly *not*.／Of course *not*.／*Not* at all. などを使う。☞Useful Expressions 13-1

3

ノート

<u>How</u> did Japan <u>grow out of</u> the ashes of war?

この章には How …? を使った表現がいくつか出てくる。よく比較して使い慣れておきたい。

例文1

How did this *change* the Japanese economy?

例文2

How did you *cope with* the shortages of materials and funds?

4

ノート

There are <u>various opinions about that, but in my view</u> the main factors were: one …

自分の意見を述べるさいの、ひとつの典型的な型。in my view は「私の考えでは」☞ Useful Expressions 12-1

Chapter

11

産業構造の変化

Changes in the Industrial Structure

資源小国日本を揺さぶった石油危機

高度成長を続けた日本経済に
冷や水を浴びせたのが、
1973年に始まる石油危機でした。
その後、日本経済は安定成長へと移行し、
産業構造が変化し始めます。

〔日本の就業人口割合の推移〕

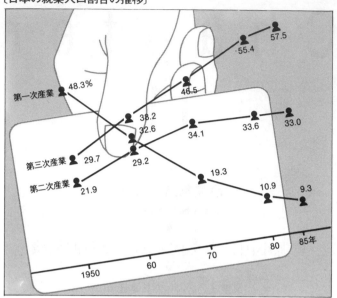

第一次産業　48.3%
第三次産業　29.7
第二次産業　21.9

38.2
32.6
29.2

46.5
34.1

55.4
33.6
19.3

57.5
33.0
10.9
9.3

1950　60　70　80　85年

Vocabulary

高度成長型	☐☐	a high growth rate type
安定成長型	☐☐	a low growth rate type
就業構造	☐☐	an employment structure
製造業	☐☐	a manufacturing sector
建設業	☐☐	a construction sector
サービス産業	☐☐	a service sector
情報関連産業	☐☐	an information-related sector
基礎素材	☐☐	basic materials
加工組立産業	☐☐	an assembly sector
精密機械	☐☐	precision machinery
生産指数	☐☐	the production index
石油消費量を節約する	☐☐	to reduce oil consumption; to cut back on oil consumption
省エネルギー型設備	☐☐	energy-saving equipment
ロボット	☐☐	a robot
NC工作機械	☐☐	a numerical control machine

〔各国の産業別就業人口割合〕

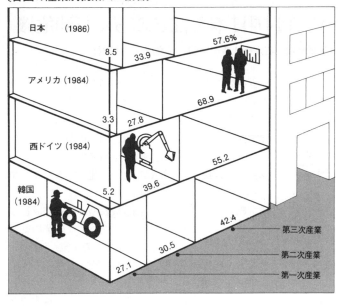

日本　（1986）　8.5　33.9　57.6%

アメリカ（1984）　3.3　27.8　68.9

西ドイツ（1984）　5.2　39.6　55.2

韓国（1984）　27.1　30.5　42.4

第三次産業
第二次産業
第一次産業

生き残りが～にかかっている	☐☐	survival depends on . . .
（企業の）買収	☐☐	acquisition
合併	☐☐	merger
金融	☐☐	financc
保険	☐☐	insurance
不動産	☐☐	real estate
先端技術	☐☐	high-tech
新素材	☐☐	new materials
セラミック	☐☐	ceramics
炭素繊維	☐☐	carbon fiber
アモルファス金属	☐☐	amorphous metals
バイオテクノロジー	☐☐	biotechnology
医療薬品	☐☐	pharmaceuticals
光ファイバー	☐☐	optical fiber
光通信	☐☐	optical communication

資源小国日本を揺さぶった石油危機

石油危機・石油輸入量の削減・貿易摩擦・新素材

・産業構造の
変化

ジョーンズ氏：戦後の日本経済の奇跡はよく知られ
ていますが、その後産業構造が大きく変化してき
ていると聞いています。いつごろからなのですか。

鈴木氏：大きく変わったのは、1973年から74年にか
けての第1次石油危機以後からです。

・石油危機

ジョーンズ氏：全体的にはどう変化してきたんです
か。

鈴木氏：簡単にいうと、高度成長型から安定成長型
へ変わったことになります。全体的な産業の就業
構造で見ますと、農業・漁業などの産業が減少し、
工業・建築業などの産業の伸びが小さくなり、情
報関連産業を中心としたサービス産業が急成長し
始めた、といってよいでしょう。一方、日本でと
くに重要なのは、製造業の構造の変化なのです。

・製造業

ジョーンズ氏：それはどういった変化なんですか。

・基礎素材
産業
加工組立
産業

鈴木氏：鉄鋼・セメント・化学などの基礎素材産業
と電気機器・自動車・精密機械などの加工組立産
業とを比較しますと、1973年から1975年以前には、
生産指数はそんなに差はなかったんです。

ジョーンズ氏：ではその後、その差が大きく開いた
というんですね。

鈴木氏：そのとおりなんです。1982年までには加工
組立産業は、1975年の水準の2倍強も成長したの
です。とくに、電気機器産業と自動車産業の構成

C h a p t e r 11

Mr. Jones: Japan's postwar economic miracle is well known, but I hear it was followed by drastic changes in the industrial structure. When did these changes begin?

Mr. Suzuki: The major ones started after the first oil crisis, between 1973 and 1974.

Mr. J: What was the general pattern of these changes?

Mr. S: Simply stated, it was a shift from a high to a low growth rate economy. Looked at from the overall employment structure, it meant fewer people engaged in farming and fishing, a slowdown in the rate of growth in employment in the manufacturing and construction sector, and the start of an upswing in the number of people in the service sector, especially the information-related areas. A particularly important aspect was the structural changes within the production sector.

Mr. J: What were those?

Mr. S: If you compare the basic material sectors like steel, cement and chemicals with the processing and assembly sectors like electrical equipment, automobiles and precision machinery, you'll find that the difference between the production indexes of the two sectors was fairly small up to the 1973 to 1975 period.

Mr. J: And it grew larger after that?

Mr. S: That's right. By 1982, the processing and assembly sector had grown to more than twice its 1975 level. The share of total production accounted for by the electrical equipment

比率が製造業のなかで急速に伸びました。

ジョーンズ氏：2倍以上も成長したのですか。その原因は何なのですか。

鈴木氏：その原因はいくつかあります。日本には天然資源がほとんどありません。人間を除けば、ミカンと温泉くらいしかないと皮肉をいう人もいますよ。ですから、1973年から74年にかけての石油危機は、日本にとっては国の生死にかかわる大問題だったんです。

ジョーンズ氏：でも、日本は見事に乗り切ったでしょう。

鈴木氏：結果的にはそうです。それで産業自体も、石油の消費を節約するために、省エネルギー型の産業に変わらなければならなかったんです。

ジョーンズ氏：その結果、どのていど節約できたんですか。

鈴木氏：1973年から1981年の9年間に20％以上も減少させたんです。GNP 当たりの石油輸入金額で比較しますと、40％も削減したんです。

ジョーンズ氏：それは大したもんですね。

鈴木氏：これと同じような働きによって、民間の設備投資でも、省エネルギー・省力化設備への投資が増えました。

ジョーンズ氏：どんな設備ですか。

鈴木氏：たとえば、IC、カラーテレビ、VTR などの生産設備です。また、ロボット、NC 工作機械の導入も行われ、生産性と品質が大きく向上したんです。鉄鋼業も連続鋳造設備などの大型省エネルギー設備を装備しました。

ジョーンズ氏：それで国際競争力がいよいよ大きくなったんですね。

・石油消費

・石油輸入量
の削減

・民間設備
投資

and automobile sectors grew particularly fast.

Mr. J: More than twice? What was behind that?

Mr. S: There were several causes. Japan has almost no natural resources. As some cynic said, aside from people, about all we've got is mandarin oranges and hot spas. So when the oil crisis hit in '73 and '74, it was a matter of life or death for Japan.

Mr. J: But you weathered it beautifully.

Mr. S: In the end, yes. To do it, our industries had to shift toward low-energy consuming sectors in order to cut back on oil requirements.

Mr. J: How much were they able to reduce oil consumption?

Mr. S: By more than 20 percent in the nine years between 1973 and 1981. In terms of the value of oil imported per million yen of GNP, the reduction was about 40 percent.

Mr. J: That's very substantial.

Mr. S: This same process also increased private plant and equipment investment, especially for energy-saving and automation equipment.

Mr. J: What kind of equipment are you talking about?

Mr. S: Production equipment for ICs, color TVs and VTRs, for instance. Productivity and quality was also greatly improved through the introduction of robots and numerical control machine tools. The steel industry installed continuous casting facilities and other large-scale energy saving equipment.

Mr. J: That also helped to boost international competitiveness.

11

Changes in the Industrial Structure

鈴木氏：そうなんです。とくに鉄鋼製品、自動車、電気・電子製品の生産性が拡大したため、アメリカや EC 諸国との貿易摩擦を引き起こす大きな原因にもなったわけです。

- 貿易摩擦

ジョーンズ氏：最近の産業の動きはどうですか。

鈴木氏：最近の日本経済の大きな流れは、知識・ソフトウエア・サービス・情報を中心とした先端技術が拡大していることです。工業・建設業など、これまでの中核だった産業が、企業体質を知識化・情報化しようと懸命になっています。生き残れるかどうかが、これにかかっているのです。

- 経済の
  ソフト化

11

産業構造の変化

ジョーンズ氏：生き残りの闘いは、アメリカでも行われています。21世紀での生き残りをかけて、企業の買収・合併が行われ、それがこのところたいへん激しくなっています。日本では産業別にはどんな産業分野がいちばん伸びているんですか。

鈴木氏：金融、保険、不動産、運輸、通信などです。

ジョーンズ氏：これから先の展望はどうですか。

鈴木氏：セラミック・炭素繊維・アモルファス金属などの新素材産業、医療・食品関連などのバイオテクノロジー、グラスファイバーによる光通信、マイクロエレクトロニクスなどの産業が、これからの産業の牽引車になるといわれています。

- 新素材

- 光通信

ジョーンズ氏：これからは従来以上に産業構造は変化するでしょうね。

鈴木氏：そのとおりだと思います。

Mr. S: Yes. The increase in productivity was especially large for steel, automotive, electrical and electronic products, and that turned out to be a major cause for trade tensions between Japan and its trading partners, particularly the U.S. and the EC countries.

Mr. J: What are the current industrial trends?

Mr. S: The main overall trend these days is expansion into high-tech sectors — with greater emphasis on knowledge, software, services and information. The industries that the economy has centered on up to now, like manufacturing and construction, are trying hard to become more knowledge and information oriented. Their survival depends on it.

Mr. J: There's a fight for survival going on in America, too. Companies are trying to ensure themselves a place in the 21st century through acquisitions and mergers. It's getting quite fierce. What sectors of Japanese business are growing the fastest today?

Mr. S: Finance, insurance, real estate, transportation and communications.

Mr. J: What's the outlook?

Mr. S: They say the future driving force behind the economy will be coming from new material sectors like ceramics, carbon fibers and amorphous metals, from biotechnology fields like pharmaceuticals and foodstuffs, from optical communications related areas such as glass and optical fibers, and from the microelectronics sector.

Mr. J: It looks like there will be even greater changes in the industrial structure.

Mr. S: It certainly does.

1

It <u>was followed by</u> drastic changes in the in-dustrial structure.

ノート

be followed by ... 「～に伴う、～のあとに来る、つぎに～が来る」

例文

The financial panic of 1927 *was followed by* the Great Depression between 1929 and 1931.　　(6)

2

<u>What was behind that?</u>

ノート

「そのうしろには何があったのか、裏には何があったのか」このまま覚えて使ってみよう。

例文

The real purpose *behind* a buffet is that it saves the hostess a lot of work.

3

You <u>weathered</u> it beautifully.

ノート

ここでの You は話の相手を含んだ日本人全体を指している。weather は動詞で「(困難なことを)切り抜ける、しのぐ」の意味にも使う。beautifully は「見事に、りっぱに」の意。

4

That <u>turned out to be</u> a major cause for trade tensions between Japan and its trading part-ners.

ノート

turned out to be ... 「～であることがわかった」

例文1

The cocktail party *turned out to be* a success.
= It *turned out* that the cocktail party was a success.

例文2

It'll *turn out to be* one of the best memories of your visit.

Chapter
12

■

日本社会の特質
Modern Japanese Society

■

国民の９割が中流意識を持っています

■

日本のなかにいるときには
意識もしなかったことなのに、
外国に出てみると、
とても貴重に思えるものがたくさんあります。
他国に類を見ない治安のよさもそのひとつです。

〔各国の犯罪情勢〕

		日本	アメリカ	イギリス	西ドイツ	フランス
殺人	犯罪率 (件/10万人)	1.5	7.9	3.2	4.5	4.9
	検挙率 (%)	97.2	74.1	76.4	94.1	83.7
強盗	犯罪率	1.8	205.4	50.0	45.8	105.6
	検挙率	78.8	25.8	22.4	49.9	21.6

(1984年)

Vocabulary

平等化(の度合い)	□□	the degree of equality among the people
華族	□□	nobility
華族制度	□□	aristocracy
なくなる・廃止される	□□	to be done away with
上流階級	□□	the upper class
中産階級	□□	the middle class
階級差	□□	class distinctions
身分差	□□	status distinctions
言論の自由	□□	freedom of speech
思想の自由	□□	freedom of ideology; freedom of thought
社会的地位	□□	social status
経営者	□□	an executive
高級官吏	□□	a high government official
国会議員	□□	a Diet member

〔日本人の生活程度の意識〕

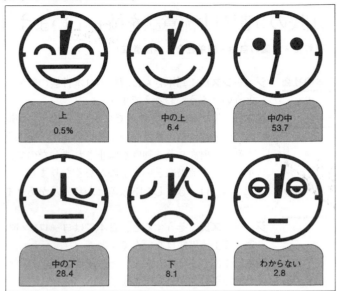

（1985年）

教育の機会が平等	□□	educational opportunities are open to everyone
他人から抜きん出る	□□	to pull ahead of others
社会に出る	□□	to go out into the world
実績を上げる	□□	to show good results
第三者の立場	□□	from the perspective of an outsider
(情報が)すぐに広がる	□□	to travel fast
(製品が)市場に普及する	□□	to penetrate the market
～の面では・という点では	□□	in terms of . . .
中流意識を持つ	□□	to put oneself in the middle class; to consider oneself middle class
殺人	□□	murder
凶悪犯罪	□□	a violent crime
繁華街	□□	shopping and amusement districts

国民の９割が中流意識を持っています

平等化・言論の自由・競争社会・中流意識

- 日本の社会

- 平等化

- 階級・身分
差

- 言論・思想
の自由

- 競争社会

ジョーンズ氏：鈴木さんは現代の日本社会の特色を
どういうふうにお考えですか。

鈴木氏：私の個人的な考えですが、「平等化」が進
んでいるのが特色ではないかと思います。第二次
大戦後、財閥や華族制度が廃止されましたので、
華族とか上流階級というものがなくなりました。
だから、はっきりした階級差とか身分差がありま
せん。

ジョーンズ氏：そうすると、日本にはヨーロッパの
ような上流階級はないんですね。

鈴木氏：ありません。また、そのほかにもいろいろ
な面で平等化が見られます。

ジョーンズ氏：たとえば？

鈴木氏：日本では言論・思想の自由が大幅に認めら
れています。これも平等化の表れではないかと思
います。

ジョーンズ氏：それでは、現在日本ではどういう
人々が社会的に地位が高いと見られているのです
か。

鈴木氏：大企業の経営者、高級官吏、一流大学教授、
医師、弁護士、国会議員などです。こうした地位
につくには、本人の努力と学歴によるところが大
きいのです。

ジョーンズ氏：そうすると、努力さえすれば、だれ
でもこうした地位につけるということですね。

鈴木氏：そうです。教育面でも、教育の機会が平等
に万人に開かれています。ですから教育での競争

C h a p t e r 12

Mr. Jones: What do you think is the most notable feature of modern Japanese society?

Mr. Suzuki: My personal opinion is that it's the high degree of equality among the people. The financial cliques and nobility were done away with after the Second World War so that we now have no aristocratic or upper class. There are no clear class or status distinctions.

Mr. J: Then you don't have an elite upper class like some European countries?

Mr. S: No. Social leveling can also be seen in many other aspects of Japan.

Mr. J: Such as?

Mr. S: We have a high degree of freedom of speech and diversity of ideology in Japan. I think this is a result of the leveling process.

Mr. J: Then what kind of people are considered to have high social status?

Mr. S: The executives of large companies, high government officials, professors in top-ranking universities, doctors, lawyers, Diet members . . . Attainment of high social status is almost always a matter of personal effort and academic record.

Mr. J: Do you mean that anyone can reach the top if he tries?

Mr. S: Yes. Educational opportunities are open to everyone on an equal basis. That's why there is so much competition in

は激しくなるんです。

ジョーンズ氏：平等だからこそ、そこから抜きん出るために、かえって競争が厳しいというのはわかります。この点は、アメリカでも似たところがありますね。

• **昇進**

鈴木氏：競争は、社会に出てからもなかなか厳しいんです。昇進していくのには、実績を上げなければなりません。会社によっては、試験に合格しなければ昇進できないところもあります。

ジョーンズ氏：第三者の立場から見ると、日本企業のなかで従業員が互いに激しく競争しているとは、なかなかわかりにくいですね。日本人は集団として固まっているように見えます。そんな競争があることは想像もできません。

• **企業間競争**

鈴木氏：企業間の競争も厳しいんですよ。たとえば製造業者は、他社よりすこしでも新しく、品質もよく、安い製品を開発しなければなりません。それはひとつには、ユーザーのほうも新しい機能とか品質に敏感なこともあるんです。しかも日本では、情報はどこにでも行き渡っています。だから新製品のニュースもすぐに広がるんです。

• **好奇心**

ジョーンズ氏：それで、日本人は新しいものが好きなんですね。

鈴木氏：そのうえ、他人より先を越したがるんですね。ですから、ものを買う場合でも、他人よりすこしでも早く、よい品質・特色のあるものを買おうとします。

ジョーンズ氏：それで、新製品が市場に早く普及するんですね。ところで、一般の日本人は、社会階層という面から自分たちをどう考えているんでしょうか。

鈴木氏：日本の総理府で、日本人の生活程度の意識

education.

Mr. J: I can see that if everyone starts out equal, then there will be more competition to pull ahead of the crowd. That's pretty much the way it works in the U.S., too.

Mr. S: The competition is tough even after a person goes out into the world. Promotions go to those with the best records. In some companies, a person will have to pass a test before he is promoted.

Mr. J: Looking at the situation from the perspective of an outsider, one doesn't get the impression that the employees of Japanese companies are competing very hard against each other. Everyone seems to be just another cog in the machine. It's hard to imagine such competition.

Mr. S: The competition between companies is also very keen. For example, manufacturers have to do everything they can to develop products that incorporate new ideas, higher quality and lower price. This is partly because the Japanese consumer is always on the lookout for new functions and better quality. What's more, information is available everywhere. News about new products travels fast.

Mr. J: And the Japanese are crazy about anything new, aren't they?

Mr. S: They also like to keep ahead of their neighbors. When they buy something, they want to be the first to get the latest, the best and the most interesting.

Mr. J: New products must penetrate the market quite quickly then. Not to change the subject, but how does the average Japanese think of himself or herself in terms of social class?

Mr. S: The Prime Minister's Office has conducted surveys

をほぼ毎年調査していますが、ここ20年以上ほとんど同じ結果が出ているんです。

ジョーンズ氏：どういう結果ですか。

鈴木氏：ほぼ90％の人が中流意識を持っているということです。自分の生活が上流だと思っている人はせいぜい１％以下なんですよ。

ジョーンズ氏：さっきの「平等化」が国民のなかに行き渡っているんですね。

鈴木氏：外国人から日本人は裕福なんだといわれても、平均的日本人は実際にどう考えてよいのかわからないんですよ。「私がお金持ち？」とひとり言をいうだけで、とても信じられないんです。

ジョーンズ氏：日本をうらやましく思っている国民は世界にたくさんいるというのにですね。

鈴木氏：日本の社会を語るときには、「安全性」についても触れておかなければいけないと思います。世界の先進諸国と比べても、殺人などの凶悪な犯罪はきわめて少ないんです。東京の繁華街はたいてい夜、女性ひとりでも歩けますしね。

ジョーンズ氏：私どもも日本に来て、街のなかの犯罪が少ないことはありがたいと思っていますよ。

about once a year over the past 20 years to find out how people view their lives. The results have almost always been substantially the same.

Mr. J: For example?

Mr. S: Almost 90 percent of the people put themselves in the middle class. Less than one percent say they are upper class.

Mr. J: The feeling of equality you mentioned earlier seems to be widespread.

Mr. S: The average person really doesn't know what to think when he reads that people in other countries think Japanese are rich. He just says to himself, "Me, rich?" and can't believe it.

Mr. J: Well, he's sure envied by a lot of people around the world.

Mr. S: Another point I think has to be mentioned when talking about the Japanese society is safety. The number of murders and other violent crimes here is much lower than in other advanced countries. A woman can feel safe walking alone at night through almost any of Tokyo's shopping and amusement districts.

Mr. J: During our stay here, we've been grateful for the lack of street crimes.

Useful Expressions ———— 12

1

<u>My personal opinion is that</u> it's the high degree of equality among the people.

ノート　　個人の意見はこれこれ、といういい方。☞Useful Expressions 10-4

例文　*In my opinion*, it's the high degree of equality among the people. ともいえる。

2

They <u>have to do everything they can to</u> develop products.

ノート　　「～するためにありとあらゆる手を打たなければならない」

例文　The farmers *had to do everything they could to* increase their harvests.　　　　　　　　　(39)

3

The Japanese <u>are crazy about</u> anything new.

ノート　　be crazy about ...　「～に夢中である、熱中している」という意味の口語表現。

例文　He *is crazy about* football.

4

We've <u>been grateful for</u> the lack of street crimes.

ノート　　be grateful for ...　「～に感謝する」

例文 1　We *are grateful* (to you) *for* your suggestion.

例文 2　I can hardly *express my gratitude* to you *for* your help.

　　　前置詞の使い方は grateful も gratitude も同じ。

Chapter

13

企業の人事管理制度

Personnel Administration at Japanese Companies

皆がいっせいに昇進するのが年功序列？

即戦力となる人間を採用するのがアメリカ式。
日本では、将来性ある人材を採用し、
自社で育てるのが一般的です。
定期採用、定期異動、定期昇給、定年制など
日本独特の制度を英語で説明するには、
どうしたらよいでしょう。

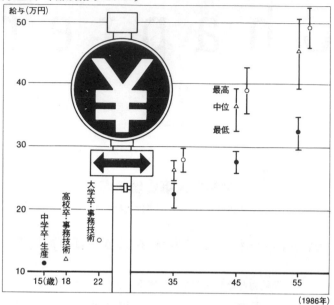

〔学歴別・年齢別給与モデル〕

給与(万円)

最高
中位
最低

大学卒・事務技術 ○
高校卒・事務技術 △
中学卒・生産 ●

50
40
30
20
10

15(歳) 18 22　35　45　55

(1986年)

Vocabulary ●

長期雇用慣行	☐☐	the long-term employment practice
定期採用	☐☐	hiring new employees at fixed times
定期異動	☐☐	carrying out personnel transfers at fixed times
定期昇給	☐☐	raising salaries at fixed times
年功序列型賃金	☐☐	a seniority-based salary system
新規卒業者	☐☐	a recent graduate
欠員(のある職位)を補充する	☐☐	to fill vacant positions
職務能力	☐☐	skills
～にピタリと対応する	☐☐	to be closely geared to . . .
長期要員計画	☐☐	the long-range personnel plan
連鎖反応的に	☐☐	in a chain reaction
勤務年数	☐☐	one's years of service
年功序列的に運用する	☐☐	to be based on seniority
民族の単一・同質性	☐☐	racial homogeneity

〔企業内の昇進基準例〕

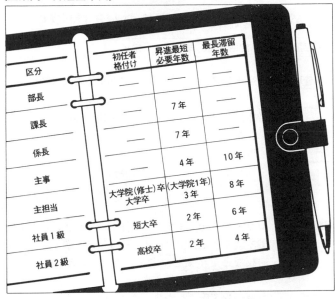

区分	初任者格付け	昇進最短必要年数	最長滞留年数
	—	—	—
部長	—		—
		7年	
課長	—		—
		7年	
係長	—		10年
		4年	
主事	大学院(修士)卒	(大学院1年)	8年
	大学卒	3年	
主担当			6年
	短大卒	2年	
社員1級			4年
	高校卒	2年	
社員2級			

能力の高い人も低い人（やる気のない人）も	☐☐ both the go-getter and the slacker
一律に昇給する	☐☐ to get the same raise
競争意識が働く	☐☐ to be motivated to compete
モラールを高めるのに役立つ	☐☐ to help to boost morale
定年	☐☐ the retirement age
平均寿命	☐☐ the average life span
年金	☐☐ a pension
年金の受給資格ができる	☐☐ to become eligible for a pension
不定期採用	☐☐ hiring on a nonregular basis
人材の条件	☐☐ personnel requirements
変動する	☐☐ to fluctuate
～重視の傾向が強まる	☐☐ to be putting more emphasis on . . .
高齢化	☐☐ aging

皆がいっせいに昇進するのが年功序列？

長期雇用慣行・定期採用・年功序列・定年

・人事管理制度

ジョーンズ氏：鈴木さん、日本企業の人事管理制度についてお伺いしたいんですが。

鈴木氏：わかりました。日本の比較的規模の大きな企業では、長期雇用慣行に基づいて、人事管理制度が組み立てられています。この主要なものが定期採用・定期異動・定期昇給・定年制などです。

・長期雇用慣行

・定期採用

ジョーンズ氏：まず、定期採用からお願いします。

鈴木氏：各企業では毎年、その年に大学・短大・高校などを卒業した者を、新入社員として4月にいっせいに採用します。

ジョーンズ氏：しかし、それで欠員のある職位に適した能力を持つ人を採用できるのですか。

鈴木氏：即戦力になる能力を持つ者を採用するというアメリカ式の採用とは考え方が違うのです。日本の企業では、多くの場合、欠員のある職位と厳密に対応させて、採用者を決めているわけではないんですよ。

ジョーンズ氏：それでは採用をどのようにして決めるのですか。

鈴木氏：各企業では、将来性が期待できる人材を採用します。それから自社にふさわしい意識・能力・意欲を持つ従業員に育成します。それに採用人員は当面の欠員補充だけ考えているわけではありません。長期要員計画や退職者数の見込みなども考えて、総合的に決めます。

C h a p t e r 13

Mr. Jones: Mr. Suzuki, would you tell me a little about personnel administration in Japanese companies?

Mr. Suzuki: I'll try. At most of the larger Japanese corporations the personnel system is structured in line with the practice of long-term employment. The main elements are the practices of hiring new employees and carrying out personnel transfers at fixed times, the practice of raising salaries at fixed times, and retirement.

Mr. J: Let's start with the hiring system.

Mr. S: Most of the companies hire only recent graduates from colleges, junior colleges or high schools, all at one time in April.

Mr. J: But with a system like that how is it possible to secure people with the ability to fill specific vacant positions?

Mr. S: The thinking is different from in the U.S. where companies try to hire people with skills that will be of immediate use in the company's actual operations. In most cases, at a Japanese company the decisions about who to employ won't be so closely geared to the positions that have to be filled.

Mr. J: Then how are hiring decisions made?

Mr. S: The companies hire people they think have good future potential. Then they put them through training aimed at remodeling them into employees with the attitude, skills and kind of drive that are best suited for the company. The company doesn't consider only the number of vacancies in deciding how many to hire. This is decided more generally on the basis of the company's long-range personnel plans and the

ジョーンズ氏：では、その新入社員をどこに配置するんですか。

鈴木氏：新入社員を配置するのにふさわしい職務にです。現在その職務についている者はほかの新しい職務に配置転換します。同時に昇進や退職補充に伴う異動などを、連鎖反応的に行います。これが一定時期に行われる定期異動なのです。

定期異動

ジョーンズ氏：すると多数の従業員が新しい職務や勤務地にいっせいに変わるわけですね。苦情はないんですか。

鈴木氏：はい、各従業員は平均して数年ごとに職務や勤務地が変わります。この場合、本人の希望もあるていど配慮されます。異動によって能力の幅や職務経験が広がり、昇進の機会にもつながります。ですから従業員からの反対はそれほど多くはありません。

ジョーンズ氏：そんなにたえず職務が変わっても給与には影響しないんですか。

鈴木氏：給与システムがアメリカと違っていますので、そういうことは起こりません。日本では、職務と給与とが直接結びついている場合が少ないのです。したがって配置転換が比較的容易にできるわけです。

ジョーンズ氏：なるほど、それでは給与はどのようにして決めるのですか。

鈴木氏：新入社員のとき初任給が決まります。その後、定期昇給によって毎年、昇給していくんです。

定期昇給

ジョーンズ氏：そうすると、年齢が増し、勤続年数が長くなるにつれて、給与が高くなりますね。そ

number of persons expected to retire.

Mr. J: Then where are all of these new employees sent?

Mr. S: To jobs that the company decides are best suited for new people. The people currently doing these jobs are transferred to new positions. At the same time, other transfers resulting from promotions or the need to fill positions vacated by retiring personnel are also carried out — in kind of a chain reaction. This is what I meant by the practice of carrying out personnel transfers at a fixed time.

Mr. J: That means that you've got many employees moving to new jobs and new locations all at once. Aren't there a lot of complaints?

Mr. S: That's right. The average employee will change his job or place of work once every few years. But some consideration is given to the person's own wishes. Such transfers help the employee to expand his abilities and broaden his working experience, and may lead to promotion. So not so many employees object.

Mr. J: Doesn't this constant moving around affect their salaries?

Mr. S: That doesn't happen here because the pay system is different from that in America. In Japan there's almost never a direct connection between the job a person does and the amount of salary he or she gets. This makes transfers relatively easy.

Mr. J: Then how are salaries set?

Mr. S: A starting salary is set at the time the person is hired. After that he gets a raise at a fixed period every year.

Mr. J: So as the person gets older his pay goes up in proportion to his years of service. Is that what you mean?

ういうことですか。

年功序列

鈴木氏：そうです。給与や昇進は、一般的に年功序列的に運用されています。これは、日本人は同質単一民族であり、教育制度も均一なので実施できるのです。職務経験の積み重ねによって職務能力もしだいに強化され、企業に対する貢献度も増大するという考え方が前提となっているといってよいでしょう。

ジョーンズ氏：定期昇給では、能力の高い人も低い人も一律に昇給するというんですか。日本の企業の従業員のモラールはひじょうに高いと聞いていますが、そんな昇給の仕方でなぜモラールが高いんでしょうね。

鈴木氏：昇給額は、個人ごとに能力・将来性などに基づいて、格差がつけられます。ですから、従業員間に競争意識が働き、それが従業員のモラールを高めるのに役立っているんです。

昇進

ジョーンズ氏：さきほど昇進も年功序列的に行われているというお話でしたね。

鈴木氏：はい、しかしだれでも一律に昇進するわけではありません。地位の高いポストになればなるほど、年齢・勤続年数が同程度の者のなかから、能力や業績の高い者が選ばれます。

定年

ジョーンズ氏：その点を私は誤解していました。ところで、何歳で定年になるのですか。

鈴木氏：従来55歳が大部分でしたが、平均寿命の伸びや、年金の受給開始が60歳であることなどから、定年を60歳に延長する企業が最近増えています。

ジョーンズ氏：日本企業の人事管理制度の概要がわかりました。

鈴木氏：もうひとつ申しますと、いままでお話しし

Mr. S: Yes. Generally speaking, salaries and promotions are based on seniority. This system is workable because of the racial homogeneity of the Japanese people and the uniform educational system in the country. It's fairly safe to assume that as they gain work experience they will become more proficient at their jobs and make a progressively larger contribution to the company.

Mr. J: About these regular wage increases, do you mean that the go-getter and the slacker both get the same raise? I know that morale is very high among Japanese workers but I don't see how it can be with a system like that.

Mr. S: The amount of increase differs from person to person depending on ability, potential and the like. The workers are motivated to compete with one another, and this helps to boost morale.

Mr. J: I thought you said that promotions are also based on seniority . . .

Mr. S: That's right. But again not everyone is promoted at the same rate. The higher the position, the more likely it is that the person selected for promotion from those of the same age and years of service will be chosen on the basis of ability and record.

Mr. J: I misunderstood the situation. What's the retirement age?

Mr. S: At most companies it used to be 55, but many are moving this up to 60 — because the life span has increased and a person becomes eligible for a pension at 60.

Mr. J: I now have a much better idea of personnel practices at Japanese companies.

Mr. S: I would like to add that the systems I just outlined for

13

Personnel Administration at Japanese Companies

たことも、最近は変化しつつあります。たとえば、定期採用以外の採用もかなりたくさん行われています。これはおもに、若年層の減少や新規事業分野への進出などのために、人材の条件が変動しているからです。また日本経済は低成長期に入っていますので、多くの企業が昇進や給与を決める場合、能力重視の傾向をいっそう強めています。さらに従業員の高齢化や定年延長などによって人件費がかさむことから、年功序列型の給与体系を見直す企業も増加しています。

主張の文化と察しの文化

英語の "Yes." や "No." は、はっきりと肯定や否定の意思表示をする言葉である。

一方、日本語の「はい」は "Yes, I agree." を意味するほかに、"I'm listening." といったニュアンスで相づちとして使われる場合も多い。

この相づちのつもりで、会語の中で "Yes. Yes." を連発すると、外国人からは自分の意見に同意したものと受けとられかねない。

同様に日本人がよくやる、首を縦に振って相手の話にうなづく相づちの動作も、外国人に対しては度を超さないように気をつけたい。「あなたの話をちゃんと聞いていますよ」ということを外国人に示すには、相手の顔をじっと見つめるようにすればよい。

もちろん外国人との会話のなかで、たとえば "Uh huh." "Really?" "You do?" "Sure." "I see." "Maybe." など、その場に見合った適切な相づちが使えれば、会話はよりスムーズに進行する。

外国人は、概して自己主張が強い。彼らの文化が「主

you have been changing recently. For example, a lot more hiring is being done on a nonregular basis — largely because there are fewer young people to chose from these days, but also because more companies are moving into new fields of business, which makes their personnel requirements fluctuate. Japan's economy is in a period of low growth, so many companies are putting more emphasis on ability in deciding promotions and salaries. Also an increasing number of companies are reviewing their seniority-based salary systems because they are feeling the squeeze of higher personnel costs brought on by the aging of their personnel and the extended retirement age.

張の文化」なのに対して、日本人の文化は、いわば「察しの文化」である。「いいえ」とはっきり否定してしまわずに、言葉を濁して婉曲に相手が察して.くれるのを待つのが、日本人の一般的な心情である。

これは単一民族である日本人が、周囲を海に囲まれた極東の島国のなかで、長い間おおむね平和に暮らしてきたのに対して、つねに異民族や外敵の脅威にさらされながら、自分の権益や安全は自分で守るしかない厳しい歴史を経て培われた、彼らの文化との違いであろう。

英語にも "No." に代えて、たとえば "I'm sorry, I can't agree with you." とか、"Sorry, that won't be possible." など、ソフトな表現の仕方もあるが、いずれにしても否定の意思表示を明確にしておかないと、しばしば誤解を生ずる原因となる。

外国人とのコミュニケーションには、日本人同士のように、相手が察してくれるのを期待するとか、以心伝心といった発想ではなく、多くの場合に彼らが「主張の文化」をバックグラウンドとしていることを念頭において、イエス・ノーの態度を明確に表明し、主張すべきことは堂々と主張して、意見の相違があれば相手を論理的に説得する努力が必要である。

Useful Expressions ——— 13

1 <u>Would you</u> tell me about personnel administration in Japanese companies?

ノート Would you . . . ? は「～していただけません、～いたしませんか」で、Will you . . . よりは丁寧ないい方。Could you . . . ? のほうがこれよりはやや丁寧。☞ Useful Expressions 1-2、9-3、10-2、17-1

例文1 *Would you* mind telling me something about Japan's postwar development?　　　　(10)

例文2 *Would you* like to take a look at it?　　　(22)

2 That <u>doesn't happen</u> here <u>because</u> the pay system <u>is different from</u> that in America.

ノート That doesn't happen because . . . 「～だから、そういうことは起こらない」be different from . . . 「～と違う」☞ Useful Expressions 20-1

例文1 That doesn't *happen* here *because* promotions are also based on seniority.

例文2 The thinking *is different from* in the U.S.　(13)

例文3 The amount of increase *differs from* person to person.　　　　　　　　　　　　(13)

3 Many companies are <u>putting</u> more <u>emphasis on</u> ability in deciding promotions and salaries.

ノート put emphasis on . . . 「～を強調する、～に重点を置く、～を重視する」in deciding promotions and salaries は when they decide promotions and salaries の意味。

Chapter
14

労使関係

Labor-Management Relations

日本では企業別組合が基本です

アメリカやヨーロッパの
産業別組合や職種別組合と違って、
日本の労働組合は企業別に組織されています。
そのため、組合側も
「企業の存続」を第一に考えて行動します。

〔主要団体別労働組合員数〕

組合員数　計 12,343（千人）

総評　4,270

同盟　2,129

新産別　62

中立労連 1,599

その他　4,820

（1986年6月）

Vocabulary

春闘	☐☐	the spring labor offensive
労使交渉	☐☐	labor negotiations
賃金引き上げ要求	☐☐	demands for higher wages
企業別に編成される	☐☐	to be organized company by company
企業別組合	☐☐	an enterprise union
職種別組合	☐☐	a craft union
産業別組合	☐☐	an industrial union
産業別組織	☐☐	industry-wide organizations; industrial federations
戦術・闘争で共同歩調をとる	☐☐	to coordinate policies and tactics
協議組織	☐☐	a council
連絡協議会	☐☐	a liaison council
基本的運動方針	☐☐	the basic policies
要求水準	☐☐	demand standard
～が交渉の焦点になる	☐☐	the negotiations focus on . . .

〔産業別単一労働組合員数および推定組織率〕

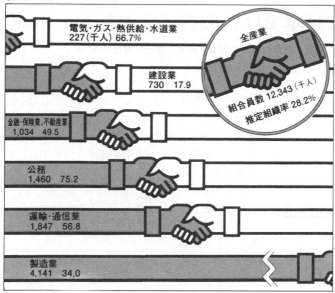

電気・ガス・熱供給・水道業
227（千人） 66.7%

全産業

建設業
730　17.9

金融・保険業、不動産業
1,034　49.5

組合員数 12,343（千人）
推定組織率 28.2%

公務
1,460　75.2

運輸・通信業
1,847　56.8

製造業
4,141　34,0

（1986年6月）

賃上げの世間相場	☐☐	the size of wage hikes at other companies in the same industry
労働組合運動	☐☐	the union's activities
組合の要求が正当なら	☐☐	if the union's demands are reasonable
事情の許す限り	☐☐	so far as the circumstances permit
～を自分たちのものだと思う	☐☐	to think of . . . as one's own
会社の実情	☐☐	the company's circumstances
良識のある考え方	☐☐	an enlightened point of view
利益配分	☐☐	dividing up profits
大幅な賃上げを獲得する	☐☐	to win big pay raises
雇用を確保する	☐☐	to maintain employment levels
企業収益性の確保	☐☐	ensuring the profitability of the company
「経済整合性路線」	☐☐	an "economy-compatible line"

日本では企業別組合が基本です

春闘・労働組合・ナショナルセンター・労使交渉

•春闘

ジョーンズ氏：先日『ジャパンタイムズ』を読んでいたら、「春闘」という記事が出ていました。労使交渉をどうして春闘というんですか。

鈴木氏：日本の労働組合は、毎年3月から4月にかけて賃金引き上げ要求を行います。労働組合と経営者は春に交渉を行うのです。そこで春闘と呼んでいるのです。

•企業別組合

ジョーンズ氏：日本の労働組合は、合衆国の組合のように職業とか産業別ではなく、企業別組合だと聞いていますが。

鈴木氏：そうなんです。日本のは企業単位に編成されている企業別組合です。

ジョーンズ氏：すると企業別組合を総合するような組織はまったくないのですか。横断的産業別組合組織のようなものは？

•産業別組織

鈴木氏：ありますよ。企業別組合が集まって産業別の組織を結成しています。たとえば鉄鋼労連、電機労連などです。これらの産業別組織は、さらにナショナルセンターに所属しています。

**•ナショナル
センター**

ジョーンズ氏：ナショナルセンターといいますと？

鈴木氏：まず、わが国最大の労働組合組織である総評（日本労働組合総評議会）、同盟（全日本労働総同盟）、中立労連（中立労働組合連絡会議）、新産別（全国産業別労働組合連合）の4団体があります。これと重複して、政策・闘争などで共同歩調をとるために結成された協議組織があります。こ

C h a p t e r 14

Mr. Jones: I saw an article in *The Japan Times* the other day about something called the "spring labor offensive." Why do you call labor negotiations a "spring offensive"?

Mr. Suzuki: Because the labor unions here make their demands for higher wages in March and April every year. Labor and management do their negotiating in the spring. So we talk about the spring labor offensive.

Mr. J: I also hear your unions are organized company by company, not by craft or industry like ours in the States.

Mr. S: Right. Each company has its own union. We have enterprise unions.

Mr. J: Aren't your individual unions tied together in any way? Aren't there any industry-wide organizations?

Mr. S: Oh, yes. In most industries the enterprise unions get together and form an industrial federation. For example, there are the Japanese Federation of Iron and Steel Workers' Unions, the Japanese Federation of Electrical Workers and so on. Then these federations are members of national centers.

Mr. J: National centers?

Mr. S: Let me explain. There are four national centers: the General Council of Japanese Trade Unions, which is the largest, the Confederation of Japan Labor Unions, the Liaison Council of Neutral Labor Unions of Japan and the National Federation of Industrial Organizations. Then, overlapping these, there are councils which were set up to coor-

れには全民労協（全日本民間労働組合協議会）や、大産業別組織としての金属労協などがあります。しかし全民労協を、87年秋にはナショナルセンターにしようという動きがあります。その場合現存のナショナルセンターは、いずれ時間をかけて連絡協議会的なものに性格を変えていくでしょう。

ジョーンズ氏：なかなか複雑なんですね。

鈴木氏：ですからたとえば、総評に加入している組合が、全民労協にも重複して加入しているという場合が多いんです。

ジョーンズ氏：なるほど。ところで上部団体と個々の組合の活動とは、どんな関係にあるのですか。

・**上部団体と企業別組合との関係**

鈴木氏：基本的な運動方針・要求水準などの大枠は、上部団体が設定します。しかし具体的な要求や労使交渉は、個々の企業別組合がそれぞれの会社に対して行います。

ジョーンズ氏：企業内の賃上げ交渉では、どんなことが争点になりますか。

・**企業内での労使交渉**

鈴木氏：各企業の業績、同業他社の賃上げ水準などの世間相場、物価動向、組合員の生活実態などです。日本では長期雇用慣行になっています。ですから経営者や管理者もかつては組合員であり、また労働組合運動の指導者であった人も多いのです。したがって経営者や管理者も、労働組合の活動が労使双方にとって重要なことはよくわかっています。ですから正当な要求には、会社の事情の許す限り、これにこたえようと努力します。

ジョーンズ氏：その条件というのがなかなか問題な

dinate policies and tactics. They are the Japanese Private Sector Trade Union Council and organizations related to major industrial sectors such as the International Metal-Workers Federation-Japan Council. But there is a movement to make the Japanese Private Sector Trade Union Council the main national center from the fall of 1987. When that happens the other organizations that were national centers will probably gradually become more like liaison councils.

Mr. J: Complicated, isn't it?

Mr. S: It may seem so, but most unions under the General Council of Japanese Trade Unions will also be members of the Japanese Private Sector Trade Union Council.

Mr. J: I see. But what do the federations do, and what do the individual unions do? What's the relationship?

Mr. S: The federations and national centers set the basic policies and demand standards. But each enterprise union makes the actual demands and does its own negotiating with its company.

Mr. J: What main points do the wage negotiations focus on?

Mr. S: Oh, the company's business results, the size of wage hikes at other companies in the same industry, living costs, the standard of living of the union members, and so on. In Japan most workers stay with the same company for their entire working life. Many on the management side were formerly union members — even union leaders. As a result, they know that the union's activities are important for both labor and management. Therefore, if the union's demands are reasonable, management will try to meet them, so far as the company's circumstances permit.

Mr. J: That's a pretty big "if."

14

Labor-Management Relations

んじゃないでしょうか。

鈴木氏：長期間会社に勤務するわけですので、組合員も基本的には会社は自分たちのものだと思っています。ですから会社の実情もよく考えて要求を提出してきます。

ジョーンズ氏：相手のことも考えたなかなか良識のある考え方のようですね。

鈴木氏：おっしゃるとおりです。もちろん会社と組合とは、利益配分の面では対立関係にあります。しかし、長期雇用慣行のもとでは、会社が配分のもとになる利益を多く上げるべきことを双方が認めています。この点では、労使は共通の基盤に立っているのです。

●組織率

ジョーンズ氏：日本の労働組合の組織率はどのくらいですか。

鈴木氏：日本には、現在全国に7万を超える労働組合があり、1,200万人を超える組合員がいます。これは、日本の全労働者数の約30％に当たります。

ジョーンズ氏：日本経済もかつては急速に高度成長しましたが、これからは難しくなっているようです。労働組合運動にもその影響が見られますか。

●運動方針の変化

鈴木氏：もちろん、あります。高度成長期には、労働組合も、ほぼ毎春、大幅な賃上げを獲得できました。しかし、1979年の第2次石油危機のあとで事情が変わりました。低成長経済下では、組合も大幅な賃上げよりも雇用の確保を重視し始めています。そして、日本経済全体の安定・発展と企業収益の確保を重視するようになりました。要求もこれに沿った形に変わってきています。これを私たちは、「経済整合性路線」に転換したといっているんです。

Mr. S: Well, since the workers are likely to be with the company for many years, they think of the company as their own. They take the company's circumstances into consideration in making their demands.

Mr. J: It sounds like an enlightened point of view.

Mr. S: You could say that. Labor and management have opposing interests when it comes to dividing up profits. But under the long-term employment system, they both realize that the company has to do well for there to be any profits to divide. They are on common ground when it comes to this.

Mr. J: What percentage of Japanese workers belong to unions?

Mr. S: There are over 70,000 unions with more than 12 million members — about 30 percent of Japan's total work force.

Mr. J: For many years the Japanese economy was expanding very rapidly but that doesn't seem possible from now on. Hasn't this had an effect on labor union activities?

Mr. S: It sure has. During the years of high growth, the unions used to be able to win big pay raises almost every spring. Things changed after the second oil crisis in 1979. With the economy growing much more slowly, the unions started putting less emphasis on large wage increases and more on maintaining employment levels. They became more concerned with the stability and progress of the Japanese economy as a whole — and with ensuring the profitability of their companies. They've changed their demands accordingly. In Japanese we say they've switched over to an "economy-compatible line."

Useful Expressions ——————— 14

1 The workers <u>are likely to</u> be with the company for many years.

ノート　be likely to . . . 「～しそうな、～らしい」

例文　He *is likely to* do very well.
　　「彼はたいへんうまくやりそうだ」

2 They <u>are on common ground when it comes to</u> this.

ノート　be on common ground 「共通の立場にいる」
when it comes to . . . 「～のこととなると」

例文1　Japanese beef is the best in the world *when it comes to* flavor.　　　　　　　　　　　　　　(16)

例文2　Japan is fifth in the world *when it comes to* the number of titles published.　　　　　　　　(20)

3 What percentage of Japanese workers <u>belong to</u> unions?

ノート　belong to . . . 「～に所属している」の使い方は次の基準によるとわかりやすい。
〈所属している――収入に無関係〉

例文1　Most Diet members *belong to* a party.　　　(8)
〈所属している――収入を得ているとき〉
　　つまり「勤めている」場合は belong to は使えない。次のように work for などを使う。
（×）He belongs to the XYZ Oil Company.

例文2　（○）He *works for* the XYZ Oil Company.

例文3　（○）He *works at* the XYZ Oil Company.

例文4　（○）He *is with* the XYZ Oil Company.

Chapter
15

企業の意思決定のしくみ

Business Decision-Making Process

まず根回し、そして稟議で決まります

欧米企業の意思決定方法は
トップダウン方式。
一方、日本の企業では
ボトムアップ方式が一般的です。
その根幹となっているのが
稟議制度です。

〔稟議書の例〕

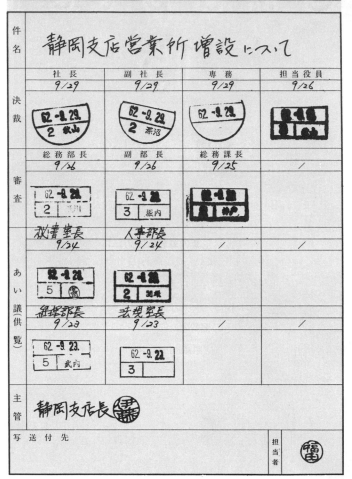

扱方標示	ファイル名	保存年限 年	施行	月 日	文書番号
	発議 昭和62年9月23日	決裁		月 日	静 第 323 号

件名　静岡支店営業所増設について

	社　長 9/29	副社長 9/29	専　務 9/29	担当役員 9/26
決裁	62 -9.29 2 武山	62 -9.29 2 深沼	62 -9.29	

	総務部長 9/26	副部長 9/26	総務課長 9/25	/
審査	62 -9.29 2	62 -9.29 3 振内	62 -9.29 1	

	秘書室長 9/24	人事部長 9/24	/	/
あい議（供覧）	62 -9.29 5	62 -9.29 2		
	経理部長 9/23	法規室長 9/23	/	/
	62 -9.23. 5 武内	62 -9.22 3		

主管　静岡支店長

写送付先　　　　　　　　　　　　　　担当者

Vocabulary

日本企業との取引が増える	☐☐	to do more and more business in [with] Japan
集団的方法	☐☐	a collective process
稟議制度	☐☐	the *ringi* system
決裁を受ける	☐☐	to get a decision
担当者・責任者	☐☐	a person in charge
起案者	☐☐	an originator
原案を文書にまとめる	☐☐	to draw up the plan in written form
起案する	☐☐	to originate a plan
A を B に回覧する	☐☐	to send around A to B
A を B に持ち回る	☐☐	to take around A to B
上位者の承認を得る	☐☐	to get the approval of one's superiors
直属の上司	☐☐	one's immediate supervisor
課長	☐☐	a manager
部長	☐☐	a general manager
関係者	☐☐	the persons concerned; those involved
ボトムアップ方式	☐☐	a bottom-up system
トップダウン方式	☐☐	a top-down system
決裁する	☐☐	to make the final decision
担当役員	☐☐	a director in charge
重要性によって違う	☐☐	to depend upon the importance of the matter
異議がある	☐☐	to run into objections; to object
廃案になる	☐☐	to be scrapped; to be withdrawn
事前のコンセンサスを得る	☐☐	to get a tacit agreement
前もっていろいろ手を打っておく	☐☐	to do groundwork before moving ahead
参画意識を持つ	☐☐	to have the feeling of participation
円滑に実施する	☐☐	to implement smoothly
責任の所在が分散する	☐☐	responsibility is diffused
企業間競争が激化する	☐☐	enterprise competition is intensified

15

Business Decision-Making Process

まず根回し、そして稟議で決まります

稟議制度・根回し・稟議制度の利点と欠点

ジョーンズ氏：鈴木さん、日本の企業では、意思決定の仕組みにひじょうに特色があると伺っています。これから日本の企業との取引がますます多くなりますので、ぜひそれを教えていただけるとありがたいんですが。

**集団的意思
決定方法**

鈴木氏：はい、喜んで。比較的規模の大きな企業では、意思決定は多くの関係者が加わって、集団的方法で行っています。これは稟議制度と呼ばれています。

稟議制度

ジョーンズ氏：稟議制度ですか。それはどんな制度ですか。

鈴木氏：そうですね、ある案件の決裁を受けようとする場合を考えてみてください。まず担当者が原案を文書にまとめます。それを回覧するか持ち歩いて、係長、課長、部長と、つぎつぎに上位者の承認を得ます。また、その案件が他部門と関係があるときは、その関係者からも同意をもらいます。そして最後に決裁者の承認を受けます。

**ボトムアッ
プ方式**

ジョーンズ氏：すると稟議制度は、アメリカのように「トップダウン方式」ではなく、「ボトムアップ方式」による意思決定方法ですね。決裁者はだれですか。

決裁者

**承認の意思
表示**

鈴木氏：決裁者は案件の重要性によって違います。最重要事項は社長が決裁します。比較的重要な事項は担当取締役になります。それ以外は部長が決裁することが多いようです。承認や同意の意思は

C h a p t e r 15

Mr. Jones: Mr. Suzuki, they tell me that Japanese companies have a very special way of reaching decisions. Since we are likely to be doing more and more business in Japan, I'd really appreciate it if you could tell me how decisions are made here.

Mr. Suzuki: I would be happy to. In the larger companies, decision making is generally a collective process involving a large number of people. We call this the *ringi* system.

Mr. J: The ringi system? What is the ringi system?

Mr. S: Let's see. Well, consider the case where someone is trying to get a decision on a new plan. The person in charge will first draw up the plan in written form. He will then take or send it around to his superiors for their approval, starting with his immediate supervisor and moving up to his manager, general manager and so on. If the plan has something to do with another division, he will also get the consent of the person concerned there. Finally, he will obtain the approval of the person who has the authority to make the decision.

Mr. J: So the ringi system of decision making is bottom-up, not top-down like the system in America. Who has the authority to make the final decision?

Mr. S: That depends on how important the matter is. If it's very important the president will decide. If it's relatively important, the director who's in charge of that part of the business will. Most other things are decided by the general mana-

稟議書に捺印することによって表示するのです。

ジョーンズ氏：決裁者のところまでいく前に、途中で上司や関係者のだれかに異議があれば、どうなりますか。

●廃案

鈴木氏：その場合には、協議して、必要があれば原案を修正します。もし承認が得られなければ、廃案になります。

ジョーンズ氏：じっさいに廃案になるものはどのくらいあるのですか。

鈴木氏：じっさいにはこんなふうに進めているのです。稟議書を作る前に、会議を開いたり、関係者に直接説明しに行ったりして、上司や関係者の了解を得ておくのです。したがって、原案を一部修正することはあっても、廃案になることはあまりありません。

ジョーンズ氏：つまり、事前のコンセンサスが成功のカギというわけですね。

●根回し

鈴木氏：そうです。日本ではこうした事前の行動を「根回し」と呼んでいます。これはもともと園芸用語なんですよ。木を移植するとき、移植しやすいように、前もって木の周囲を掘って、一部の根を切っておくことなんです。ビジネスでは、何かを行う場合に、前もっていろいろ手を打っておく、という意味に使っています。

ジョーンズ氏：稟議制度には、ほかのシステムと比べてどんな利点があるのですか。

●稟議制度の
利点

鈴木氏：ふつう3つの利点があります。第1に、その案件に関係のある人々の意思を聞き、多くの人が目を通すので、安全な意思決定ができます。第2に、関係者が参画意識を持つので、決定事項を

ger. Approval is shown by the person putting his seal on the plan.

Mr. J: What happens if the person presenting the plan runs into objections from one of his superiors or someone else before he reaches the officer who can give final approval?

Mr. S: Then there are discussions and, if necessary, the plan is revised. If approval can't be obtained for the revised plan, it's scrapped.

Mr. J: What's the percentage of abandoned plans?

Mr. S: Let me explain. Usually what happens is this: before the plan is drawn up, the person pushing it will explain it to everyone concerned at conferences and through personal contact. In this way, he tries to get the tacit agreement of his superiors and the others involved. So even if it should be necessary to partially revise the plan after it is written up, there is very little possibility of it having to be withdrawn.

Mr. J: What you are saying is that the key to success is in getting a consensus beforehand.

Mr. S: That's right. Our word for this kind of groundwork is "*nemawashi*." Nemawashi is a gardening word that means to prepare a tree for transplanting by digging around it and cutting some of the roots. In business it means the groundwork done before moving ahead with a plan.

Mr. J: Do you think the ringi system has advantages over other systems?

Mr. S: Yes, I think there are three main ones. First, it provides a safe way of making decisions because it allows the persons concerned with the plan to express their opinions on it, and also assures that the plan will be reviewed by a large number

円滑に実施しやすくなります。第3に、若手社員も起案者として企画に参画するため、企業運営に対する関心が強くなります。

ジョーンズ氏：しかしこの方法では、意思決定までに時間がかかり過ぎませんか。

稟議制度の欠点

鈴木氏：はい、その点がこの制度の欠点のひとつでしょう。また、責任の所在が分散しがちなことも欠点といえましょう。ですから、日本のこうした意思決定方法を知らない外国のビジネスマンが、日本人と仕事をしたり交渉をしたりするときに、しばしばイライラする原因になるようですね。

ジョーンズ氏：まさにそうなんですよ。アメリカの企業では、責任、権限が明確に決まっていて、権限の範囲内であれば、責任者がただちに決断を下しますからね。それで、日本の企業の内部では、そうした欠点については何か改善する動きはあるのですか。

意思決定方法の改善

鈴木氏：はい、最近では多くの企業がシステムを改善しようとしています。国際化が進むとともに、企業間競争も激しくなってきているので、どうしても意思決定のスピードアップを図る必要が出てきているからです。

of people. Second, those who approve the plan will have the feeling of participation in formulating it, and this makes it possible to implement the plan more smoothly. Third, it gives the younger employees an opportunity to participate in business planning as originators, which makes them more interested in the company's operations.

Mr. J: But doesn't it take a long time to get a decision?

Mr. S: Yes, that's no doubt one of the weak points. Also it tends to diffuse responsibility. Therefore, when foreign businessmen who are unfamiliar with the Japanese method of decision making work or negotiate with their Japanese counterparts, they often feel frustration.

Mr. J: I'll bet! In American companies responsibility and authority are clearly defined, and the person in charge can immediately decide on anything that comes within his authority. Are there any Japanese companies trying to eliminate these shortcomings of the system?

Mr. S: Yes, many of them are trying to improve their systems. With increasing internationalization and intensifying competition, they are feeling a real need to speed up decision making.

1

ノート

例文

I'd appreciate it if you could tell me how decisions are made here.

I'd appreciate it if ... は「～していただけるとありがたい」。覚えておくと便利なやわらかい表現。

I *would appreciate it if* you *would* do me a favor.

2

ノート

例文1

例文2

The plan has something to do with another division.

have something to do with ...「～に関係がある、かかり合いがある」

His success seems to *have something to do with* his character.「彼の成功はどうも彼の性格と関係がありそうだ」

否定文では、have nothing to do with ... か do not have anything to do with ... ／疑問文では do [does] ... have anything to do with ... を使う。

She *had nothing to do with* him.
＝She *did not have anything to do with* him.

3

ノート

例文

The key to success is in getting a consensus beforehand.

the key to ...「～のカギ、手がかり、秘訣」be in ... ing「～することにある」

This is *the key to* the problem.
「これが問題を解くカギだ」

Chapter
16

労働時間と賃金水準
Working Hours and Salary Levels

賃金は国際水準以上なのですが……

働きバチといわれる日本人。
確かに欧米に比べて、平均的には
労働時間が長く、有給休暇も少ないようです。
一方、平均賃金は、円高の影響もあって
いまや世界最高水準に達しています。

〔週当たりの実労働時間（製造業・生産労働者）〕

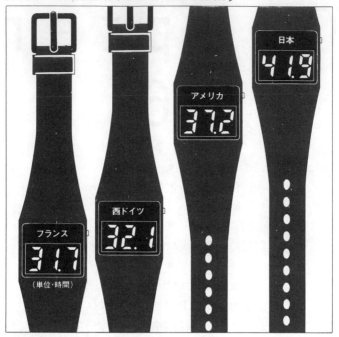

日本 **41.9**
アメリカ **37.2**
西ドイツ **32.1**
フランス **31.7**

（単位・時間）

（1984年）

Vocabulary

仕事中毒（の人）	□□	workaholic
統計によると	□□	according to the statistics
週平均労働時間が42時間である	□□	to spend an average of 42 hours a week on the job
企業（規模）による格差が大きい	□□	to be different depending on the size of the firm
休日	□□	a day off
週休2日制を実施する	□□	to implement the five-day work week
有給休暇	□□	paid vacations; paid days off
長期休暇制	□□	a practice of taking long vacations
数日の連続休暇を与える	□□	to give several days in a row off
〜を奨励する	□□	to encourage ...
交代で休暇をとる	□□	to take vacations in turns

〔物価水準の国際比較（小売価格）〕

	東京	ニューヨーク	ロンドン	パリ
食パン	100	62	94	91
牛肉	100	34	105	67
キャベツ	100	66	175	249
背広	100	76	114	131
カラーテレビ	100	31	116	147
ガソリン	100	28	133	140
電話料（区域内）	100	125	150	213

（食料品：1986年10月／その他：1987年1月）

年収	☐☐	an annual income
賞与	☐☐	an annual bonus
毎月支払われる賃金	☐☐	monthly pay
為替レート	☐☐	the exchange rate; the value of the yen against foreign currencies
付加給与	☐☐	fringe benefits
社宅（制度）	☐☐	a company housing (system)
保養所	☐☐	recreation facilities
恵まれている	☐☐	to be well-off
世界最高水準である	☐☐	to be the top by world standards
生活必需品	☐☐	daily necessities
ドルが下がる	☐☐	the dollar goes down against the yen
しぶしぶ認める	☐☐	to be forced to admit

16

Working Hours and Salary Levels

賃金は国際水準以上なのですが…

週労働時間・有給休暇・賃金格差・福利厚生

ジョーンズ氏：アメリカの新聞やテレビで、日本人は働きバチだの、仕事中毒だのという報道をときどき見かけましたが、実態はどうなんですか。

週労働時間

鈴木氏：統計によりますと、日本の企業労働者の週当たりの平均労働時間数は42時間弱になっています。欧米諸国は40時間を下回っています。ですから日本人はいくらか働き過ぎているという結果になりますね。日本では、従業員1,000人以上の企業では、40％が労働時間が40時間未満です。それに対して、従業員1,000人未満の企業では、90％以上が40時間以上の労働時間となっています。企業規模による格差が大きいのが特徴です。

ジョーンズ氏：休日はどのくらいあるのですか。

週休2日制

鈴木氏：現在、少なくとも部分的に週休2日制を実施している企業は、全企業の50％を、労働者数では70％を、それぞれ超えています。しかし、完全週休2日制を行っている企業は10％未満で、労働者数では30％未満です。週休2日制を実施する企業は、すこしずつ増加しています。しかし、この実施についても、企業規模による格差が大きいのが実情です。

年次有給休暇

ジョーンズ氏：日本の労働者は、有給休暇はとれるのですか。

鈴木氏：はい、2年目からは6日間とれます。最高20日与えられることになっていて、平均は労働者ひとり当たり約15日です。しかし、休暇の平均消

C h a p t e r **16**

Mr. Jones: Every now and then U.S. newspapers and TV will have an article or program on how hard the Japanese work, and they often call the Japanese workaholics. What's the real story?

Mr. Suzuki: Well, according to the statistics, workers at Japanese companies spend an average of just under 42 hours a week on the job. In Europe and America, the figure is less than 40 hours. So I guess we are working a bit too much. At 40 percent of Japanese companies with 1,000 or more employees, the working time is set at less than 40 hours a week. But at 90 percent of the companies with less than 1,000 employees, it's 40 hours or more. So you see there's a big difference depending on the size of the firm.

Mr. J: How many days off do the workers get?

Mr. S: At present, more than 50 percent of the companies have at least partially implemented the five-day work week, and these companies account for over 70 percent of all employed workers. But less than ten percent give their employees two days off every week and these companies account for less than 30 percent of all workers. Although the number of companies implementing five-day work weeks is gradually increasing, there is again a considerable difference between different sized enterprises.

Mr. J: Do Japanese workers get paid vacations?

Mr. S: Yes, from their second year they get six days. The maximum is 20 days and the average is 15. But on the whole, workers take only 60 percent of their vacation time. This is

化率は60％ていどです。これは日本人の一部に働くのが好きな人がいることもありますが、それよりも仕事が忙し過ぎて、休暇を思うようにとれない人がいることが原因のようです。

長期休暇制

ジョーンズ氏：長期休暇制はありますか。

鈴木氏：産業によっては、いっせいに数日の連続休暇を与えるところはあります。しかし、長期休暇制度を奨励している企業は、私は知りません。もしあったとしてもきわめてまれでしょう。私の会社などでは、夏期には交代で、せいぜい1週間前後まとまった休暇をとるていどです。

ジョーンズ氏：賃金はどのくらいですか。

年収

賃金格差

鈴木氏：日本の給与所得者の平均年収は、約350万円くらいです。ただし賃金も、大企業と中小企業との格差が大きいんです。たとえば、従業員30人未満の企業の平均賃金は、従業員1,000人以上の企業の平均賃金の2分の1ていどです。年収には通常毎月支払われる賃金のほかに、年に2回支給される賞与が含まれます。

賞与

ジョーンズ氏：平均年収が約350万円とすると、日本の平均賃金はけっして低くはありませんね。

鈴木氏：為替レートの関係で、単純に比較することは難しいですね。しかし、日本の賃金は円高の影響もあって低いどころか世界各国のなかでも、最高水準のグループに入っているのは確かです。

ジョーンズ氏：賃金以外の付加給与はどうですか。

福利・厚生施設

退職金

鈴木氏：現金で支払われる賃金のほかに、社宅や保養所などの福利・厚生施設が充実しています。さらに退職時には退職金を支給する企業もたくさんあります。また、退職金の一部または全部を年金

partly because there are some Japanese who simply enjoy working, but an even bigger reason is that many of them are too busy to take as many days as they'd like.

Mr. J: Is there a custom of taking long vacations?

Mr. S: In some industries, everyone is given several days in a row off at the same time but I don't know of any company that systematically encourages long vacations. If there are any, they must be very few in number. Where I work, we take our summer vacations in turns and can only get about a week at the most.

Mr. J: What are salaries like?

Mr. S: The average is about 3.5 million yen a year. But there is a big difference between pay at large and small companies. For example, the average pay at companies with less than 30 employees is about half of that at companies with 1,000 or more workers. Ordinarily, a worker's annual income includes two annual bonuses in addition to his monthly pay.

Mr. J: If annual incomes average about 3.5 million, it's pretty hard to say that salaries are low here.

Mr. S: Comparisons are hard to make because they are influenced by the value of the yen against foreign currencies. Today though, with the yen so strong, wages here are far from low compared with other countries. In fact, they are among the highest anywhere.

Mr. J: Aside from salaries, what fringe benefits do workers receive?

Mr. S: There are well developed company housing systems and recreation and welfare facilities. Many companies give their employees retirement pay, and some pay part or all of this as a pension.

で支給する企業もあります。

ジョーンズ氏：日本人はずいぶん恵まれているんですね。

鈴木氏：いやいや。一般の日本人は、恵まれているという実感はありませんよ。日本人のなかで、世界最高水準に近いという感じを持っている人は少ないでしょう。日本では生活必需品が高いですからね。むしろ、日本人の気持ちにあるのは「中流意識」でしょう。

ジョーンズ氏：このまえ日本に来たときと比べて、ドルの価値が大幅に下がってしまったので、ますます日本の商品が高く見えますよ。

鈴木氏：とくに外国から来た人はそうでしょうね。

ジョーンズ氏：生活必需品といえば、お宅の奥さんに家内がデパートを案内してもらった話を聞きましたよ。家内は日本の牛肉はアメリカの5倍もすると驚いていました。

鈴木氏：確かに高いですね。だけど、日本の牛肉も高級品になると味はそうとうなもののようですよ。松阪牛や神戸牛はとくに有名です。テキサスから来た友人が、テキサスの牛肉よりおいしいとしぶしぶ認めていましたよ。

ジョーンズ氏：テキサスの人がいうのでは、そうとうなもんですね。まさか、そのテキサスの人は舌がおかしかったんじゃないでしょうね。

鈴木氏：いやいや。こんど一度、奥様とご一緒に神戸牛のステーキ・ディナーにご招待しましょう。

Mr. J: You Japanese are quite well-off, I'd say.

Mr. S: Well, I don't know about that. The average Japanese certainly doesn't consider himself well-off. There are very few who think of themselves as being near the top by world standards. For one thing, the price of necessities is very high here. Most Japanese probably consider themselves middle class.

Mr. J: The dollar has gone down a lot against the yen since the last time we were here, so for us Japanese products seem higher than ever.

Mr. S: For someone visiting from overseas, that's probably true.

Mr. J: Regarding the price of necessities, my wife was telling me about your wife taking her around to one of the department stores. She said the price of beef was five times what it is in America.

Mr. S: Yes! But Japanese beef is the best in the world when it comes to flavor. Matsuzaka beef and Kobe beef are especially famous. One of my friends who came here from Texas was forced to admit it was better than anything he'd tasted at home.

Mr. J: That is something, getting a Texan to say that! Are you sure there wasn't something wrong with his taste buds?

Mr. S: Nothing at all. Let me convince you by taking you and your wife out for a Kobe steak dinner.

1

<u>What's the real story?</u>

ノート　「本当の話［真相］はどうなのか」いろんな場面で使える表現。

2

<u>This is partly because</u> there are some Japanese who simply <u>enjoy working.</u>

ノート　this is partly because . . . 「これは一部には～のためである」enjoy . . . ing「～を楽しむ」

例文　（○）I *enjoy listening* to good music.
（×）I enjoy to listen to good music.

3

That is <u>something</u>.

ノート　「それはなかなかのものだ、たいしたことだ」参考までに、つぎのようないい方もある。

例文　That's *going some*.
＝That's quite a concession to make.
　　「これはそうとうな譲歩ですな」

4

<u>Are you sure</u> there wasn't something wrong with his taste buds?

ノート　Are you sure . . . ?「本当に確かなんだろうね」この場合「まさか～ではなかったんだろうね」という気持ち。

例文　*Are you sure*?
　　「本当ですか」

Chapter

17

■

小集団活動
Small Group Activities

■

日本製品の品質を支える小集団活動

■

小集団活動は、
高品質の日本製品を生み出す源泉であり、
生産性や従業員のモラールを高める
重要な柱と考えられています。
そのため外国人の関心も高く、
しばしば質問を受けることがあります。

〔QCサークル活動の目的とテーマ〕

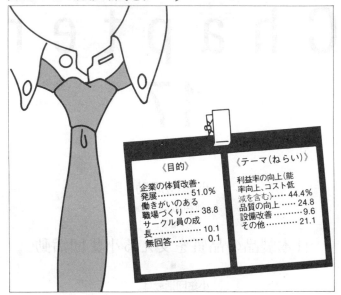

《目的》

企業の体質改善・発展‥‥‥‥‥ 51.0%
働きがいのある職場づくり ‥‥‥ 38.8
サークル員の成長‥‥‥‥‥‥ 10.1
無回答‥‥‥‥‥ 0.1

《テーマ(ねらい)》

利益率の向上(能率向上、コスト低減を含む)‥‥‥ 44.4%
品質の向上‥‥‥‥ 24.8
設備改善‥‥‥‥‥ 9.6
その他‥‥‥‥‥‥ 21.1

Vocabulary

〜によるところが大きい	□□	to have a lot to do with ...
従業員の高いモラール	□□	the good morale of workers
品質管理	□□	quality control
QCサークル活動	□□	quality control activities
ZD運動	□□	zero defect activities
自主管理活動	□□	*jishu kanri* activities
自律的管理	□□	workers' self-administration
全社的に展開する	□□	to carry out company-wide
全社的品質管理（TQC）	□□	total quality control; TQC systems
自発的・自主的に作る	□□	to form voluntarily
就業時間内[外]に	□□	during [outside] working hours
問題の解決を図る	□□	to find solutions to problems
原価低減	□□	cost reduction
品質向上	□□	quality improvement

〔自主管理活動のしくみ〕

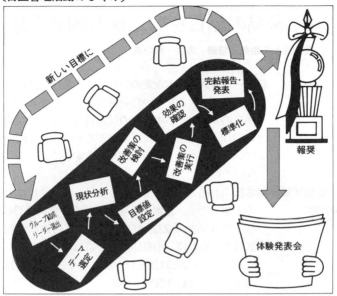

生産性向上	☐☐ productivity improvement
安全性の向上	☐☐ safety improvement
業務(効率)改善	☐☐ operational efficiency improvement
目標と方針	☐☐ aims and policies
職場の活性化	☐☐ creating a vigorous working atmosphere
能力の向上	☐☐ upgrading worker skills
意欲の向上	☐☐ increasing workers' desire to work
役割意識を持つ	☐☐ to feel one has a special role to play
一体感	☐☐ a sense of unity
マンネリ化する	☐☐ to get into a rut
目標の設定	☐☐ setting objectives
効果の検討	☐☐ evaluating the result
成果発表会	☐☐ a meeting for announcing the results
積極性がある	☐☐ to have a positive attitude
参考になる	☐☐ to be informative

日本製品の品質を支える小集団活動

小集団活動の種類・経緯・方法・問題点

ジョーンズ氏：日本企業のいわゆる小集団活動につ
いて、ぜひお話を伺いたいのですが。日本製品の
品質のよさや、日本企業の従業員のモラールが高
いのは、小集団活動によるところが大きいと聞い
ています。たいへん関心がありますので、もっと
伺いたいんです。

● 小集団活動
の種類

鈴木氏：お聞きになっていることは、基本的にはそ
のとおりです。日本では現在、多くの企業で QC
サークル活動・ ZD 運動・自主管理活動などの
名称で、いわゆる小集団活動が盛んに行われてい
ます。自主管理とは従業員が主体となって行う「自
律的管理」という意味です。

ジョーンズ氏：小集団活動は、どんなきっかけから
始まったのですか。

● 小集団活動
が始まった
経緯

鈴木氏：もとはといえば、第二次世界大戦後アメリ
カから導入した品質管理の思想が発端です。この
活動は、初めは製造部門だけに限られていました。
その後、全社的な品質管理活動を展開しなくては
その目的は達成できないことがわかったのです。
そこで全社的品質管理 (TQC) として、日本の多
くの企業で、従業員の参加を得て発展しました。
そしてとくに、現場の作業を中心とした小集団活
動が、盛んに行われるようになりました。日本で
は現在約1,000万人近くが、小集団活動に参加し
ているといわれています。

ジョーンズ氏：そんなに大勢の人が参加しているん
ですか。具体的にどんなことをするのですか。

● 小集団活動
の進め方

鈴木氏：典型的な例では、職場に 5 人ないし10人て

C h a p t e r 17

Mr. Jones: I wonder if you'd be able to tell me something about what you call the "small group activities" at Japanese companies. I've been told that these activities have a lot to do with the high quality of Japanese products and the good morale of workers here — and I'm very interested in learning more.

Mr. Suzuki: What you heard is basically true. Activities of this type are common at many Japanese companies under such names as quality control activities, zero defect activities and *jishu kanri* activities. Jishu kanri means something like "workers' self-administration."

Mr. J: How did these concepts get started in the first place?

Mr. S: The original idea was brought in from America after the Second World War. In the beginning the activities were restricted to the manufacturing department. But later it was realized that the objectives could be met only if quality control was carried out company-wide. Many firms developed total quality control or TQC systems with the cooperation of their workers. At any rate, small group activities, especially on the shop floor, have become very widespread. Today, there are nearly ten million workers participating in such activities throughout the country.

Mr. J: As many as that? What are the actual activities?

Mr. S: Well, in the typical case, five to ten workers at the same

いどのグループを自主的につくり、従業員が自発的・自主的に毎月2、3回、1回当たり1時間前後就業時間内または外に会合を開きます。目的は職場内の問題の改善を行うことです。

ジョーンズ氏：どんな問題をとりあげるのですか。

鈴木氏：原価低減や品質向上に関するもののほかに、作業の安全性の向上の問題などが中心になります。しかし問題は幅広くとりあげられています。

ジョーンズ氏：小集団活動が従業員の自発的・自主的活動であるという点で、たいへん興味がありますね。ところで、職場の長の役割と小集団活動とは、どんな関係になるのですか。労働組合からの反対はないのですか。

小集団活動のテーマ

鈴木氏：小集団活動でとりあげるテーマは、その職場の全体の目標や方針に結びついています。そして、グループが自主的に選び、職場の長が承認します。また、職場の長は、小集団活動が円滑にはかどるように、必要に応じて積極的にバックアップします。

ジョーンズ氏：なるほど。

小集団活動の効用

鈴木氏：それに、小集団活動は、生産性・品質向上や業務の改善だけでなく、職場の活性化や、従業員の能力・意欲の向上にも、おおいに役立っています。

ジョーンズ氏：それはどうしてですか。

鈴木氏：従業員の意識は、上司の命令よりも自分たちが設定した目標に集中するわけです。職場の各メンバーは役割意識を持っています。ですから、目標がチャレンジングであれば、各人は能力を向上させようと努力し、それによって働きがいも出てきます。さらに職場の一体感も出てきます。したがって、組合は小集団活動に反対していません。

job site will voluntarily form a group that meets for an hour two or three times a month. The meetings may be either during or outside of working hours. The purpose is to find solutions to problems relating to their work.

Mr. J: What kind of problems do they take up?

Mr. S: Cost reduction, quality improvement and safety are probably the main ones. But a wide range of other subjects are also discussed.

Mr. J: The voluntary or spontaneous side of it is very interesting to me. What kind of relationship is there between the foreman and the group? And doesn't the union object?

Mr. S: The objectives of the groups are related to the aims and policies of the shop as a whole. The group selects its own topics and the foreman approves them. When necessary, the foreman will actively give the group his support.

Mr. J: I see.

Mr. S: Besides helping to improve productivity, quality and operational efficiency, the activities also do a lot toward creating a more vigorous working atmosphere, upgrading worker skills and increasing the workers' desire to work.

Mr. J: How do you explain that?

Mr. S: The workers' mentality isn't so much focused on orders of their superiors as on achieving the goals that they have set for themselves. Each feels he has a special role to play. If the goal is challenging, the individual workers will try to develop their own skills and therefore will get more satisfaction from their work. A stronger sense of unity will develop between the workers. Therefore, the unions don't object.

ジョーンズ氏：とすると小集団活動は、企業にとっても従業員にとっても、たいへん望ましい活動なわけですね。しかし問題点もあるんでしょうね。

鈴木氏：もちろん問題点もあります。おもな問題点としては、活動を続けていくうちに、新しいテーマの設定がしだいに難しくなることです。活動がしだいにマンネリ化しやすいのです。それに目標設定や活動方法、効果の検討などを行うのが、仕事の合間になってしまうことです。

ジョーンズ氏：小集団活動を、円滑かつ効果的に進めていくためには、どんな条件が必要ですか。

鈴木氏：まず必要なことは、経営トップが従業員の成果に強い関心を示すことです。たとえば、経営トップは成果発表会などに積極的に出席すべきです。つまり小集団活動に強い関心と期待を持っていることを、機会あるごとに従業員に明確に示すことが大切です。つぎの要素としては、従業員側に、小集団活動を自主的に推進できる能力があることが必要です。つまり従業員の教育水準が高く、向上意欲が強く、と同時に積極性があることです。もうひとつは、従業員の自由意思に基づいて、小集団活動を運営することが必要です。この点では日本の企業の長期雇用慣行が大きな強みになっていると思います。これによって従業員は企業に対して、自分たちの会社であるという意識を持てるようになるんです。

ジョーンズ氏：たいへん参考になりました。

Mr. J: It appears that the small group activities are beneficial to both the company and the workers. But there must be problems.

Mr. S: Oh, sure there are. The main one is probably that it becomes more and more difficult to think up new topics. It's easy for a group to get in a rut. Then the only opportunity the group has to set its objectives, work out its methods and evaluate the results is between jobs.

Mr. J: What are the minimum conditions that must be met before these activities can move ahead smoothly and effectively?

Mr. S: One thing that is necessary is for the top management to show that they are seriously interested in what the workers have accomplished. For example, they should make it a point to come to meetings where the groups announce their results. In other words, they should use every opportunity to show that they care about what's happening. Another factor is that the workers themselves must be capable of pushing ahead with the activities on their own. That means the workers must be fairly well educated, be improvement-minded and have a positive attitude. It's also imperative that the workers be able to pursue small group activities freely as they see fit. In these aspects, I think the long-term employment policy of Japanese corporations is a big asset. It tends to make the workers feel that they are the company.

Mr. J: This has been extremely informative.

1

I wonder if you'd be able to tell me something about it.

ノート

I wonder if you *would be able to* [*could*] ... は丁寧で、「〜させていただいてよろしいでしょうか、〜させていただけないでしょうか」の意味。I wonder ... だけよりもやわらかいいい方。

例文1 I *wonder if you could* teach us a few things.　(27)

例文2 Mr. A and I *were wondering if you would* care to join us — that is, if you haven't planned anything.

2

It appears that they are beneficial to both the company and the workers.

ノート It appears that ... は「〜のようだ、〜らしい」。

例文1 *It appears to me that* everything is symbolic.
　「何もかもみんな象徴的のようですね」

例文2 *It appears that* the storm has calmed down.
　「あらしは静まったようだ」

3

It's easy for a group to get in a rut.

ノート 「グループが型にはまってしまうのは簡単だ→すぐ簡単にグループは型にはまってしまう」for ... が to ... の意味上の主語になっている。

例文 *It's* impossible *for* her *to* go there.
　「彼女がそこに行くなんて不可能だ」

Chapter
18

日本人の余暇

How Japanese Spend Their Free Time

海へ山へ参加型の遊びが増えています

休みの日はもっぱらテレビとごろ寝
というサラリーマンが多い一方で、
最近の円高によって
海外に出かける人もますます増加しています。
経済の発展は、日本人の余暇の過ごし方にも
影響を及ぼしています。

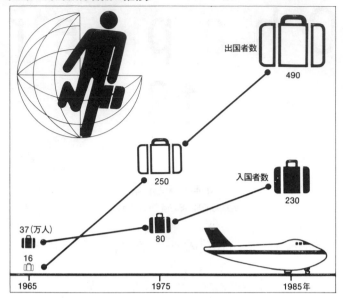

〔日本の海外旅行者数の推移〕

出国者数
490

入国者数
230

250

80

37（万人）

16

1965　　　　　　1975　　　　　　1985年

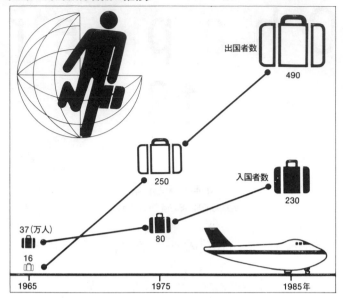

Vocabulary

酒場	☐☐	a tavern
こざっぱりした	☐☐	nice and cozy
本音を出す	☐☐	to let one's hair down
意見を交換する	☐☐	to exchange information and opinions
伴奏だけを演奏する	☐☐	to play only the accompaniment
自慢のノドを競う	☐☐	to show off one's vocal skills
寝ころがって本を読む	☐☐	to lounge around reading a book
ボンヤリしてうたた寝をする	☐☐	to doze off
碁を打つ・碁をやる	☐☐	to play *go*
碁盤・361個の目の盤	☐☐	a board with a grid having 361 inter-sections
石を相互に置く	☐☐	to take turns placing stones
（将棋の）こま	☐☐	a piece
相手の王将を追い詰める	☐☐	to try to capture the opponent's king

■ 海へ山へ参加型の遊びが増えています **Vocabulary**

〔おもな余暇活動への参加率〕

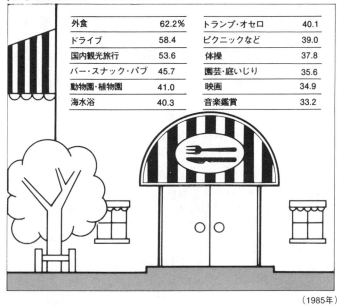

外食	62.2%	トランプ・オセロ	40.1
ドライブ	58.4	ピクニックなど	39.0
国内観光旅行	53.6	体操	37.8
バー・スナック・パブ	45.7	園芸・庭いじり	35.6
動物園・植物園	41.0	映画	34.9
海水浴	40.3	音楽鑑賞	33.2

(1985年)

18

How Japanese Spend Their Free Time

違った動きをする	□□	to make different moves
麻雀	□□	mah-jong
～という点では	□□	when it comes to . . .
熱中して時間を長くかける	□□	to be absorbed for hours
(麻雀の)パイ	□□	a tile
パイをとったり捨てたりする	□□	to pick up and discard tiles
上がり役をつくる	□□	to get a winning combination
役づくり	□□	building up a good hand
ゴルフセット	□□	a set of golf clubs
お金がかかる	□□	to cost
ビジネスの社交上	□□	for the purpose of business socializing
ゴルフ会員権	□□	a golf club membership
全国高校野球大会	□□	the high school baseball championship

海へ山へ参加型の遊びが増えています

カラオケ・テレビとごろ寝・麻雀・ゴルフ・海外旅行

酒

鈴木氏：ここがいわゆる「スナック」です。西洋の酒場のようなものです。スタイルは洋風と和風が入り混じっています。

ジョーンズ氏：小ざっぱりして感じがいいですね。

鈴木氏：日本のサラリーマンは、「飲み屋」と呼ぶ日本風の酒場やこうしたスナックに、仕事からの帰りによく立ち寄ります。くつろいで酒を飲み、本音を出したり、仕事に関する情報や意見を交換したりします。

ジョーンズ氏：ほら、むこうでマイクを持って歌いだした人がいますよ。

カラオケ

鈴木氏：あれはカラオケといいます。よくご覧になると、マイクがテープレコーダーとアンプのセットにつながっているのがおわかりでしょう。カラオケは伴奏だけを演奏しますから、歌う人は歌詞を歌うんです。店にはカラオケテープと歌の本を置いています。そこで、こうして自慢のノドを競う人でにぎわうというわけです。

ジョーンズ氏：鈴木さんは休みの日はどんなふうにして過ごしていますか。

**テレビと
ごろ寝**

鈴木氏：きのうの日曜日は、寝ころがって本を読んだり、ボンヤリしてうたた寝したり、テレビで野球を見たりしていました。日本のサラリーマンに比較的多い、暇な時間の過ごし方だと思います。それから夕方近くに近所の友達が訪ねて来て、碁を打ちました。

碁

ジョーンズ氏：アメリカで碁をやる友人がいますが、さっぱりわかりません。どんなゲームですか。

C h a p t e r 18

Mr. Suzuki: This is what we call a "*sunakku.*" It's a kind of tavern. The style is a mixture of Western and Japanese.

Mr. Jones: It seems pleasant enough. Nice and cozy.

Mr. S: Office workers often drop in places like this — or Japanese-style drinking places called "*nomiya*"— on their way home from work. They relax, have a few drinks, let their hair down and exchange information and opinions about their jobs.

Mr. J: Look, some guy's just picked up a microphone and started to sing.

Mr. S: That's what's called a "*karaoke.*" If you look closely, you'll see that the mike is connected with a tape recorder and amplifier combination. The karaoke plays only the accompaniment and the singer sings the words. The management supplies the tapes and song books. A lot of Japanese enjoy showing off their vocal skills this way.

Mr. J: What do you do on your days off, Mr. Suzuki?

Mr. S: Well, yesterday, Sunday, I lounged around a while reading a book, dozed off a few times, watched some baseball on TV. . . I think napping and watching TV is a fairly popular way of spending free time among Japanese office workers. Then a friend may drop by in the afternoon for a game of *go*.

Mr.J: I have a friend back home who plays go, but I don't know anything about it. What kind of game is it?

鈴木氏：361個の目のある正方形の盤の上でやるんです。2人の対局者が、白と黒の石を交互に置いていきます。その石で囲みとった目の数の多いほうが勝ちです。碁は最近アメリカでも人気が上がっていると聞いています。愛好者の数も増えていますし、碁クラブもつぎつぎとできているようですよ。日本ではほかに将棋も人気があります。

•将棋

ジョーンズ氏：将棋というのはどんなゲームですか。

鈴木氏：将棋も2人でやるゲームです。81個の区画がある盤の上で、交互にこまを動かして相手の王将を追い詰めたほうが勝ちとなるのです。いろんな種類のこまがあって、いろんな動きができます。

ジョーンズ氏：チェスと似ているんでしょうか。

鈴木氏：そうです。しかし将棋の場合は、相手からとったこまを自分のこまとして、ふたたび使えるんです。

•麻雀

ジョーンズ氏：麻雀も盛んだと聞いていますよ。

鈴木氏：熱中し時間を長くかけることでは、麻雀がいちばんかもしれません。4人が136個のパイを使ってやるんです。そのパイを捨てたりとったりして、14個のパイを早くよい組み合わせにすることを競うゲームです。役づくりの面白さの点ではジンラミーに似ています。

•ゴルフ

ジョーンズ氏：私はチェスとかトランプのようなゲームはあまり好きではないんですが、ゴルフはよくやります。日本でも愛好者は多いようですね。

鈴木氏：確かに多いです。私の読んだ調査によると、40代のサラリーマンの80％以上がゴルフセットを持っているといわれています。

ジョーンズ氏：しかし日本でゴルフをやると、ずいぶんお金がかかるのにはびっくりしました。

Mr. S: It's played on a board marked with a grid having 361 intersections. Two players take turns placing black and white stones on the intersections. The one who can enclose the larger number of intersections with his stones is the winner. I hear go is also becoming popular recently in America. The number of players is increasing and a lot of go clubs are springing up. Another popular game here is *shogi*.

Mr. J: How is shogi played?

Mr. S: Shogi is also a game between two players. They take turns moving their pieces around on a board with 81 squares trying to capture each other's kings. There are different kinds of pieces that can make different moves.

Mr. J: Is it something like chess?

Mr. S: Yes, but in shogi you can use the pieces you take from your opponent as your own.

Mr. J: I hear mah-jong is also popular.

Mr. S: It's probably number one when it comes to getting people completely absorbed for hours on end. It's played by four people with 136 pieces called tiles. The players pick up and discard the tiles, trying to get a winning combination of 14 before anyone else does. A lot of the fun comes from trying to build up a good hand — like gin rummy.

Mr. J: I'm not so keen on games like chess and cards. I like golf. There seem to be a lot of golfers in Japan, too.

Mr. S: Oh, yes. A survey I read about found that more than 80 percent of the office workers in their forties have a set of golf clubs.

Mr. J: I was surprised by how much it costs to play golf here.

鈴木氏：ゴルフはビジネスの社交上やることも多い
のです。日本は土地の価格が高いこともあり、ゴ
ルフ会員権も高価です。個人の費用でやるにはか
なり高い遊びです。とくにアメリカやヨーロッパ
と比べたらなおさらです。

野球

ジョーンズ氏：見るスポーツとしても、自分でやる
スポーツとしても、野球は最も人気のあるスポー
ツのひとつだそうですね。

鈴木氏：プロ野球は2リーグ12球団があってたいへ
ん盛んですし、学生や社会人野球のファンも大勢
います。たとえば春と夏には、全国高校野球大会
で国中が沸き返ります。また、社会人チームの全
国大会もあります。これは、メンバーが同じ事業
所とか、工場から出てきますので、「職場チーム」
といったほうがいいかもしれません。私の会社で
も、少なくとも1チームは毎年出場します。

人気のある
スポーツ

ジョーンズ氏：そのほかには、どんなスポーツに人
気がありますか。

鈴木氏：ジョギングとボウリング、水泳、スキーに
人気があります。見るほうではサッカー、ラグ
ビー、バレーボールなどです。

旅行

ジョーンズ氏：レジャー活動として旅行はどうです
か。

鈴木氏：神社仏閣にもうでたり、温泉地へ行く人が
多いですよ。最近とりわけ増えているのは海外旅
行です。とくに若い人や年配の人たちで、海外に
観光に行く人が多いのには驚きます。

ジョーンズ氏：それは日本の経済的な発展に関係あ
るのでしょうね。

鈴木氏：そうです。日本人は自由時間を過ごす方法
にはこと欠きません。古いものと新しいもの、日

Mr. S: Golf is usually played for the purpose of business socializing. Partly because land prices are high, golf club memberships are quite expensive. For someone playing at his own expense, it's a pretty costly game. Much more so than in America or Europe.

Mr. J: I've been told that baseball is one of the most popular sports — for both participants and spectators.

Mr. S: Professional baseball is very popular, and we have 12 teams in two leagues. School and company teams also have a lot of fans. For example, every spring and summer the whole country goes wild over the high school championships. There is also a national playoff for company teams — or I should say "workplace teams" because the members usually come from the same office or factory. At least one team from my company joins the meet every year.

Mr. J: What other sports are popular?

Mr. S: Jogging, bowling, swimming and skiing are quite popular. And other popular spectator sports include soccer, rugby, volley ball . . .

Mr. J: Is there much interest in traveling as a leisure activity?

Mr. S: There have always been people who like to make the rounds of the shrines and temples, and go to the hot spas. Recently, the number of people taking trips overseas has been increasing. I'm amazed by how many young and elderly people are going on overseas trips these days.

Mr. J: That no doubt has something to do with Japan's economic prosperity.

Mr. S: It does. The Japanese have never had a scarcity of ways to spend free time. There are old ways, new ways, traditional

本独自のものと外国からのものなど、さまざまな
遊び方があります。しかし近年経済力を増すにつ
れ、多様な時間の過ごし方が現れました。とくに
若い人たちがそうで、それも自分でやるタイプの
遊びが多いんです。

ジョーンズ氏：たとえばどんなものでしょうか。

鈴木氏：登山や釣りは以前からやる人はいました
が、とりわけ最近は一般化して愛好者が増えまし
た。新しいタイプのスポーツではサーフィン、ウ
インドサーフィン、スキューバダイビング、ハン
ググライダー、スカイビングなどがあります。

このあいだはどうも……

　日本人は、他人から厚意を受けたり世話になったりし
たときは、次に会った機会に「この間はどうも」と礼を
述べる。さらにこの言葉は、人間関係を良好に維持する
ための再会のあいさつとしても、しばしば用いられる。

　一方、欧米人は、たとえばプレゼントをもらったさい
には、その場で包装を開いてゼスチャーたっぷりに喜ぶ
が、彼らが礼をいうのはたいていそのとき限りで、次に
再会したときには、そのことについて何の反応もなく、
日本人としては、どこかもの足りない感じがして拍子抜
けしてしまうことがよくある。

　しかしこれは、別に彼らに感謝の気持ちが薄いわけで
はなく、謝意を言葉に表すのは通常一回限りというのが
彼らの習慣なのである。

　したがって、欧米人に対して「この間はどうも」のつ
もりで、たとえば

"Thank you for the other day."

などといっても、彼らは何についてお礼されているのか、

Japanese ways and ways introduced from overseas. But as
the economy has grown stronger, the variety in activities has
increased even further. This is particularly true with young
people, and they are going into more participation-type activities.

Mr. J: Like?

Mr. S: Mountain climbing, fishing. . . These have long been
popular, but more and more people are getting involved.
Then there are newer sports like surfing, windsurfing, scuba
diving, hang-gliding, skydiving . . .

当惑してしまうようだ。

　欧米人にも、再会したときに感謝の気持ちを表すこと
がまったくないわけではないが、その場合には、

"Thank you very much for the nice pendant you pre-
sented me last week."

などのように、何に対するお礼かを明確に表現する。

　また日本人は、人間関係を円滑に保つために「すみま
せん」という言葉をよく使う。たとえば、相手に対して、
①謝るとき②ものを尋ねたり、頼んだりするとき③好意
に感謝するとき、などである。

　「すみません」に対応する英語表現として、"I'm sorry." とか "Excuse me." などが思い浮かぶが、①につい
ては "I'm sorry." "Excuse me." とも使用可能である。②
については "Excuse me." は使えるが、"I'm sorry."とは
いわない。③については "Excuse me." "I'm sorry."とも
使えない。

　したがって、日本語の「すみません」の感覚で、軽々
しく "I'm sorry." というと、自分の落度を認めたことに
なるし、落度もないのにやたらに "I'm sorry." を使うと、
外国人からは卑屈な態度と受けとられかねない。

1 This is <u>what we call</u> a "sunakku."

ノート　　what we call「いわゆる」

例文 1　That's *what's called* a "karaoke." (18)

例文 2　We've had *what we call* the 6-3-3 system. (21)

2 They <u>let their hair down</u> and exchange information.

ノート　　let one's hair down は「髪をほどいてたらす」から口語で「打ち解ける、くつろぐ」の意味。

3 <u>I'm amazed by</u> how many young and elderly people are going on overseas trips these days.

ノート　　be amazed は「(感心して) 驚く」、be surprised は「(思いがけないことに) 驚く」、be astonished は「(きわめて大きく) 驚く」ときに使う。

例文 1　We *were very surprised at* the news.
　　　「ニュースに (接して) 驚く」

例文 2　We *were surprised by* the attack.
　　　「われわれは不意の攻撃を受けた」

例文 3　I *was astonished at* her behavior.
　　　「彼女の行為にはびっくり仰天した」

4 This <u>is</u> particularly <u>true with</u> young people.

ノート　　be true with ...「～について当てはまる」be true of といういい方もある。

例文　It *is true of* animals.

Chapter
19

平均寿命と人口増加率

Life Expectancy and Population Growth

日本は世界一の長寿国になりました

世界一の長寿国となった日本は、
欧米先進諸国の2〜4倍のスピードで
高齢化社会へと移行しています。
老人問題は
今後の日本の最重要課題といえます。

〔平均寿命の国際比較〕

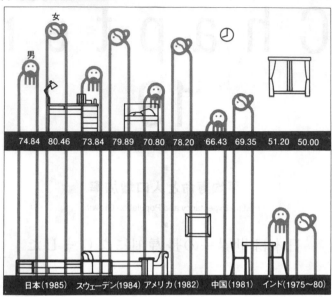

| 女 |
| 男 |

| 74.84 | 80.46 | 73.84 | 79.89 | 70.80 | 78.20 | 66.43 | 69.35 | 51.20 | 50.00 |

日本(1985)　スウェーデン(1984) アメリカ(1982)　中国(1981)　インド(1975〜80)

Vocabulary

老人問題	☐☐ the problems of the elderly
国際シンポジウム	☐☐ an international symposium
世界一の長寿国	☐☐ the country where people have the longest life expectancy
食生活が豊かになる	☐☐ to be able to eat well
栄養のバランスがとれている	☐☐ to get a balanced diet
低カロリー食品	☐☐ low calorie foods
衛生観念を持つ	☐☐ to learn about the importance of hygienic practice
医療制度	☐☐ a medical system
平均寿命	☐☐ the average life expectancy
出生率	☐☐ the birth rate
死亡率	☐☐ the death rate
ガン	☐☐ cancer
脳卒中	☐☐ stroke

〔各国の年齢階層別人口構成〕

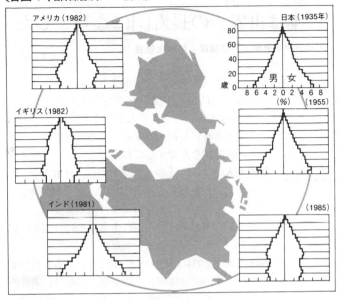

心臓病	☐☐	heart disease
成人病	☐☐	diseases of adults
～を克服する	☐☐	to get . . . under better control
私の記憶に間違いなければ	☐☐	if my memory serves me right
高齢化社会に移行する	☐☐	to become a nation of old people
予測する	☐☐	to predict
～が不安になる	☐☐	to be anxious about . . .
老後をどうする	☐☐	how to spend one's old age
寝たきり老人	☐☐	a bedridden elderly person
生産年齢人口	☐☐	people in their productive years
負担が増える	☐☐	to have a bigger burden
老齢者を扶養する	☐☐	to support the aged
老齢年金	☐☐	an old-age pension
保険料	☐☐	a premium
年金加入者	☐☐	a pensioner

日本は世界一の長寿国になりました

平均寿命と死因・人口構成・高齢化社会

ジョーンズ夫人：私どもの泊まっているホテルで、先日老人問題の国際シンポジウムが開かれていて、各国からたくさんの人が集まっていましたよ。そのとき耳にしたんですが、日本は世界でも指折りの長寿国なんですってね。

平均寿命

鈴木夫人：はい、そのとおりですわ。日本人の平均寿命は、現在およそ男子が75歳、女子が80歳で、男女とも世界一の長寿国になったそうです。

ジョーンズ夫人：日本人が長生きなのには何か特別なわけがあるんでしょうか。

鈴木夫人：それには、いくつか原因があると思います。まず国民全体の食生活が豊かになり、栄養のバランスがとれていることです。それから教育水準が高く、病気に対する知識や衛生観念が広く普及しています。また医療制度や医療サービスが充実していることでしょう。

ジョーンズ夫人：バランスのとれた食品といえば、日本の低カロリー食品は最近、ダイエットしたいというアメリカ人にとても人気がありますのよ。

鈴木夫人：そうだそうですね。

ジョーンズ夫人：それにしても、日本人の平均寿命は急激に伸びているようですね。これからまだ、伸びるんでしょうか。

鈴木氏：平均寿命の伸びは、高齢者死亡率が低くなってきたことが最も大きな理由です。最近では平均寿命の伸びは鈍くなっていますが、平均寿命は男女ともあと6、7年は伸びるだろうという専門家の説があります。ただし、ガン・脳卒中・心

C h a p t e r **19**

Mrs. Jones: A few days ago, at our hotel there was an international symposium on the problems of the elderly. People were there from all over the world. I just happened to hear someone say that the Japanese have the longest life expectancy in the world.

Mrs. Suzuki: It's true. The average life span is 75 for men and 80 for women. That makes Japan first in the world.

Mrs. J: Are there any specific reasons for this?

Mrs. S: There are several I think. Japanese are now able to eat well and get a balanced diet. Through education the people have learned a lot about diseases and how important hygienic practices are. Also Japan now has a medical system that provides excellent medical services.

Mrs. J: Speaking of a balanced diet, did you know that low-calorie Japanese foods have recently become very popular in the U.S. among people who want to lose weight?

Mrs. S: Yes, I read about that.

Mrs. J: We were told that the increase in life expectancy here has been very rapid. Do you think it will continue?

Mr. Suzuki: A lower death rate among old people is the biggest cause of the longer life expectancy. The rate of increase has slowed recently but some specialists say that it may rise another six or seven years. For that though, it'll be necessary to get cancer, stroke and heart disease under better control.

臓病などの成人病が克服できればの話ですがね。

ジョーンズ夫人：日本では、どんな病気で亡くなる人が多いんですか。

鈴木氏：いまお話ししたものです。ガン・脳卒中・心臓病、この順です。これらの病気による死亡率は、全体のほぼ70％にも達しています。

ジョーンズ氏：それはアメリカでもほぼ同じですね。ところで人口増加率はどのくらいですか。

鈴木氏：私の記憶に間違いがなければ、1981年から1985年までの人口増加率は3.4％でしたから、年平均0.7％ぐらいですね。日本の人口は現在約1億2100万人です。1872年には約3,500万人でした。ですから、この100年余りの年平均増加率は、ほぼ1％というところでしょうか。

ジョーンズ夫人：それでは、人口増加率はむかしも最近もあまり大きな変化はありませんね。

鈴木氏：はい。とくに第二次大戦後は出生率はかなり減少しましたが、死亡率も減少しました。その結果、人口増加率はあまり変化していません。

ジョーンズ氏：出生率と死亡率がともに減少しているとすると、人口の高齢化が進んでいるわけですね。

鈴木氏：そのとおりです。日本人の人口構成は1985年には、15歳未満が22％、15歳以上64歳までが68％、65歳以上が10％でした。これが1950年には、それぞれ35.4％、59.7％、4.9％でした。このことからも日本は急速に高齢化社会に移行していることがわかります。

ジョーンズ氏：それはたいへんなスピードですね。これからもそんなスピードで高齢化が進むのでしょうか。

鈴木氏：厚生省の見通しによると、そのようです。

Mrs. J: What are the main causes of death in Japan?

Mr. S: The ones I just mentioned. Cancer, stroke and heart disease. In that order. They account for nearly 70 percent of deaths.

Mr. Jones: That's almost exactly the same as in the U.S. How fast is the population growing?

Mr. S: If my memory serves me right, the population grew 3.4 percent between 1981 and 1985. That's about 0.7 percent a year. The present population is 121 million. In 1872 it was about 35 million. So the average over the past 100 years or so has been about one percent a year.

Mrs. J: It's been about the same over all those years?

Mr. S: Yes. The birth rate fell considerably after the Second World War, but so did the mortality rate. As a result, the population growth rate didn't change much.

Mr. J: If the birth rate and the death rate both went down, that means you've got an aging society.

Mr. S: Exactly. In 1985, 22 percent of the population was under 15 years old, 68 percent was between 15 and 64, and 10 percent was over 65. In 1950 these figures were 35.4 percent, 59.7 percent and 4.9 percent. From that you can see that Japan has quickly become a nation of old people.

Mr. J: That's a very rapid rate of change. Do you expect the population to go on aging at that rate?

Mr. S: Projections made by the Ministry of Welfare would

65歳以上の人口は2000年には16.2％、2020年には23.5％になると予測しています。人口は、欧米先進諸国の２倍ないし４倍のスピードで高齢化することになります。

・高齢化社会の問題

ジョーンズ夫人：長寿はいいですけれども、高齢化が進むと、いろいろな社会的問題が起きてきますよね。アメリカでも高齢化は、大きな課題のひとつになっています。

鈴木夫人：日本でもこの問題について関心が高まっています。自分の老後をどうすればよいか、家族のなかに寝たきり老人が出たらどうするかなど、多くの人たちの不安が増えています。

鈴木氏：人口の高齢化の影響は個人レベルだけではありません。社会、経済に大きな影響があります。たとえば、生産年齢層による高齢者扶養の負担が増えますし、労働人口も高齢化するでしょう。したがって、老人問題は今後、日本の最重要課題に数えられるといえましょう。

・老齢年金

ジョーンズ氏：アメリカでは65歳になると老齢年金がもらえる制度があるんですが、日本ではどうなっていますか。

鈴木氏：はい、日本にも老齢年金の制度があります。特例を除いて、25年以上、保険料を積み立てた年金加入者には、65歳から支給するのが原則になっています。現在は労働人口と高齢者の比率が７対１くらいですが、今後これが４対１とか３対１になるのは避けられません。この制度も先行きたいへんのようです。

make you think so. The prediction is that people over 65 will make up 16.2 percent of the population by the year 2000 and 23.5 percent by 2020. The population is aging two to four times faster than in industrially advanced countries in the West.

Mrs. J: It's nice for people to have long lives, but when old people start accounting for a larger and larger percentage of the population, it causes a lot of social problems. It's a big topic of discussion in the States, too.

Mrs. S: Concern about the problem is growing here. Many people are becoming more anxious about how they will spend their old age, or what they would do if one of the older members of the family should become bedridden.

Mr. S: An aging population affects not only the individual. It also has a big effect on the society and economy as a whole. For example, people in their productive years will have a bigger burden of supporting the aged and the age of the labor force will also increase. I think problems concerning old people will become some of Japan's biggest challenges.

Mr. J: In the U.S., people are eligible for social security from 65. How about here?

Mr. S: We also have an old-age pension system. There are some special exceptions, but the rule is that a person who pays premiums for 25 years or more can start getting a pension from 65. Right now there are seven working people for every pensioner but this is certain to become four to one or even three to one. So the pension system has some hard going ahead.

1 Are there any specific <u>reasons for</u> this?

2 What are the main <u>causes of</u> death in Japan?

ノート a reason は「理由（自分の行動や意見を説明する理由、訳、いい分）」。a cause は「原因（ある結果をもたらす事情、原因）」。

原因が単純な場合は cause を使うが、原因が複雑な場合は be responsible for ... が使われる。

例文 What's *responsible for* the upsurge of the dollar?
「ドルの高騰の原因は何か」

3 <u>Speaking of</u> a balanced diet, Japanese foods have become very popular in the U.S.

ノート speaking of ... 「～といえば」の意の慣用表現。talking about ... ／ speaking about ... なども使われるが、speaking of ... がいちばんポピュラー。

例文 *Speaking of* semiconductors, I hear there is a big push in the development of VLSI.　　　(23)

4 <u>If my memory serves me right,</u> the population grew 3.4 percent.

ノート 「記憶が正しければ」の基本的な口語表現。

例文 *If my memory serves me right*, I am sure he is 80 years old this year.

Chapter

20

■

マスコミ

Mass Communications

■

日本は情報の輸入超過国です

■

日本のマスメディアの双璧は新聞とテレビ。
とくに新聞はたいへんユニークで、
発行部数が200万部を超える新聞が
5紙もある国は、ほかに例がありません。
全国ネットのテレビ局も多く、
長時間にわたって多彩な放送を行っています。

〔各国のおもな新聞の発行部数〕

NEWS PAPER

プラウダ（ソ連）10,700

読売新聞（日本）8,924

朝日新聞（日本）7,591

人民日報（中国）5,700

毎日新聞（日本）4,180

デイリー・ミラー（イギリス）3,169

サンケイ新聞（日本）2,017

日本経済新聞（日本）2,281

ニューヨーク・デイリー・ニューズ（アメリカ）1,353

ニューヨーク・タイムズ（アメリカ）963

朝刊（千部）

（1985年）

20

マスコミ

Vocabulary

普及率	☐☐	the number published per capita
全国紙	☐☐	a national paper
高級紙	☐☐	a quality paper
大衆紙	☐☐	a popular paper
国際的なニュース（取材）	☐☐	international coverage
夕刊大衆紙	☐☐	a popular evening paper
スポーツ紙	☐☐	a sports sheet
地方紙	☐☐	a local newspaper
テレビを見る	☐☐	to watch TV
NHK テレビ	☐☐	the NHK main channel
NHK 教育テレビ	☐☐	the NHK educational channel
公共的法人により運営される	☐☐	to be run by a public corporation
（収入を）コマーシャルに依存している	☐☐	to rely on commercials

〔各国の書籍出版点数〕

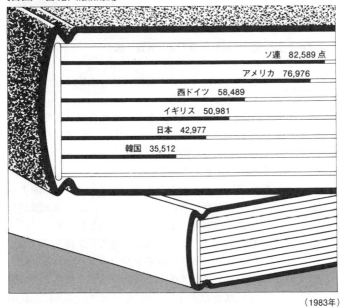

ソ連	82,589 点
アメリカ	76,976
西ドイツ	58,489
イギリス	50,981
日本	42,977
韓国	35,512

（1983年）

全国にわたる	□□	nationwide
キー局	□□	a key station
地方局のネットワーク	□□	a network of local affiliates
独自の番組づくり	□□	own programming
根強い人気	□□	dcep-rooted popularity
深夜のディスクジョッキー	□□	late-night disk jockey shows
音楽番組紹介の雑誌	□□	a music guide
いやされることのない渇き	□□	unquenchable thirst
定期刊行物	□□	a periodical
多様化	□□	diversification
（雑誌が）廃刊になる	□□	to go out of business
漫画	□□	a cartoon
広告収入	□□	advertising income

日本は情報の輸入超過国です

全国紙と大衆紙・テレビ・ラジオ・書籍・広告

・新聞

ジョーンズ氏：日本の新聞の発行部数はそうとう多いんだそうですね。

鈴木氏：ええ、人口当たりの普及率は世界でいちばん高いようです。日本の新聞には、アメリカと比べると大きな違いがいくつかあるようです。

ジョーンズ氏：どんな違いですか。

・全国紙

鈴木氏：日本の大手の新聞は、アメリカの新聞よりも発行部数が多いんです。日本には、全国紙が5紙あります——朝日、毎日、読売、サンケイ、日経の5紙です。それぞれ朝刊と夕刊を発行していますが、朝刊だけでも200万部から800万部以上発行されています。これらだけで、日本全国の総発行部数の55％くらいになります。つぎに、日本の場合は、アメリカほど高級紙と大衆紙がはっきり分かれていません。とくに上位3紙は、高級紙でありながら、一般大衆にも合った記事のとりあげ方もしています。また、アメリカの新聞はローカルなニュースの比重が大きいのですが、日本のほうが国際的なニュースが多いようです。

ジョーンズ氏：このまえ東京駅で、ビジネスマンの帰宅時間にぶつかりました。駅の売店には、新聞を円筒状に盛りあげてありました。なかなか、たいへんな数でしたよ。

・夕刊大衆紙

鈴木氏：あれは、だいたい夕刊大衆紙とスポーツ紙が多いんです。ビジネスマンが会社からの帰りに電車のなかで読んでいます。さっきいいました全

Chapter 20

Mr. Jones: I've heard that a large number of newspapers are published in Japan.

Mr. Suzuki: That's true. They say the number published per capita is the highest in the world. Also there are several big differences between Japanese and American papers.

Mr. J: Such as?

Mr. S: The largest Japanese papers have a much larger circulation than any papers in the U.S. We have five national papers — the *Asahi*, *Mainichi*, *Yomiuri*, *Sankei* and *Nikkei*. They all put out morning and evening editions and the circulations of their morning papers alone range between two and eight million. That by itself accounts for 55 percent of the total number of newspapers distributed. Another thing is that the dividing line between quality papers and popular papers isn't as sharp as it is in America. Take the three papers with the biggest circulations for example. All three are quality papers, but they also carry some sensationalism as well. Also Japanese papers give less weight to local news than American ones, and have broader international coverage.

Mr. J: I was at Tokyo station the other day about the time the office crowds were coming through on their way home. The newsstands had newspapers rolled one inside another and sticking up in the air like telescopes. There were really a lot of them.

Mr. S: Most of those are the popular evening papers and sports sheets. They are read mostly by office people in the train on the way home. Then in addition to the national papers I

国紙以外に、大小の地方紙が80紙くらいあります。

• テレビ

ジョーンズ氏：テレビはどうですか。東京にはケーブルテレビでないテレビキー局がどのくらいあるんですか。

鈴木氏：現在、東京では7局が放送していますので、外国の大都市に比べると多いですね。

• テレビ
視聴時間

ジョーンズ氏：あんなに放映していて、日本人は一日何時間くらいテレビを見ているんですか。

鈴木氏：ある調査によると、10歳以上の人間で平均3時間見ているようです。5年前と比べるとだんだん減ってきています。

ジョーンズ氏：意外と少ないんですね。アメリカでは1日に6時間から7時間という数字が出ています。昨晩気づいたのですが、CM が入らない放送があるんですね。

鈴木氏：NHK テレビと NHK 教育テレビには CM は入りません。公共企業体が経営し、テレビのある各家庭からの受信料で運営されているからです。この2局以外は民間放送局のテレビなので、CM 放映料で運営されています。

ジョーンズ氏：テレビも新聞みたいに、全国放送なんですか。

鈴木氏：NHK の2局はそうです。ほかの民間放送は、東京と大阪の局がキー局となって、地方の局をネットワークに収めています。地方局も独自の番組を制作しています。

• ラジオ

ジョーンズ氏：ラジオはどうなんですか。

鈴木氏：とくに若い人たちの間でなかなか根強い人気があるんです。彼らはとりわけ FM の音楽番組や深夜のディスクジョッキーを聞いています。本屋に行くと、FM の番組紹介の雑誌も何誌か

mentioned earlier, there are some 80 local newspapers of various sizes.

Mr. J: How about television? How many ordinary broadcast channels do you have in Tokyo?

Mr. S: Tokyo has seven channels. That's the same or more than most other major cities.

Mr. J: How much TV does the average Japanese watch anyway?

Mr. S: According to one survey, ten-year-old children and up watch an average of three hours a day. But it's been going down little by little over the past five years.

Mr. J: That's not so much. I hear it's six or seven hours a day in America. I noticed last night that some channels don't have advertising.

Mr. S: The NHK main channel and the NHK educational channel don't. They are run by a public corporation, and every household with a TV set has to pay a fee to support them. All of the other channels rely on commercials for their income.

Mr. J: Is TV nationwide like the newspapers?

Mr. S: The two NHK channels are. The other big commercial channels have key stations in Tokyo and Osaka and each of these has a network of local affiliates. The local stations also do some of their own programming.

Mr. J: What about radio?

Mr. S: It still has a lot of deep-rooted popularity, especially among young people. They particularly like the FM music programs and late-night disk jockey shows. You'll find several weekly FM music guides at the book stores.

あります。

ジョーンズ氏：書籍や雑誌・週刊誌もたくさん発行
されているようですね。

書籍

鈴木氏：書籍の発行点数は世界でも5位なのです
が、ここ数年はいくらか下降ぎみのようです。

ジョーンズ氏：アメリカでも同じようですよ。

鈴木氏：およそ120年前に日本が世界の国々に門戸
を開いて以来、国民は世界から情報を輸入するの
に熱心だったのです。情報に関しては、輸入超過
国です。日本のもので外国語に翻訳されたものは、
輸入の10分の1くらいしかないんです。しかし、
書籍そのものの貿易では、1983年に初めて、輸入
よりも輸出が上回ったんです。だけど、新聞・雑
誌・その他の定期刊行物では輸入のほうが、輸出
の2倍くらいあります。

雑誌

週刊誌

ジョーンズ氏：雑誌や週刊誌はどうなんですか。

鈴木氏：雑誌と週刊誌は多様化しています。だけど
種類が多くなるにつれて、廃刊になるものも多く
なっています。最近は文字よりも写真、イラスト、
漫画を中心にした週刊誌が増えているんです。

広告

ジョーンズ氏：現在、広告費はメディア別ではどん
な割合になっていますか。

鈴木氏：金額では、やはり、いちばん多いのはテレ
ビで、全体の35％になります。ついで、新聞29％、
雑誌7％、ラジオ5％、それ以外はその他です。

ジョーンズ氏：広告費は伸びていますか。

鈴木氏：年々上昇していますよ。広告費は10年前の
2倍以上になっています。

Mr. J: Japan seems to publish a lot of books and magazines, too.

Mr. S: Japan is fifth in the world when it comes to the number of titles published. I hear the number's been dropping slightly over the past few years though.

Mr. J: It's the same in the States.

Mr. S: Ever since Japan opened itself up to the rest of the world about 120 years ago, the people have had an unquenchable thirst for information from overseas. Japan imports much more information than it exports. For every ten foreign books that are translated into Japanese, only about one is translated the other way. As for the actual number of copies going in and out of the country though, book exports overtook imports for the first time in 1983. But when it comes to newspapers, magazines and other periodicals, imports are about twice exports.

Mr. J: What's the magazine situation?

Mr. S: There's been great diversification. But as the number of titles has increased, the number going out of business has also increased. The recent trend has been toward weekly magazines that are short on words and long on photos, illustrations and cartoons.

Mr. J: How do the different media rank in advertising income?

Mr. S: As you might expect, TV is top with 35 percent. Newspapers get 29 percent, magazines seven percent and radio five percent. The rest goes to miscellaneous media.

Mr. J: Are the sums involved increasing?

Mr. S: Yes, steadily. Media advertising income has doubled in the past ten years.

Useful Expressions —————— 20

1

There are several big <u>differences between</u> Japanese <u>and</u> American papers.

ノート　difference between A and B「A と B との間の違い」☞Useful Expressions 13-2

例文1　The temperature *difference between* the north *and* south must be rather large.　　　(1)

例文2　There is a *difference* of 20 pounds *between* the two.

2

Japan <u>seems to</u> publish <u>a lot of</u> books and magazines.

ノート　seem は主観的な場合、look は客観的な場合に用いられる。天候など客観的な事実には look を使うのが普通。

例文1　It *looks like* rain.

例文2　It *seems* likely to rain.

　seem のほうが主観的な感想を表している。a lot of はアメリカでもイギリスでも、口語で頻繁に使われている。従来 a lot of は肯定文で使い、否定文、疑問文、条件文では many や much を使うといわれていたが、現在、口語ではそうした用法もそれほど厳密ではなくなっている。否定・疑問・条件文などでも a lot of はそうとう使われている。

例文3　There were really *a lot of* them.　　　(20)

例文4　It still has *a lot of* deep-rooted popularity, especially among young people.　　　(20)

Chapter
21

教育
Education

日本の教育はどうも知育偏重ですね

教育の普及率、水準の高さからすれば
日本の教育は世界屈指のものです。
しかし、「知識習得に偏っている」「没個性的」
という批判もあり、
個性を伸ばし、創造性を開発する教育へと
内容の変化が求められています。

〔日本の学校体系図〕

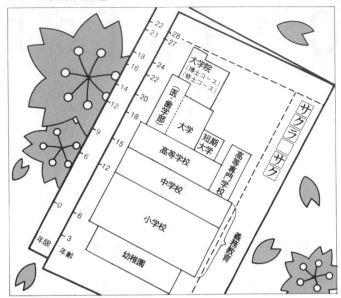

Vocabulary

義務教育	□□ compulsory education
小学校	□□ an elementary school
中学校	□□ a middle school; a lower secondary school; a junior high school
6-3-3制	□□ the 6-3-3 system
医学部	□□ a medical college
歯学部	□□ a dental college
２年制短期大学	□□ a junior college
高等専門学校	□□ a technical college
情報処理技術者	□□ a data processing specialist
専修学校	□□ a vocational school
二の次になる	□□ to take second place
高等学校長の推薦文	□□ the recommendation of one's high school principal
人物全体	□□ the total individual
～を総合的に審査する	□□ to make a thorough study of . . .

〔各国の高等教育進学率〕

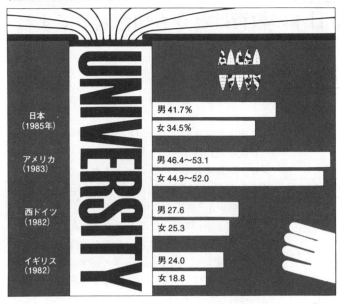

日本 (1985年)	男 41.7%	
	女 34.5%	
アメリカ (1983)	男 46.4〜53.1	
	女 44.9〜52.0	
西ドイツ (1982)	男 27.6	
	女 25.3	
イギリス (1982)	男 24.0	
	女 18.8	

卒業生・出身者	☐☐	a former student
全国共通一次試験	☐☐	the preliminary standard college entrance examination
2次試験	☐☐	the secondary examination
予備校	☐☐	a preparatory school
塾	☐☐	a cram school
コミュニティー・カレッジ	☐☐	a community college
あらゆる年齢の人々	☐☐	people of all ages
進級する	☐☐	to pass one's course
文科系	☐☐	the humanities
いいかげんな講義をする	☐☐	to conduct a sloppy course
宿題をどんどん出す	☐☐	to pile on the homework
大学院生	☐☐	a postgraduate student
有名な伝統ある学校	☐☐	a famous, long-established school

日本の教育はどうも知育偏重ですね

教育制度・進学率・大学入試・塾

● 義務教育

ジョーンズ夫人：アメリカでは州によって義務教育の年限が違います。日本ではどうですの。

鈴木夫人：日本では、小学校と中学校が義務教育で、6歳から15歳までの9年間ですわ。

ジョーンズ夫人：そのあとはどうなってますの。

● 教育制度

鈴木夫人：この図をご覧になってください。1947年以来、6-3-3制になっていますの。小学校6年、中学校3年、高等学校3年です。大学は4年です。大学院は修士課程が2年、その上の博士課程は3年になります。ただし、医学・歯学は学部が6年で、修士課程がなく、大学院は4年間の博士課程だけになりますの。ですから博士号をとるのに10年かかることになります。さらに、2年制の短期大学、中学卒業後5年間教育を行う高等専門学校があります。このほかにも、美容師、理髪師、調理師、会計士、デザイナー、情報処理技術者などを養成するための、いろいろな種類の専修学校があります。これらの学校はたいてい義務教育を終了した人か、高校を卒業した人が入学します。最近、こうした専修学校も人気が高まっています。

● 専修学校

ジョーンズ氏：現在の義務教育の就学率や進学率はどうなっていますか。

● 進学率

鈴木氏：義務教育の就学率は100％です。高校への進学率はおよそ94％、短期大学・大学へは約37％です。いずれも該当する年齢人口に対する割合です。ですから、高校へ入学するのは、現実には当

C h a p t e r 21

Mrs. Jones: In the States the number of years of compulsory education differs from state to state. What's the situation here?

Mrs. Suzuki: Elementary school and middle school are compulsory. That's nine years, from age 6 to 15.

Mrs. J: What follows that?

Mrs. S: Here, look at this chart. From 1947 we've had what we call the 6-3-3 system. Six years of elementary school, three of middle school and three of high school. College is four years. It takes two years to get a master's degree and another three for a doctorate. Medical and dental college courses are six years. There are no master's courses for medicine or dentistry, though. Only four-year doctor courses, so it takes ten years to get a doctor's degree. We also have two-year junior colleges and technical colleges with five-year programs for middle school graduates. There are also many kinds of vocational schools for people who want to become beauticians, barbers, cooks, accountants, designers, data processing specialists and the like. Most of the students entering these schools are middle school or high school graduates. These vocational schools are becoming more popular recently.

Mr. Jones: What percentage of children actually complete their compulsory education, and what percentage continue their education beyond that?

Mr. Suzuki: Everyone completes compulsory education and 94 percent go on to high school. Thirty-seven percent go on to college or junior college. These are percentages of the total number of persons in the age group concerned, so you can

たり前になっているのがおわかりいただけると思います。

ジョーンズ夫人：世界の小学校・中学校の学力検査の結果を見ますと、アメリカと比べて、日本はそうとうレベルが高いようですね。とくに算数・数学などは。

鈴木夫人：確かにそのようですわ。

日本の教育

鈴木氏：その点がよしあしなんですよ。日本の教育全体にいえることですが、どうも日本では知識習得面があまりに重く見られ過ぎるんですよ。個性を伸ばしていく教育面が二の次になります。

ジョーンズ氏：それはどういうところから来ているんでしょうかね。

大学入試

鈴木氏：教育に対する伝統的考えがあるんじゃないでしょうか。私の考えでは、大学の入学試験が大きくかかわっていると思います。その問題の根源には、よい大学に入れば、よい職業に就きやすくなるということがあります。

ジョーンズ氏：それはアメリカでもほぼ同じですよ。よい大学を卒業すれば、よい職業に就ける可能性が高いのは当たり前です。

鈴木氏：ところが、日本の大学入学者の選抜が、1回か2回の試験でほぼ決まってしまう点が問題なんです。アメリカの大学の選抜方法はどうなっていますか。

アメリカの選抜法

ジョーンズ氏：アメリカの場合は、高校時代の成績、課外活動と大学入学学力テスト（**SAT**や**ACT**）などの点数、高等学校長の推薦文などを考慮します。つまり人物全体を見るんです。

鈴木氏：選抜するまでに半年くらいじっくり時間をかけて、総合的に審査するようですね。

ジョーンズ氏：はい、そのとおりです。ハーバード

see that high school attendance has practically become the norm.

Mrs. J: Achievement tests given at elementary and middle schools throughout the world show that the level of educational achievement in Japan is higher than in America. Especially in arithmetic and mathematics.

Mrs. S: That's what I hear.

Mr. S: There's good and bad to that. One thing that you can say about Japanese education as a whole is that there is too much emphasis on acquiring factual knowledge. Development of individuality takes second place.

Mr. J: Where does that come from?

Mr. S: Partly from the traditions in education, I think. My feeling is that the university entrance examinations have a lot to do with it. The root of the problem is that if a person can get into a good university, he or she will have an easier time getting a good job.

Mr. J: It's pretty much the same in America. It's only natural for a graduate from a good college to have a better chance of landing a good job.

Mr. S: The problem in Japan is that whether a person will be able to get into a university or not depends almost totally on one or two tests. How do schools decide who to admit in the U.S.?

Mr. J: American universities consider the person's high school record, his extracurricular activities, his SAT or ACT score, the recommendation of his high school principal . . . They look at the total individual.

Mr. S: I hear they take around half a year to make a thorough study of the applicant's qualifications.

Mr. J: Yes, that's true. At some schools like Harvard, the ap-

225

大学などは、入学志願者の面接を卒業生のビジネスマンに委託して、広い視野から志願者を判定しているようです。

・日本の
大学入試

鈴木氏：日本の場合も、試験以外に高校の成績などもいちおう審査の対象にはなります。しかし現実には、国公立の場合は全国共通一次テストと各大学の2次試験の成績だけをもとにしています。私立はその大学独自の試験の成績で決まってしまいます。

鈴木夫人：それで、いきおい入学試験を目指して勉強することになるんですわ。有名大学の志願倍率は、どうしても高くなります。

ジョーンズ夫人：大学入試に落ちた学生はどうするんですか。

・予備校

・浪人

鈴木氏：たいていは予備校という大学の受験準備のための学校に入って、翌年の受験を目指すんです。こういう学生を「浪人」と呼んでいます。これは、もともとは「主人のいないサムライ」という意味です。有名大学の入学者のおよそ半数は、1年くらい浪人を経験した学生なんです。

ジョーンズ氏：高校をよけい1年なり2年やるのと同じですね。

・塾

鈴木氏：そうなんです。浪人しないで有名大学に入るためにも、小学校のときから、子供を塾に通わせ始める両親もそうとういるんです。小学生全体の25％は夕方、塾に通っています。小学校6年生と中学生は半数が塾に行っています。

ジョーンズ夫人：日本の子供って、勉強だけしかやっていないみたいですのね。

鈴木氏：そうかもしれません。アメリカの大学への

plicants are interviewed by former students of the school who are now in business positions — to give a broader perspective to the selection process.

Mr. S: Japanese universities are also supposed to consider the applicant's high school record. The fact of the matter is that the national universities choose people solely on the basis of the preliminary standard college entrance examination, and the secondary examination held at each university. The private universities do it on the basis of their own tests.

Mrs. S: Students therefore all tend to study only to pass the entrance examinations. The number of applicants at famous universities is much higher than the number that can be accepted.

Mrs. J: What happens to the ones who don't get in?

Mr. S: Most of them go to preparatory schools that specialize in examination test training, and study for the next year's tests. These students are called "*ronin*," a word that originally meant "masterless *samurai*." About half the students at the famous universities have spent a year or more as a ronin.

Mr. J: That amounts to adding an extra year or two onto high school.

Mr. S: Exactly. A lot of parents start sending their kids to cram schools from the time they are in elementary school — so they will be able to get into a famous college without spending time as a ronin. A quarter of all elementary school students go to evening cram schools. About half of the sixth graders go, as well as half the middle school students.

Mrs. J: It sounds like Japanese children do nothing but study.

Mr. S: That's about the size of it. In America what percentage

**●アメリカの
大学進学率**

進学率はどのくらいになっているんですか。

ジョーンズ氏：50％ちょっとです。これは男女とも
ほぼ同じです。日本ではいかがですか。

鈴木氏：女性の大学への進学率は年々増えています
が、まだ男性のほうが多いんです。

ジョーンズ氏：合衆国の場合、この50％という数字
は、進学該当年齢に対する比率です。ですから大
学で学んでいる人はもっと多いでしょう。コミュ
ニティー・カレッジが発達しておりますので、あ
らゆる年齢の人々が勉強できるようになっていま
す。また、大学で資格をとれば、昇進にも有利に
なります。 ですから、会社を辞めて、大学なり
大学院に行き直す人もいます。

**●大学での
勉強方法**

鈴木氏：日本では、学生は大学に入るには懸命に努
力しなければなりませんが、いったん入学してし
まうと、進級するにはそれほど勉強する必要はな
いんです。とくに文科系ではそうなんです。入学
した者はだれでもほぼ卒業します。そんなに猛勉
強しなくても、落第する心配はないんです。

ジョーンズ氏：その点アメリカの大学はかなり厳し
いですね。教授もいいかげんな講義をしていたの
では生徒が来なくなって、職を失ってしまうから
です。学生に宿題をどんどん出して、真剣に実力
をつけようとするんです。

●大学院

鈴木氏：また、ハーバード大学にしても MIT にし
ても、大学院のほうが学生数が多いんですね。

ジョーンズ氏：そうなんです。有名な伝統ある大学
では、大学院が最も重要な部門になっています。

鈴木氏：日本の大学も大学院をもっと充実する必要
があると私もつねづね思っているんですよ。

of high school graduates go on to college?

Mr. J: Just over 50 percent. It's about the same for boys and girls. How about in Japan?

Mr. S: More girls are entering universities these days, but the number of boys is still larger.

Mr. J: In regard to the U.S., when I say 50 percent, that's 50 percent of the college entrance age group. The total number entering college is much larger. Community colleges are well developed and they are open to people of all ages. A college degree also gives a person a better chance for advancement in his work, so there are quite a few people who quit their jobs to go back to college or to take postgraduate courses.

Mr. S: In Japan, students have to work hard to get into college, but once they are in, they don't have to study very much to pass their courses. This is especially true in the humanities. Anyone who gets into a university will almost always graduate. He doesn't have to worry about failing even if he doesn't study so hard.

Mr. J: Things are much harder at American universities. A professor who conducts a sloppy course will lose his students, even his job. The teachers pile on the homework and make a real effort to teach the subject.

Mr. S: At schools like Harvard and MIT I hear there are more postgraduate students than undergraduate students.

Mr. J: That's right. The postgraduate programs are the most important part of the famous, long-established schools.

Mr. S: I've always thought that Japanese schools should do more to develop their postgraduate courses.

1

What <u>follows</u> that?

ノート　「その次は何ですか」順序を尋ねるさいの決まり表現。☞Useful Expressions 11-1

2

There's <u>good and bad</u> to that.

ノート　「それにはよしあしがあるんですよ」

3

<u>My feeling is that</u> the university entrance examinations <u>have a lot to do with</u> it.

ノート　「私の感じでは〜なんですよ」☞Useful Expressions 12-1

have a lot to do with ... 「〜とおおいに関係がある」☞Useful Expressions 15-2

4

She will <u>have an easier time getting</u> a good job.

ノート　have an easy time ... ing 「〜することを楽々と手に入れる」反対は have a hard time ... ing 「〜してひどい目に合う、苦労して〜する」

5

Most of them go to preparatory schools that <u>specialize in</u> examination test training.

ノート　specialize in ... 「〜を専門にする、得意とする」

6

<u>That's about the size of it.</u>

ノート　口語の決まり表現。「まあそんなところです」

Chapter
22

家庭生活
Home Life

妻が財布のひもを握っています

日本の多くの家庭では、
妻が家計を預かっています。
このことは、
外国人には意外と知られていないので、
説明すると、たいへん驚くようです。

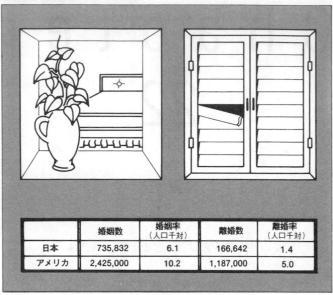

〔婚姻率・離婚率の日米比較〕

	婚姻数	婚姻率 （人口千対）	離婚数	離婚率 （人口千対）
日本	735,832	6.1	166,642	1.4
アメリカ	2,425,000	10.2	1,187,000	5.0

（1985年）

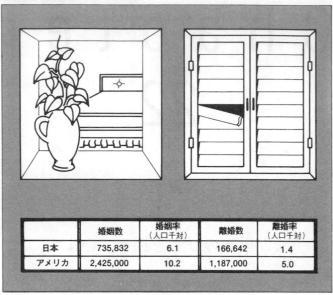

22

家庭生活

Vocabulary

お見合いで結婚する	☐☐	to marry through a go-between
進める	☐☐	to arrange
仲人	☐☐	a go-between
紹介する	☐☐	to introduce
しばらく交際する	☐☐	to go out together for a while
恋愛になる	☐☐	to fall in love
利点	☐☐	an advantage
客観的に判断できる 　第三者	☐☐	someone who is able to judge things objectively
性格	☐☐	personality
趣味	☐☐	an interest
職業	☐☐	an occupation
関係のない分野	☐☐	different walks of life
魅力的	☐☐	attractive
離婚率	☐☐	the divorce rate
平均家族数	☐☐	the average family size

妻が財布のひもを握っています   **Vocabulary**

〔家庭内での決定権にみる日米比較〕

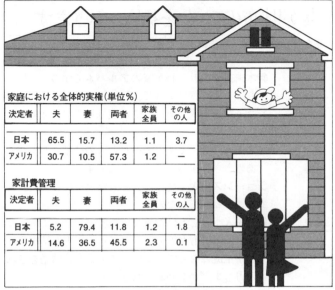

家庭における全体的実権（単位%）

決定者	夫	妻	両者	家族全員	その他の人
日本	65.5	15.7	13.2	1.1	3.7
アメリカ	30.7	10.5	57.3	1.2	—

家計費管理

決定者	夫	妻	両者	家族全員	その他の人
日本	5.2	79.4	11.8	1.2	1.8
アメリカ	14.6	36.5	45.5	2.3	0.1

（1982年）

３世代家族	☐☐	a three-generation family
両親と子供だけの核家族	☐☐	a family made up of just parents and children
スープのさめない距離に	☐☐	close enough to bring over some soup before it cools
既婚婦人	☐☐	a married woman
司法官	☐☐	a judge
企業経営者	☐☐	a person operating one's own business
行政管理職	☐☐	a person going into government
管理職的な仕事	☐☐	an executive position
男性が強い社会	☐☐	a male-oriented society
生活費を管理する	☐☐	to have control over the household accounts
財布のひもをがっちり握る	☐☐	to keep a firm hand on the purse strings
家計費	☐☐	money to take care of the house

妻が財布のひもを握っています

見合い・結婚年齢・家族構成・女性の仕事

鈴木夫人：これ、わが家のアルバムですの。奥様、
ちょっとご覧になって。

ジョーンズ夫人：あら、これ奥様とご主人様ではな
いかしら。

鈴木夫人：そうですの……私どもの結婚式ですわ。
あのときはずっと若かったんですのよ。

ジョーンズ夫人：奥様は、どんなふうにご主人にお
会いになりましたの。

見合い

鈴木夫人：私どもはお見合いで結婚したんです。最
近は、男性も女性も、自分で選んだ方と結婚する
のが主流になっています。でも見合い結婚をされ
る方もまだかなりおられますわ。

ジョーンズ夫人：お見合いって、どういうふうに進
めるんですの。

鈴木夫人：仲人という間をとり持つ紹介者が、結婚
を希望する男性と女性を、お食事をとりながら、
紹介することが多いようです。ご両親がご一緒さ
れることもあります。男女双方とも関心があれば、
このあと、しばらく交際して結婚するかどうかを
決めます。これがきっかけとなって恋愛が始まる
こともありますわ。

ジョーンズ夫人：なかなか興味あるやり方ですね。

見合いの利点

鈴木夫人：見合い結婚には、大きくいって、利点が
2つあります。まず、冷静にお互いの性格、趣味、
職業などを判断できる第三者が2人を引き合わせ
てくれること。それに、お互いにそれ以前には関
係のなかった分野から広く相手を見つけることが
できる点ですわ。

C h a p t e r 22

Mrs. Suzuki: This is our family photo album. Would you like to take a look at it?

Mrs. Jones: Yes, I would . . . Ohhh, that's you and your husband, isn't it?

Mrs. S: Yes . . . Our wedding. We were much younger then.

Mrs. J: How did you meet your husband?

Mrs. S: We were married through a go-between, but these days most men and women marry someone they've found by themselves. There are a lot of arranged marriages even these days, though.

Mrs. J: How are they arranged?

Mrs. S: Well, the go-between introduces the boy and the girl to each other, frequently over dinner. The parents often go along too. If both parties are interested, the couple will then go out together for a while and eventually decide whether or not to get married. This gives them a chance to fall in love.

Mrs. J: It sounds very pragmatic.

Mrs. S: Broadly speaking, I think arranged marriages have two advantages. One is that the couple is brought together by someone who is able to judge things like personality, interests and occupation objectively. The other is that it gives people from completely different walks of life a chance to meet each other.

見合いの利点

ジョーンズ夫人：とくに、広い範囲から相手を見つけられるのは魅力的ですね。

鈴木夫人：見合い結婚のよい面は、離婚率の低いことにも一役買っているかもしれませんわ。日本の離婚率は、人口1,000人対比でせいぜい1、2件で、ここ10年ほどはそんなに変わっていません。

結婚年齢

ジョーンズ夫人：日本のお若い方たちは何歳くらいで結婚するんですか。

鈴木夫人：結婚の平均年齢は、男性が28歳で、女性が26歳です。

ジョーンズ夫人：アメリカでは、男性がほぼ24歳で、女性が22歳のようですわ。

家族構成

鈴木夫人：奥様、この写真をご覧になって。子供たちを連れて、昨年夏にグアム島に行ったときの写真ですわ。男の子2人は大学生で、下の女の子は高校生ですの。

ジョーンズ夫人：立派なお子さんたちですね。5人家族でいらしたのね。私どもは子供は2人ですの。

鈴木夫人：そうでしたの。日本の平均の家族数は、3.4人になっています。むかしは3世代の家族が一緒に住んでいたんですが、最近は両親と子供だけの核家族が増えているんです。確かにご主人の

核家族

ご両親とは一緒に住みたくないという奥さん方が多くなっているようです。年寄りと若い世代の人が「スープの冷めない距離」に住むのがいいといわれていますが、住宅事情が許せば、それが理想的でしょうね。これが私が勤めていたときの写真です。

ジョーンズ夫人：あら、いまとちっともお変わりありませんのね。日本の女の方って、いつまでもお若いんですね。

鈴木夫人：お褒めにあずかって光栄ですわ。

Mrs. J: The opportunity of being able to choose someone from a larger circle of people would be attractive.

Mrs. S: The merits of the arranged marriage system may have something to do with the low divorce rate in Japan. Out of a thousand couples, only one or two break up each year. And this has been fairly constant over the past ten years.

Mrs. J: At what age do Japanese young people usually get married?

Mrs. S: On the average 28 for men and 26 for women.

Mrs. J: In America I think it's 24 for men and 22 for women.

Mrs. S: See this picture? This was taken on a trip we made to Guam with our children last summer. Our two sons are both in college and our daughter's in high school.

Mrs. J: Fine looking children. So there are five of you? We have two children.

Mrs. S: Really? The average family size in Japan is 3.4. In the past there were many three-generation families living together but the number of families made up of just parents and children has been increasing recently. There seem to be a lot of wives these days who say that they'd rather not live with the husband's parents. We have an expression that says that the older and younger generations should live close enough together to bring over some soup before it cools. I guess that would be ideal if the housing situation permitted it. Here, this is a picture of me when I was working.

Mrs. J: You haven't changed a bit. Japanese women never seem to age.

Mrs. S: You flatter me.

22

Home Life

女性の仕事

ジョーンズ夫人：日本では、女性はどのくらいお仕事をされていますの。

鈴木夫人：働く年齢の女性のおよそ半分が働いています。そのうちの70％が既婚婦人です。

ジョーンズ夫人：そんなに働いておられるんですか。どんな職業が多いのですか。

鈴木夫人：学校の先生には女性が多いのですが、そのほか、司法官、企業経営者、行政管理職も増えています。だけど、まだアメリカに比べると、管理職的な仕事は数が少ないでしょう。

ジョーンズ夫人：日本はまだ、男性のほうが強い社会なのかしら。

**家庭内の
主婦の権限**

鈴木夫人：いいえ、そうともいえません。家庭のなかのことは、主婦のほうが夫以上に役割を果たして、責任を持っています。夫が勤め人の場合、給料は大部分妻に渡してしまう人が多いんです。日常の生活費の管理には、妻が権限を持っています。私どもも、夫は「おまえがわが家の財布のひもをがっちり握り過ぎている」と小言をいっています。（笑い）

ジョーンズ夫人：まあ、それは意外でした。アメリカでは、主婦が必要な家計費を夫から受けとるのが普通です。

Mrs. J: Do a lot of Japanese women have jobs?

Mrs. S: Half of women of working age do. And 70 percent of them are married.

Mrs. J: I didn't realize there were so many working women. What kind of jobs do they have?

Mrs. S: Well, there are a lot of female teachers in Japan, but more and more women are also becoming judges, operating their own businesses, going into government and politics . . . Compared with the U.S., though, the number of women in executive positions is still small.

Mrs. J: Would you call Japan a male-oriented society?

Mrs. S: No. In the home the housewife usually has more authority and responsibility than her husband. And in most families where the husband is the wage earner, he will turn his whole salary over to her. The wife has control over the household accounts. For example, my husband often complains that I keep too firm a hand on the purse strings. (Laughs)

Mrs. J: I'd've never dreamed that it was that way. In America, many husbands just give their wives enough money to take care of the house.

22

Home Life

Useful Expressions ———— 22

22

Useful Expressions

1

These days most men and women marry someone they've found by themselves.

ノート

these days「近ごろは」by oneselfとfor oneself
はいくらか感じの違いがある。

by oneself は「（自分に利益をもたらす意味がな
く）独立で」、むしろ alone（単独で）に近い。for
oneself は「（自分の利益のために）自分で」の意
味が強い。

2

The couple will then go out together for a while.

ノート

go out は、未婚の男女の初期の浅い交際や長期
に渡る交際を指した「つき合い」に使うことが多い。

例文

Are you *going out* with Mary?
「いまメアリーとつき合っているのかい」

3

Broadly speaking, I think arranged marriages have two advantages.

ノート

broadly speaking「大ざっぱにいえば、大筋では」
の意。generally speaking「一般的にいって」とと
もに、覚えておいてよい語句。

4

You flatter me.

ノート

「まあうれしいことをいってくれますね（お口が
お上手ですね）」次のようないい方もよくする。

例文

Flattery will get you nowhere.
「お世辞いったってだめだよ」

240

Chapter
23

交通と通信

Transportation and Communications

日本の鉄道はすべて民営になりました

日本の国内交通は、現在、
旅客・貨物ともに自動車が第1位を占めています。
明治のころから人々に親しまれてきた国鉄は、
巨額な累積赤字を解消するために
1987年から7社に分割され民営となりました。

〔日本の国内輸送の割合の変化〕

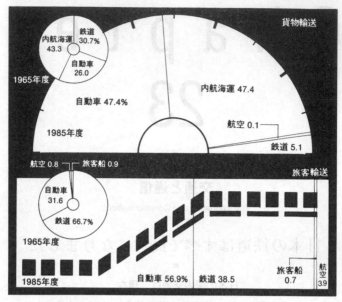

貨物輸送

鉄道 30.7%
内航海運 43.3
自動車 26.0
1965年度

自動車 47.4%
内航海運 47.4
航空 0.1
鉄道 5.1
1985年度

旅客輸送

航空 0.8　旅客船 0.9
自動車 31.6
鉄道 66.7%
1965年度

自動車 56.9%　鉄道 38.5　旅客船 0.7　航空 3.9
1985年度

Vocabulary

新幹線	□□	a bullet train; the Shinkansen
地下鉄網	□□	a subway system
通勤鉄道網	□□	a commuter system
人口の少ない地方	□□	the less heavily populated areas
旅客輸送	□□	passenger transportation
〜を二分している	□□	to share . . . equally
国営鉄道	□□	the state-operated railroad
民営化する	□□	to privatize
累計赤字	□□	a tremendous (accrued) debt
斜陽の	□□	to be on the decline
国内郵便	□□	domestic mail
舗装する	□□	to pave
高速道路	□□	an expressway
自動車産業国	□□	a leading producer of automobiles
外航海運	□□	overseas shipping business
世界的な不況	□□	global depression

〔各国の電話機数（100人当たり）〕

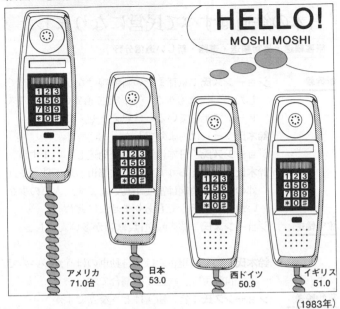

HELLO!

MOSHI MOSHI

23

Transportation and Communications

アメリカ
71.0台

日本
53.0

西ドイツ
50.9

イギリス
51.0

(1983年)

重量トン	□□	deadweight ton
過剰	□□	excess
バルクキャリアー	□□	a bulk carrier
航空貨物	□□	air cargo
事務機器	□□	an office machine
半導体	□□	a semiconductor
人工衛星による通信技術	□□	satellite communications
通信網を総合する	□□	to integrate the communications network
公営の電話会社	□□	the state-run telephone company
自由化する	□□	to deregulate
～を融合した分野	□□	fields that integrate . . .
データ通信	□□	data communications
ビデオテックス	□□	videotex
付加価値通信網	□□	value-added networks; VAN

日本の鉄道はすべて民営になりました

旅客輸送・貨物輸送・道路・新しい通信分野

新幹線

ジョーンズ氏：京都までの新幹線はなかなか快適でしたよ。揺れも少ないし、とても200kmのスピードで走っているとは思えませんでした。

鈴木氏：それは何よりでした。

ジョーンズ氏：日本は鉄道網が発達していますね。

鈴木氏：そのとおりですね。大都市の地下鉄網や近郊の通勤鉄道網は密度が高いんです。人口の少ない地方ではそうでもありませんけどね。

旅客輸送

ジョーンズ氏：旅客輸送は、鉄道が多いんでしょう。

鈴木氏：いや、現在では、自動車のほうが多いのです。自動車6、鉄道4の割合です。

貨物輸送

ジョーンズ氏：貨物輸送はどうなんですか。

鈴木氏：鉄道の比率は驚くほど低いのですよ。鉄道と航空を合わせてせいぜい5％強です。残りを内航海運と自動車で二分しているといった状況です。ただし、航空の場合は、総送送量は少ないのですが、着実に伸びています。

ジョーンズ氏：アメリカでは、貨物輸送はまだ40％近くは鉄道に頼っています。もっとも、旅客輸送となると、鉄道は1％もないんです。

鈴木氏：アメリカで、鉄道の貨物がまだそんなにあるとは気づきませんでした。日本では、鉄道の営業路線はかつては国営が4、民営が1の割合だったのです。しかし、国営鉄道は巨額な累積赤字を

国鉄民営化

抜本的に解決するために、1987年に民営になりました。

ジョーンズ氏：アメリカでも、鉄道は斜陽産業で、

C h a p t e r 23

Mr. Jones: We had a lovely ride down to Kyoto on the bullet train. It was so smooth we couldn't believe that we were traveling at 200 kilometers per hour.

Mr. Suzuki: Glad to hear it.

Mr. J: Japan certainly has a well-developed railway system.

Mr. S: I guess we do. The subway and commuter systems in and around the large cities are very close-knit. It's different in the less heavily populated areas, though.

Mr. J: Railways seem to be the main form of passenger transportation.

Mr. S: Not really. Recently more people travel by car. I think it's six to four in favor of cars.

Mr. J: What about freight?

Mr. S: A surprisingly small percentage goes by rail. Rail and air combined account for a little over five percent. Ships and trucks share the remainder about equally. Though the amount of air cargo transport is small, it's growing steadily.

Mr. J: In America, railroads still carry about 40 percent of the freight. Of course when it comes to passenger transport, they handle less than one percent.

Mr. S: I didn't realize that trains were still so big in cargo transport in the U.S. Until recently, we had about four kilometers of state-operated railroad to every kilometer of private railroad. But in 1987 the state-run railway was privatized in an attempt to clear up its tremendous debt.

Mr. J: Railways are also on the decline in the States, and have

道路

いろいろと問題を抱えていますよ。いまでは、アメリカの国内郵便はほぼ全部、航空便になってしまっていますしね。ところで、5年前より日本の道路はたいへんよくなりましたね。

鈴木氏：年々よくなっています。主要な道路はほぼ舗装されています。しかしアメリカと比べると道路の幅も狭いし、高速道路も不足しています。土地の値段が高いものですから、思うようにはかどらないんですよ。

自動車

ジョーンズ氏：車の数もそうとう増えているようですね。なにしろ日本は世界でもトップクラスの自動車生産国ですからね。

鈴木氏：人口4人に対して1台くらいになっています。アメリカはどうなっていますか。

ジョーンズ氏：1.4人に1台の割ですから、一家に1台以上あるわけですね。日本の外航海運は盛んなんでしょう？

外航海運

鈴木氏：日本は周囲を海に囲まれていますので、海運は重要なんです。しかし、さまざまな問題があって、業界の状況はたいへん厳しいようです。とくに、荷動きの量が減っているうえに、船腹量が過剰なのが大きな原因なんです。

ジョーンズ氏：確かに、海運は世界的に不況のようですね。先日読んだビジネス週刊誌にも、世界でタンカーだけでも1億重量トン、バラ積み船のバルクキャリアーで5,000万重量トンも過剰になっているという記事が出ていましたよ。

航空貨物

鈴木氏：そのようですね。その半面、日本でも航空貨物の輸送売上は年々増えています。これには、事務機器や半導体のような小型のものも、航空便で運ばれるようになったこともあります。

a lot of problems. Nearly all domestic mail goes by air now, you know. One thing I noticed here this time is that the roads are much better than they were five years ago.

Mr. S: They've been getting better every year. Most main roads are paved now. But they're much narrower than in the U.S., and we don't have enough expressways. Progress is slow because of the high price of land.

Mr. J: The number of cars has increased greatly, too. You can tell Japan is one of the world's leading producers of automobiles.

Mr. S: There's about one car for every four people. How about in the States?

Mr. J: It's one car per 1.4 persons, more than one car per family. Regarding shipping, does Japan do much overseas shipping business?

Mr. S: The country is surrounded by water so sea transport is of course important. But there are a lot of problems and the business environment is very severe. The main sources of trouble are a decline in the amount of cargo being handled and excessive capacity.

Mr. J: I know there's a global depression in merchant shipping. I read in a business magazine the other day that worldwide there's a 100 million deadweight ton excess in tanker capacity and a 50 million ton excess in bulk carrier capacity.

Mr. S: So I hear. On the other hand, though, the amount of air cargo business has been increasing every year in Japan. It's partly because there are many more small items like office machines and semiconductors that can be carried by air these days.

・通信網の
統合

ジョーンズ氏：半導体といえば、超 LSI の開発や光ファイバー通信・人工衛星による通信技術が大幅に進展していますね。こうした技術の応用によって通信網の統合が日本でも進んでいるようですね。

・通信の
自由化

鈴木氏：そのとおりです。日本では、1985年に公営の電話会社が民営化され、通信の自由化が実現したわけです。いよいよ通信分野は多様化してきますね。

ジョーンズ氏：これからとくにどんな分野が進展すると見られているんですか。

・新しい
通信分野

鈴木氏：さまざまな予想が出ていますので、なかなか難しいのですが、やはり通信とコンピューターを融合した分野だと思います。

ジョーンズ氏：具体的には？

鈴木氏：データ通信、電話回線を結んで文字・図形情報を送るビデオテックス、付加価値通信網といっている VAN（Value-Added Network）が伸びるのではないかといわれています。なかでも、VAN サービスに期待がかかっているようです。

Mr. J: Speaking of semiconductors, right now I hear that there is a big push in the development of VLSI, optical communications and satellite communications. I hear Japan is also moving ahead with the application of these to integrate its communications network.

Mr. S: That's right. We used to have a state-run telephone company but that was privatized in 1985, so the communications field is deregulated now. From now on we'll be seeing a lot of diversification.

Mr. J: What fields do you expect to see progress in?

Mr. S: All kinds of predictions are being made and it's not easy to say, but I think fields that integrate communications and computer technology will advance quickly.

Mr. J: Like?

Mr. S: Data communications, videotex, value-added networks or VANs as they are called. VANs are considered especially promising.

1

ノート

例文

It was <u>so</u> smooth we couldn't believe that we were traveling at 200 kilometers per hour.

　so ... that ... 「ひじょうに〜なので〜」の that は口語では省かれることがある。上例は It was so smooth (that) we couldn't believe ... と that が省かれたもの。

The box was *so* heavy (that) we couldn't move it.

2

ノート

Railways <u>are on the decline</u> in the States.

　be on the decline 「下り坂である、衰えている」

3

ノート

例文

There's about <u>one car for every four people</u>.

　この for は、each や every や数詞の前に用いて、対比・割合を示し「〜に対して」。

For every six who attended the meeting, there were two who did not.

4

ノート

<u>There is a big push</u> in the development of VLSI.

　there is a big push 「大きな前進（努力）がある」、つまり「〜の開発に大きな力を入れている」。ちなみに VLSI は <u>V</u>ery <u>L</u>arge <u>S</u>cale <u>I</u>ntegration の略。

5

ノート

<u>From now on</u> we'll be seeing a lot of diversification.

　from now on 「これからは、今後は」

Chapter
24

日本の技術力
Japan's Technological Strength

日本人の特性と技術力との深い関係

高品質の日本製品と、それを支える技術力は
現在、世界中で高く評価されています。
それだけに外国人の興味や関心も高く、
その要因について
質問されることがよくあります。

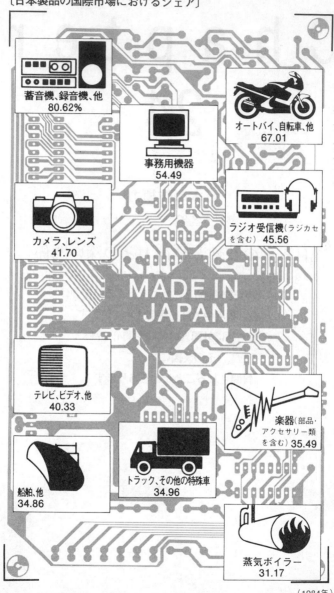

〔日本製品の国際市場におけるシェア〕

蓄音機、録音機、他
80.62%

事務用機器
54.49

オートバイ、自転車、他
67.01

カメラ、レンズ
41.70

ラジオ受信機（ラジカセを含む）45.56

MADE IN
JAPAN

テレビ、ビデオ、他
40.33

楽器（部品・アクセサリー類を含む）35.49

船舶、他
34.86

トラック、その他の特殊車
34.96

蒸気ボイラー
31.17

（1984年）

Vocabulary •——————————————

日本の工業製品	☐☐	Japanese industrial products
～について高い評価をする	☐☐	to have a very high opinion of . . .
画面が鮮明である	☐☐	the picture is sharp
故障の心配がない	☐☐	to be trouble-free
燃費がよい	☐☐	to get excellent gas mileage
日本人の特性	☐☐	characteristics of the Japanese people
細やかな細工品	☐☐	a finely crafted thing
茶器	☐☐	a tea utensil
異質なものを結合する	☐☐	to combine unrelated things
技術を組み合わせる	☐☐	to integrate techniques
メカトロニクス	☐☐	mechatronics（日本でできた英語）
密接な関係	☐☐	a close connection
生産現場	☐☐	a shop-floor
大学卒の従業員	☐☐	a university-educated employee
直接得た技術	☐☐	first-hand knowledge
力を発揮する	☐☐	to make a significant contribution
自動化	☐☐	automation
技術の改善	☐☐	a technical improvement
意思疎通	☐☐	communication
反映する	☐☐	to reflect
大学卒の技術者	☐☐	an engineer out of college
～に配置される	☐☐	to be assigned to . . .
～を誇りに思う	☐☐	to feel pride in . . .
生産現場の従業員	☐☐	an employee on the shop-floor
不良品の絶滅	☐☐	elimination of defective products
品質をつくり込む	☐☐	to build the quality into the product
完全主義者	☐☐	a perfectionist
独創的な技術開発	☐☐	the creation of original technology
研究開発の分野	☐☐	the field of R&D
努力を強化する	☐☐	to redouble efforts
阻害する	☐☐	to stifle

24

Japan's Technological Strength

日本人の特性と技術力との深い関係

高品質を支える技術力の要因・今後の展開

**・日本製品の
品質のよさ
の評判**

ジョーンズ氏：日本の工業製品は、アメリカ人も高い評価をしていますよ。ちょっと前ですが、息子が、現在わが家で使用中のテレビの映像がよくないから、そろそろ買い替えたらどうかというんです。そしてそのときには、画面の鮮明な日本製のテレビがいいと、盛んに勧めていました。

鈴木氏：それは日本人としてたいへんうれしいお話ですね。私もこの間アメリカに行ったとき、アメリカの友人から、近いうちに現在乗っている車を買い替えたいと思っている。そのさい、故障が少なく、燃費もよいと評判が高い日本車にしたいと思っているが、あなたはどの車種を推薦するかという質問を受けましたよ。

**・工業製品の
品質のよさ
技術力の
高さ**

ジョーンズ氏：そうですか。ところで鈴木さん、日本の工業製品の品質のよさや、技術力の高さを支えているおもな要因は何でしょうかね。ちょうどよい機会ですから、あなたのご意見を伺わせていただけませんか。

鈴木氏：そうですね。それには、いくつかの要因があると思います。それに、これらの要因は日本人の特性と密接に関連していると思います。

ジョーンズ氏：それは興味深いですね。ぜひ聞かせてください。

**・小型化した
ものを精緻
に作る能力**

鈴木氏：まず第1に、日本人はむかしから茶器の細やかな細工や盆栽に見られるように、小型化したものを精緻に作ることを得意としています。この日本人の特性が現在、小型乗用車、ヘッドホンステレオ、カメラ、電子時計、**LSI** などの製品に

C h a p t e r 24

Mr. Jones: You know we Americans have a very high opinion of Japanese industrial products. Not so long ago, our son told us we should get a new TV pretty soon because our picture tube is going. He insisted that we should buy a high-resolution Japanese model because the picture is so sharp.

Mr. Suzuki: As a Japanese, I'm always happy to hear such stories. When I was in America the last time, one of my friends told me he was planning to buy a new car. He'd decided to get a Japanese model because he'd heard so many good things about their being trouble-free and getting excellent gas mileage. He asked me what Japanese make I'd recommend.

Mr. J: Is that right? But tell me, what do you think are the main factors behind Japan's ability to produce high quality industrial products and maintain such high technical standards? I think this'd be a good chance to get your thoughts on the subject.

Mr. S: Well, there are several, I think. I believe they are all closely related to characteristics of the Japanese people.

Mr. J: That's interesting! I'd like to hear more about that.

Mr. S: Well, first, the Japanese have long been skillful at making small, finely crafted things — as you can see from our tea utensils and *bonsai*. I think this trait shows up in products like compact cars, headphone stereos, cameras, electronic watches, LSIs and the like. Second we are traditionally good

**技術を組み
合わせ応用
する能力**

発揮されていると思います。それから第2は、日本人は伝統的に異質なものを巧みに結合する才能があり、違った分野の技術の組み合わせや応用に優れています。この特性が、最近の技術では機械と電子技術を組み合わせたメカトロニクスの分野で、おおいに生かされています。とりわけ、VTR、複写機、ファクシミリなどの製品に生かされています。

ジョーンズ氏：なるほど、日本の技術は日本人の特性と密接に関係があるというわけですね。

**大学卒技術
者の生産現
場への投入**

鈴木氏：はい、そのとおりです。第3に考えられるのは、日本では生産現場を大切にしています。大学卒の技術者を、生産現場にも技術スタッフとしてたくさん配置します。彼らには現場から直接得た技術がありますので、自動化や技術の改善などに、なおさら力を発揮するわけです。開発・設計部門と生産現場との意思疎通も密接になっていますので、現場からの意見や提案も、開発・設計部門によく反映されています。

ジョーンズ氏：その点はアメリカとは大きく事情が違いますね。大学卒の技術者が生産現場に配置されることはまずありません。日本では、生産現場に配置された技術者から苦情は出ないのですか。

鈴木氏：いいえ、まったく逆です。生産現場に配置されることを誇りに思っている技術者が多いんですよ。それに生産現場と開発・設計部門間の人事異動も、たえず行われています。

ジョーンズ氏：そうですか。

小集団活動

鈴木氏：第4に、日本ではとくに生産現場の従業員が、自主的に運営する QC サークル・ZD 運動

at combining unrelated things — integrating and applying techniques from different fields. This talent shows up very strongly in the area of mechatronics, which combines mechanics with electronics. Particularly in such products as video tape recorders, copiers and facsimile machines.

Mr. J: Hmmm. What you are saying is that there's a close connection between Japanese technology and the nature of the Japanese people.

Mr. S: Exactly. The third factor I can think of is the importance attached to what happens on the shop-floor in Japan. Large numbers of university-educated employees are assigned to white-collar jobs at the factories. The first-hand knowledge they acquire allows them to make a more significant contribution, such as to automation and other technical improvements. Also good communication between people on the shop-floor and those in the development and design divisions assures that the ideas of those who work at production are reflected in development and design decisions.

Mr. J: That's quite different from what goes on in the States. There engineers out of college are never assigned to jobs on the shop-floor. Don't the engineers who are given such jobs complain?

Mr. S: No, quite the contrary. Most of them feel pride in their assignment. Then too, there's an almost constant interchange of personnel between the factory and the development and design divisions.

Mr. J: I see.

Mr. S: Fourth is the fact that Japanese employees, especially those on the shop-floor, voluntarily organize themselves into

などを行っていることが挙げられます。いずれも生産の各段階の従業員で構成する小集団活動で、不良品の絶滅やコスト切り下げの努力が真剣に進められています。先日もお話ししましたので、覚えていらっしゃると思います。まさに製品の品質をつくり込むといった意気込みで行われているんです。日本人には完璧志向があるという人もいます。第5に、日本では、国土が狭いわりに交通・情報網が発達しており、そのうえ、国民の大多数の生活レベルが中産化しています。ですから、新製品の国内普及が早く、ユーザーの要求も早く高度化するんです。そのため各メーカー同士も互いに競い合って、製品の開発・改善の努力をいつも続けています。第6に、最後の要素として考えられるのは、日本の長期雇用慣行です。短期的に業績を上げることだけにとらわれないで、新設備の設置や技術改善などが割合たやすくできることも挙げられます。

●交通・情報網の発達

●新設備の設置と技術改善

●今後の技術力強化

●独創的な技術開発

ジョーンズ氏：よくわかりました。では、今後の日本の技術力強化について、あなたはどのようなお考えをお持ちですか。

鈴木氏：これまで日本は、独創的な技術開発の面では、実績が少なかったと思います。しかし、最近ではご承知のとおり、超LSI、光通信システム、ニューセラミックスなどの先端技術で、日本が世界をリードするものも出てきています。今後はとくに研究開発の分野では、ともすると独創的発想を阻害するおそれのある「集団的思考」に改革を加えながら、新技術の研究・開発を促進する努力を強化していくだろうと思います。

groups for promoting quality control and realizing zero defects. These are small groups consisting of the workers at each stage of production, and they take cost reduction and the elimination of defective products very seriously. We talked about them the other day. Remember? The attitude is one of actually building the quality into the product. Some say we Japanese are perfectionists. The fifth factor is that for its small size Japan has highly developed transportation and communication systems, and that on top of this, most Japanese enjoy middle-class living standards. As a result, new products penetrate the market quite rapidly and consumers quickly develop sophisticated tastes. Therefore, the manufacturers are constantly working to develop and improve their products ahead of the competition. The sixth and final factor I can think of is Japan's long-term employment system. This frees the company from having to focus solely on short-term results and makes it relatively easy to introduce new equipment and technical improvements.

Mr. J: I follow you. But what do you see as the likely course of future technological development in Japan?

Mr. S: Well, I feel that up to now Japan has made rather few advances in the creation of truly new and original technology. But this is changing, and as you know Japan is now a world leader in a number of high-tech fields like VLSIs, optical communication systems and fine ceramics. I think that especially in the field of R&D we may see redoubled efforts to promote the development of new technology being paralleled by changes aimed at modifying the Japanese "group-think" mentality that so often tends to stifle creative thinking.

Useful Expressions ———— 24

1 We <u>have a very high opinion of</u> Japanese industrial products.

ノート　このopinion は「評価、(善悪などの)判断」。

例文　They *have a poor opinion of* the new method.
「彼らは新方式をあまり評価していない」

2 He <u>insisted</u> that we should buy a Japanese model.

ノート　insist that ... 「〜を主張する、いい張る」この形式以外には、insist on ... の形でよく使う。

例文　He *insisted on* climbing Mt. Fuji.

3 <u>What do you think are</u> the main factors behind Japan's ability?

ノート　What do you think のあとの語順は、文法上からいえば are が文末になるはずだが、the main factors ... が長いので慣用的にareがさきに来ている。

例文　*What do you think is* the most notable feature of modern Japanese society? (12)

4 We <u>are good at</u> combining unrelated things.

ノート　be good at ... が正しい用法で be good in ... は使わない。なお反対は be poor at ... 。☞Useful Expressions 38-3

ただし、strong ／ weak の場合は、それぞれ be strong *in* ... ／ be weak *in* ... 。

例文　Tom *is strong in* mathematics.
「トムは数学が得意だ」

Chapter 25

日本語

Writing System and Language

日本語は縦にも横にも書けるんですね

日本の経済力・技術力が
世界の注目を集めるにしたがって、
日本語を学ぶ外国人の数も増えています。
漢字・ひらがな・カタカナという
3つの文字体系を持つ日本語のユニークさに
ひかれる人も多いようです。

日本の文字

25

日本語

KANJI			
阿	米	川	山
阿	米	川	山
象	木	川	山
象	木	川	山

HIRA GANA			
衣	宇	以	安
む	宇	い	あ
え	う	い	あ

KATA KANA			
江	宇	伊	阿
エ	ウ	イ	ア
エ	ウ	イ	ア

Vocabulary ●

縦に書く	☐☐	to write vertically
横に書く	☐☐	to write horizontally
四角く複雑である	☐☐	to be angular and quite complicated
わりに簡単である	☐☐	to be rather simple
観察眼のある	☐☐	to be perceptive
漢字	☐☐	a *kanji* character
体系が違う	☐☐	to belong to different systems
気が遠くなる	☐☐	to be mind-boggling
〜から伝来する	☐☐	to come from . . .
古代中国漢王朝	☐☐	the Han dynasty of ancient China
意味がある	☐☐	to have one's own meaning
表意文字	☐☐	an ideogram
峰	☐☐	a peak
面白い	☐☐	to be fascinating
立つ	☐☐	to stand up
〜の一部をとって作られる	☐☐	to be formed by extracting one element from . . .
名詞	☐☐	a noun
動詞	☐☐	a verb
形容詞	☐☐	an adjective
活用語尾	☐☐	an ending
外来語	☐☐	a word borrowed from a foreign language
ビジネス文書	☐☐	business writing
数字	☐☐	the Arabic numerals
AとBを併記する	☐☐	to include A and B
〜と親戚である	☐☐	to be related to . . .
アルタイ系の	☐☐	Altaic
有力な説	☐☐	a widely accepted theory
重要言語	☐☐	an important language
日常会話	☐☐	daily conversation

日本語は縦にも横にも書けるんですね

漢字・ひらがな・カタカナ・日本語の学習

● **縦書きの**
日本語

ジョーンズ夫人：日本の新聞は縦に書いてあります
のね。

鈴木夫人：ええそうです。右から左へ読むんですよ。

ジョーンズ夫人：私には、このなかに文字が2種類
あるように見えますけど。四角い複雑な文字と、
丸くてわりに簡単な文字と。

● **漢字**
ひらがな
カタカナ

鈴木夫人：そのとおりですわ。奥様よく観察なさっ
ていらっしゃいますね。ほら、ご覧になって。こ
の最初の字は漢字、3番目の字はひらがなです。
文字の体系が違うんです。それに、カタカナとい
う体系もあるんですのよ。

ジョーンズ夫人：まあ、では、3種類のアルファベッ
トのようなものがあるんですね。

鈴木夫人：おっしゃるとおりですわ。3種類の違っ
た文字があるんです。でも、それぞれの体系の文
字数は、英語のアルファベットより多いんです。

ジョーンズ夫人：どのくらいあるんですの。

鈴木夫人：ひらがなとカタカナはそれぞれ46文字あ
ります。漢字は……大きな辞書にはおよそ5万字
くらい載っています。

ジョーンズ夫人：まあ、気が遠くなりそうですわ。
日本人はそれを全部学校で習いますの。

鈴木夫人：それはとても無理ですわ。学校で習うの
は日常使う2,000字くらいです。それから一般の
新聞や雑誌に出てくる漢字は3,000字くらいかし
ら。

● **漢字の歴史**

ジョーンズ夫人：それでもたいへんな数ね。この間
の歴史のお話のなかで、ご主人が日本の文字は中

C h a p t e r 25

Mrs. Jones: I see your newspapers are written vertically.

Mrs. Suzuki: That's right. We read the lines from right to left.

Mrs. J: I've noticed two types of letters. Some of them are angular and quite complicated. The other ones are rounded and rather simple.

Mrs. S: Right! You're very perceptive. Here, let me show you. These first two letters are *kanji* characters and this third one is a *hiragana* character. They belong to different systems. We also have another system called *katakana*.

Mrs. J: You mean you have three alphabets?

Mrs. S: Yes, three different types of characters. But each type has more letters than the English alphabet.

Mrs. J: How many?

Mrs. S: The hiragana and katakana alphabets each have 46 characters. And the kanji characters . . . A large dictionary will probably give around 50,000.

Mrs. J: That's mind-boggling. Do you learn all of those at school?

Mrs. S: That wouldn't be possible. In school we learn about 2,000 of the most common ones. Most ordinary newspapers and magazines are written in about 3,000 characters, I think.

Mrs. J: Even that's a lot. When we were talking about Japanese history the other day, your husband said that

国から朝鮮を経て伝わったのだとおっしゃいましたね。

鈴木夫人：ええ、そうです。4世紀ごろから伝来したんです。「漢字」という言葉は、「漢の文字」という意味です。漢というのは中国の古代漢王朝のことですわ。漢字が中国で使われるようになったのは、3,000年以上もむかしからなんです。

ジョーンズ夫人：3,000年以上むかしに、いまでも使える文字が発明されていたなんて、素晴らしいことですわ。漢字はひと文字ずつで何か意味がありそうですね。

● 漢字の性格

表意文字

象形文字

鈴木夫人：鋭いご明察ですわ。ひらがなとカタカナは、アルファベットと同じで音を表すだけですけれど、漢字は表意文字なんです。たとえば、これは山、これは川、これは木ですわ。

ジョーンズ夫人：私にはさっぱり……。

鈴木夫人：この本をちょっとご覧になって。これは3つの山の峰に見えません？　これは川の水が流れる様子、こちらはこうして木の幹と枝と根でしょう？

ジョーンズ夫人：なんて面白いんでしょう。ものの形がそのまま文字になっているんですね。

鈴木夫人：ええ、そうです。これは象。

ジョーンズ夫人：えっ、象？　象の絵には見えませんわ。

鈴木夫人：ほら、こうして象の絵をかいて縦にすると、この字に近くなるでしょう。

ジョーンズ夫人：ほんと、こんどはわかりましたわ。ところでひらがな、カタカナはどうしてできたのでしょう。

● ひらがな・

カタカナの

成立

鈴木夫人：ひらがなは9世紀ころの平安時代に漢字

Japanese writing came from China through Korea.

Mrs. S: Yes, in around the fourth century. "Kanji" means "letters from *Kan*." Kan is our word for the Han dynasty of ancient China. The first kanji characters appeared in China more than 3,000 years ago.

Mrs. J: Letters invented more than 3,000 years ago still in use today — it's amazing. I get the feeling that each of the kanji characters represents something — has its own meaning.

Mrs. S: You are very perceptive. The hiragana and katakana characters are like English letters. They only represent sounds, whereas the kanji characters are ideograms. Look. This character means mountain, and this is river, and this is tree.

Mrs. J: I don't . . .

Mrs. S: Look at this book. Don't you see the three peaks of the mountain? The flow of the river? The trunk, branches and roots of the tree?

Mrs. J: How fascinating! The letter comes from the shape of the thing.

Mrs. S: Yes. Here, this is the character for elephant.

Mrs. J: Elephant? I don't see a picture of an elephant.

Mrs. S: Look. If I draw an elephant like this and then turn it till it's standing up — doesn't it resemble this letter?

Mrs. J: Yes, now I see it! Where did the hiragana and katakana alphabets come from?

Mrs. S: The hiragana characters were devised from kanji char-

から作られたのです。ひとつひとつのひらがなは、古代日本語に近い発音の漢字を簡略化したものです。ひらがなはもともと女性専用の文字でした。カタカナはずっと後代になって、同じ音の漢字の一部分をとって作ったんです。

ジョーンズ夫人：でも、3種類の文字をどう使い分けるんですか。

鈴木夫人：漢字は名詞、動詞・形容詞の語幹など文章の重要部分に使います。ひらがなは動詞や形容詞の活用語尾などに使います。カタカナは中国語以外の外来語を書くのに多く使います。

●横書き

ジョーンズ夫人：文章は横にも書くんですよね。

鈴木夫人：そうです。もともと日本語は縦書きなんですが、ビジネス文書は数字や英語を併記する必要がありますので、横書きが多いようです。

ジョーンズ夫人：日本語はどの言語の親戚なんですか。

鈴木夫人：私の習ったところでは、アルタイ系で朝鮮語と同系だろうという説が有力です。でも学問的にはまだ証明されてないということですわ。

**●日本語の
学習**

ジョーンズ夫人：日本語は、最近は世界の重要言語のひとつになっていると思いますわ。アメリカでも日本語学習が盛んですよ。やはり、日本の経済・技術力がだんだん大きくなったので、日本のことを知りたい人が増えてきているんですね。

鈴木夫人：そのようですね。中国やヨーロッパ、オーストラリアでも盛んなようですわね。

acters in the Heian period. Each letter is a simplification of a kanji character with a pronunciation similar to a syllable of ancient Japanese speech. Hiragana characters were originally used only by women. The katakana characters were formed much later by extracting one element from a similar sounding kanji character.

Mrs. J: How do you decide which alphabet to use?

Mrs. S: Kanji characters are used for the most important elements of the sentence — the nouns, verb roots, adjective roots . . . Hiragana characters are used for the verb and adjective endings. Katakana characters are used mostly for writing words we've borrowed from languages other than Chinese.

Mrs. J: I'm sure I've also seen Japanese written horizontally, haven't I?

Mrs. S: Yes, we write that way, too. Japanese writing is designed to be written vertically but most business writing is done horizontally, because it's easier to include Arabic numerals and English words that way.

Mrs. J: What languages is Japanese related to?

Mrs. S: I was taught that it belongs to the Altaic and Korean family of languages. That's the most widely accepted theory. But they say this has never been proved.

Mrs. J: I feel Japanese has become one of the important languages in the world. Interest in learning Japanese is quite high in America. I feel it's Japan's present economic power and technology that have made people want to know more about the country.

Mrs. S: I suppose so. I hear there is also increasing interest in China, Europe and Australia.

ジョーンズ夫人：私も日本語習おうかしら。でも、とても難しそうですわね。

鈴木夫人：実際にはそんなに難しくないんですのよ。会話でしたらむしろやさしい言葉だといいますわ。外国の方でも、1年くらい勉強すると日常会話はおできになる方がたくさんいらっしゃいますもの。日本にいる間にぜひお始めになるとよろしいわ。私が学習のお手伝いをいたしますわ。

ジョーンズ夫人：ドウモ、アリガトウ。

言葉と文化の相関関係

　日常われわれは、「おはようございます」「こんにちは」「こんばんは」というあいさつを、たんに朝・昼・夕の時間の違いだけで使い分けているのではない。

　たとえば、「おはようございます」は、ひじょうに広範囲に使える言葉で、家族や友人はもちろん、見知らぬ人に向かっていっても、けっしておかしくない。

　しかし、「こんにちは」や「こんばんは」は、毎日顔を合わせている家族同士では、まず使わない。ごく親しい友人に対しても「こんにちは」とあいさつするのは、なんとなくよそよそしい印象を相手に与える。「やあ」「どうも」「しばらく」などのほうが、親しみがあって適切な場合が多い。

　同様に英語でも、朝のあいさつは "Good morning."、昼は "Good afternoon."、夕方は "Good evening." だと一本調子に、相手の見境なしに使っていると、いつまでたっても改まった感じで、親交を深めるうえで阻害要因になりかねない。

　したがって、外国語を使いこなすには、どんな状況のときにその言葉が使えるのか、その国の文化と関連づけて適切に理解しておく必要がある。

Mrs. J: Maybe I should start to learn, but it seems so difficult.

Mrs. S: It's not really so hard. For just a conversational knowledge, it's probably easier than most languages. Many foreigners are able to get along in daily conversation after about a year of study. You should start studying while you are here. I'd be glad to help.

Mrs. J: *Domo arigato*.

また外国人に日本の事柄を説明するさいには、双方の文化で共通に認識し合えることをベースにして類似点と相違点を説明していくアプローチが、相手にとって理解しやすく、効果的なことが多い。

たとえば次のAとBの文は、ともに大福もちの説明である。

A Daifukumochi is a sweetmeat made of beans which have been cooked with sugar and mashed. It's covered with soft and sticky rice which has been steamed and pounded. It's round in shape, about two inches in diameter.

B Daifukumochi looks like a white marshmallow, but is about three times larger. It's made of rice which has been steamed and pounded, and it's filled with bean-jam. The jam is sweeter and a little thicker than regular jam.

現物をまったく知らない外国人が聞いて理解しやすいのは、彼らがよく知っているマシュマロやジャムを例にとって説明しているBのほうであろう。またBでは最初に「大福もちはホワイトマシュマロに似ている……」と切り出しているが、このように、まず全体像を説明し、そのうえで部分や具体的内容を解説していく手順も、異文化の外国人の理解を早めるコツである。

Column

1

<u>Let me show you</u>.

ノート

　「私にあなたに示させてください」→「ちょっと
ご覧になって」という感じ。

例文

Let me see.「ええと、はてな（何か思い出そうと
したり、とっさに答えが出てこない場合）」

2

<u>That's a lot</u>.

ノート

　「そんなに多くですか」→「それはたいへんです
ね」の感じ。このほか「それはたいへんですね」と
いういい方には、*That's a job*, isn't it?（親しみを
込めたり、皮肉っぽい感じで）とか *That's a lot of
work*.「大事な仕事で（たいへんな様子を率直に）」
などがよく使われる。

3

<u>It's</u> Japan's present economic power and
technology <u>that</u> have made people want to
know more about the country.

ノート

　これも強調構文。☞Useful Expressions 3-3

4

Many foreigners <u>are able to get along</u> in
daily conversation after about a year of
study.

ノート

　be able to ... は未来形・完了形とともに使うこ
とが多いが、能力を強調する気持ちのときは現在時
制でも使う。can よりもやや改まった感じ。また
can と違って、be able to ... は普通は生物（とく
に人間）が主語になる。

（×）This law is able to be evaded.

Chapter

26

日本文学
Japanese Literature

俳句は世界でいちばん短い詩です

日本の伝統的文学の基調となるものは、
自然と融和する心と
移ろいゆくものに対する美意識
であるといわれています。
ここでは、日本文学を外国人に説明するための
いくつかのヒントを挙げてみました。

〔翻訳言語数の多い日本文学作品〕

順位	作家名	原書名	翻訳された言語の数
1	川端康成	雪国	9
2	安部公房	砂の女	8
	川端康成	古都	
4	三島由紀夫	宴のあと	7
5	川端康成	山の音	6
	三島由紀夫	金閣寺	
		潮騒	
	谷崎潤一郎	細雪	
9	芥川龍之介	羅生門	5
	遠藤周作	海と毒薬	
	井上靖	猟銃	
	三島由紀夫	仮面の告白	
		午後の曳航	
	大江健三郎	個人的な体験	
	谷崎潤一郎	蓼喰ふ虫	
		鍵	
17	芥川龍之介	河童	4
	井伏鱒二	黒い雨	
	川端康成	みづうみ	
		千羽鶴	
	谷崎潤一郎	春琴抄	
		瘋癲老人日記	
	松本清張	点と線	
24	安部公房	他人の顔	3
		燃えつきた地図	
		箱男	
	遠藤周作	沈黙	
	川端康成	伊豆の踊り子	
	太宰治	斜陽	
		人間失格	
	夏目漱石	こころ	
		吾輩は猫である	
		門	
	野間宏	真空地帯	
	深沢七郎	楢山節考	
	三浦綾子	塩狩峠	
	三島由紀夫	春の雪	
		真夏の死	

(1987年)

Vocabulary •——————————————————

世界一短い型の詩	☐☐	the world's shortest poetry form
17音	☐☐	seventeen syllables
不思議にも	☐☐	mysteriously
奥深い	☐☐	profound
イメージの豊かな表現	☐☐	expressions with rich images
約束事	☐☐	a convention
和歌集	☐☐	an anthology of *waka* poems
畳の上に並べる	☐☐	to spread out on the floor
小説	☐☐	a novel
日記	☐☐	a diary
随筆	☐☐	an essay
宮廷	☐☐	the Imperial Court
女性遍歴	☐☐	love affairs
頂点	☐☐	an apex
王朝文学	☐☐	*Heian* court literature
教養	☐☐	cultural accomplishments
伝統的な衣装	☐☐	traditional garment
神子(みこ)	☐☐	a shrine maiden
栄華を極める	☐☐	to revel in glory
世界観	☐☐	a view of the world
仏教思想に根ざした	☐☐	to be rooted in Buddhist concepts
町人文学	☐☐	townsmen's literature
人間の欲望	☐☐	human lust
庶民の夢	☐☐	fantasies of the common man
義理と人情	☐☐	love and duty
社会のおきて	☐☐	obligations
ノーベル文学賞	☐☐	the Nobel prize for literature
西欧と交流を深める	☐☐	to develop deeper relations with the West
近代化の道を歩む	☐☐	to move ahead with modernization
～に応じて	☐☐	in parallel with . . .
多様性	☐☐	diversification

26

Japanese Literature

俳句は世界でいちばん短い詩です

俳句・和歌・万葉集・源氏物語・江戸文学

ジョーンズ氏：日本には世界一短い型の詩があるそうですね。

俳句

鈴木氏：はい、俳句のことをおっしゃっているんですね。確かに俳句は17音しかありません。

ジョーンズ氏：そんなに短い句でどうやって内容が表現できるんでしょうね。

鈴木氏：これでたいへん奥深い世界を表現できるから不思議なんです。そのためには、作者は無駄のない、イメージの豊かな言葉を選びます。それに、作者と鑑賞する人の間にある種の約束事が必要なんです。

ジョーンズ氏：どんな約束ですか。

季語

鈴木氏：たとえば、詩のなかにはかならず季節を表す言葉が入っています。たとえば、「天の川」という言葉を見れば、俳句に心得のある読者は瞬間にこれで夏の夜の情景を思い浮かべます。読む者は、全体の意味を理解するために、こうした約束事を知っておく必要があります。

ジョーンズ氏：俳句の歴史は古いんですか。

俳句の歴史
松尾芭蕉

鈴木氏：いえ、そう古くありません。俳句が独立した詩として完成したのは17世紀です。松尾芭蕉という詩人が、静けさのなかの美しさを追求して、俳句を芸術的に深いものにしたのです。

ジョーンズ氏：独立したということは、俳句は何かほかの詩から生まれたということですか。

和歌・短歌

鈴木氏：そうなんです。31音節からできている短歌という和歌の一種があります。俳句はじつはこの

C h a p t e r 26

Mr. Jones: The Japanese have the world's shortest poetry form, don't they?

Mr. Suzuki: Yes, if you mean *haiku*. A haiku poem has only 17 syllables.

Mr. J: I don't see how you can get much meaning into such a short verse.

Mr. S: Mysteriously though, the haiku poets are able to put profound meaning into their poems. For this, they have to be very economical in their use of words and choose expressions with rich images. A kind of an understanding between the poet and the reader is also necessary.

Mr. J: What kind of understanding?

Mr. S: For example, every poem has a word symbolizing the season of the year. The word "Milky Way," for instance, immediately paints the scene of a summer evening in the mind of an experienced haiku reader. The reader has to know these conventions to understand the full meaning.

Mr. J: Does the haiku form have a long history?

Mr. S: No, not so long. It was established as an independent form in the 17th century. It was perfected by a poet named Basho Matsuo whose pursuit was to express the beauty of silence. He's the one who gave haiku deep artistic significance.

Mr. J: When you say it was established as an independent form, do you mean it grew out of some other form of poetry?

Mr. S: Yes, that's right. There is a poetic genre called *waka* which includes a 31-syllable poem style known as *tanka*.

　　　　　　　短歌の上半分が独立して詩になったんです。

ジョーンズ氏：すると、和歌の歴史のほうが古いんですね。

鈴木氏：そうです。ずっと古いんです。日本でいちばん古い歌集は7世紀か8世紀のものです。これは『万葉集』といって、上は天皇から下は名もない庶民までの4,500首のいろんな歌が収められています。これを読むと当時の日本人のおおらかな心がよくわかりますよ。

ジョーンズ氏：和歌は万葉集の頃がいちばん盛んだったんですか。

鈴木氏：いえ、その次の平安時代です。

ジョーンズ氏：和歌はいまも詠まれていますか。

鈴木氏：ええ、詠まれています。天皇から一般国民まで広い層の愛好者がいますよ。それから平安時代の有名な和歌100首をカードにして、2組でとり合う百人一首というゲームも、新年に広く一般家庭で行われています。カードを畳の上に並べて、読み手が歌を読みあげると、ゲームをやっている人がすばやくカードを見つけてとる遊びです。このほかに優れた小説や日記、随筆も多く書かれました。その代表作は何といっても『源氏物語』でしょうね。紫式部という女流作家が書いたんです。

ジョーンズ氏：話には聞いたことがありますが、読んだことはないんです。

鈴木氏：当時の宮廷に生まれた光源氏という貴公子の、貴族社会を舞台にした恋物語、もっとはっきりいえば女性遍歴を描いた長編物語です。これは王朝文学の傑作といわれていて、当時の貴族の生活や趣味や教養、それに独特の美しさの感じ方な

Haiku is the first half of the tanka form made into an independent poem.

Mr. J: So waka is older.

Mr. S: Yes, much older. The oldest anthology of waka poems we have comes from the seventh or eighth century. This is the *Manyoshu* and contains 4,500 waka poems on a great variety of subjects written by all ranks of people — from emperors to commoners. It gives an excellent picture of the serene, uninhibited attitude of the people of that time.

Mr. J: Was it around the time the *Manyoshu* appeared that the waka poetry reached its peak?

Mr. S: No, that was in the next period — the Heian period.

Mr. J: Are waka poems still popular?

Mr. S: Yes, there are still many devotees — including the Emperor and people from all walks of life. There is a popular game played in homes throughout the country at the beginning of the new year using 100 cards each having a waka poem from the Heian period written on it. The cards are spread out on the floor and when the reader starts reading that verse, the players try to find it and pick it up before anyone else. There are also a lot of famous novels, diaries and essays that come from the Heian period. Probably the most famous is *Genji Monogatari*, or *The Tale of Genji*, written by a woman named Murasaki Shikibu.

Mr. J: I've heard about it, but never read it.

Mr. S: It's a love story set in the Imperial Court during the time of Prince Hikaru Genji. More precisely, it's a long novel about Prince Genji's love affairs with the court women. *Genji Monogatari* is considered to be the apex of Heian court literature and gives a superb portrayal of the

**王朝文化と
日本文化**

どがよくわかるんです。王朝文化は、日本風といわれるものの基調になっていて、いまも日本人の生活のなかに生きているんです。

ジョーンズ氏：たとえばどんな形でですか。

日本の着物

鈴木氏：日本の伝統的な衣装である着物がそうなんです。現在の着物は、平安時代の貴族の下着から発達したものです。平安時代の貴族の衣装に近いものは、いまでも結婚式などの機会に神社に行くと、神官や神子（みこ）が着ているのが見られますよ。

ジョーンズ氏：その次の時代の文学にはどんなものがありますか。

平家物語

鈴木氏：その次は武士時代で、その前半の代表作は、『平家物語』です。

ジョーンズ氏：これもその時代の歴史や文化に基づいて書かれているんですか。

鈴木氏：そうです。これは平家一門の栄華の様子と滅亡の姿を描いたものです。平家は平安時代最後の統治者で、同時に最初の武家政治の担い手でもあったのです。このなかには、ひとつの基調となる考え方が流れているんですよ。

ジョーンズ氏：どんな考え方ですか。

**仏教思想
無常観**

鈴木氏：人間の世界の物事はすべて移り変わっていく、栄華を極めた者もいつかはかならず滅びるときが来る、という仏教思想に根ざす世界観があるんです。

ジョーンズ氏：武士時代には何か新しい動きがあったんですか。

鈴木氏：武士時代の後半の江戸時代には、商人階級がしだいに経済力をつけて、それまでの文学とは

life, interests, cultural accomplishments, and unique aesthetic sense of the Heian nobility. The Heian court established the tone of Japanese culture and its influence is still strong in our lives, even today.

Mr. J: Can you give me an example?

Mr. S: One would be our traditional garment — the *kimono*. The kimono worn today developed from the undergarments worn by the nobility in the Heian period. We can still see kimonos like the nobles wore in the Heian period when we go to a shrine to attend a wedding ceremony. They are worn by the priest and the shrine maidens.

Mr. J: What type literature did the next period produce?

Mr. S: Next came the feudal age. *Heike Monogatari* or *The Tale of Heike*, is typical of the literature of the first half of this period.

Mr. J: Was this also based on the history and culture of the time?

Mr. S: Yes. It tells the story of the splendor, downfall and final ruin of the Heike clan. They were the last rulers during the Heian period and the first rulers of the feudal period. It has a definite philosophical theme running through it.

Mr. J: Which is?

Mr. S: That everything in man's world is subject to change, that those who revel in glory will certainly someday be deposed. This is a view of the world rooted in Buddhist concepts.

Mr. J: Were there any new trends during the feudal period?

Mr. S: During the latter part of this period, meaning the Edo period, the merchant class gradually gained economic power

町人文学

違った、「町人文学」がたいへん盛んになりました。代表的作家としては、まず井原西鶴が有名ですね。

ジョーンズ氏：その作品にはどんな特徴があるんですか。

鈴木氏：彼の作品は、町人の生活に身近な題材を選んでいます。たとえば、金もうけとか女遊びというような人間の欲望をありのままに描いているんです。いってみれば、庶民の夢を物語のなかで見せてくれたので人気があったんです。もうひとりの代表的人物は近松門左衛門です。

ジョーンズ氏：彼はどんな作品を書いたんですか。

鈴木氏：彼は義理と人情をテーマにしたドラマを書いたんです。つまり、恋人同士は人間としての愛情と社会のおきてとの矛盾に悩んだ揚げ句、最後の解決として心中を選ぶんです。そして彼の作品は歌舞伎や人形浄瑠璃でも上演され、たいへんな人気でした。ところでジョーンズさん、日本に、ノーベル文学賞受賞者がいるんですが、ご存じですか。

ジョーンズ氏：そうですか。それは知りませんでした。だれですか。

川端康成

鈴木氏：川端康成です。1968年のことです。彼は新しい感覚で日本の自然や日本人の美しさを描こうとした作家で『伊豆の踊子』なんかが有名です。

**日本の近代
文学の初め**

ジョーンズ氏：日本の近代文学はどんなふうにして始まったんですか。

鈴木氏：いつかお話ししたように、明治以降、日本は西欧との交流を深めて、近代化の道を歩みだしました。この流れに沿って、まずロシア、ドイツ、イギリス、フランスなどの西欧諸国の文学作品が

and a new type of literature known as the "townsmen's literature" flourished. The leading writer was Saikaku Ihara.

Mr. J: What distinguished his works?

Mr. S: He chose subjects that were closely related to the lives of townspeople. He wrote of gambling and womanizing, for example, and described human lust in plain language and with considerable realism. He was popular because he wrote stories in which he developed the fantasies of the common man. Another famous writer of the period was Monzaemon Chikamatsu.

Mr. J: What were his works like?

Mr. S: He wrote dramas on the theme of love and duty — plays about lovers torn between their love and their obligations, who find suicide the only solution. His works were performed as both *kabuki* and *ningyojoruri* plays, and were extremely popular. Did you know that one Japanese novelist won the Nobel prize for literature?

Mr. J: Really? No, I didn't. Who's that?

Mr. S: Yasunari Kawabata, who won it in 1968. Kawabata expressed in a fresh way the beauty of Japan's natural surroundings and its people. One of his famous works is *Izu no Odoriko*, or *The Izu Dancer*.

Mr. J: Where did modern Japanese literature develop from?

Mr. S: We spoke the other day about how starting from the Meiji period, Japan developed deeper relations with the West and moved ahead with modernization. In parallel with this, translated literature was introduced from Russia, Ger-

つぎつぎと紹介されましてね。坪内逍遙によって
シェークスピア全集なんかも翻訳されたんです。
100年にわたるこうした外国文学の影響と日本社
会の変化に応じて、日本文学はひじょうに多様性
を持つようになりました。戦後はヘミングウェイ、
スタインベック、フォークナーなどアメリカの作
家の作品も、本や映画でつぎつぎと紹介され、戦
後の日本文学はたいへん影響を受けましたよ。

謙譲の美徳は通じません

　日本語の「どうぞよろしく」は、かならずしも相手の
助力を期待しているとは限らず、たんなるあいさつにす
ぎないことも多い。これを無理やりに英語で表現しよう
として、
　　"Please help me if you can." とか、
　　"Please give me your special consideration."
などといったりすると、外国人には、自主性のない、ひ
じょうに人頼みの態度という印象を与える。そればかり
か、「こっそり自分だけ特別扱いしてもらおうとしてい
るのではないか」などと、あらぬ誤解を招きかねない。
　ビジネスの場などでよく使われる「善処します」とい
う言葉も、文字どおりの意味とは限らず、遠回しの否定
に用いられることもしばしばある。本当にアクションを
とるのならよいが、その場しのぎに、
　　"I'll give the matter careful consideration." とか、
　　"I'll take a positive attitude toward it."
などと発言すると、後日思わぬトラブルの原因となるの
で注意したい。
　また外国人を家庭に招待して、いざ食事を始めるとい
うときになって、日頃の習慣から「何もありませんが」

many, England, France and other Western countries. For example, most of Shakespeare's plays were translated into Japanese by Shoyo Tsubouchi. Over the past 100 years, the influence of foreign literature and changes in society have caused a tremendous diversification in Japanese literature. Since the end of the war, works of American writers such as Hemingway, Steinbeck and Faulkner have been introduced to Japan both in translated books and as movies, and have had a very large influence on postwar Japanese literature.

26

Japanese Literature

Column

のつもりで、

"Sorry, we have nothing to serve you."

などとゆめゆめいわないこと。外国人には、「こんなに
ごちそうが用意されているのに、なぜそんな発言をする
のか理由がわからない」ということになる。

贈り物をするさいにも、われわれ日本人は「つまらな
いものですが」と言葉を添えて相手に贈呈する。これを
直訳調に、

"This is a trivial thing."

などというと、彼らにしてみれば「つまらないものをな
ぜわざわざくれるのか」と感じてしまう。

たとえば英語にも、

"This is just a little something."

"This is nothing much."

などという表現はあるが、手をかけた料理をすすめると
きや、それなりの贈り物をするときには使わない。

「何にもありませんが」にしても、「つまらないもの
ですが」にしても、日本語では言外に含まれている「……
がお気に召せば幸いです」というニュアンスを、英語で
は明確に表現して、

"I hope you'll like it."

"I thought you might like it."

などとするのが適切である。

1

The Japanese <u>have the world's shortest</u> poetry form.

ノート 「世界最小（大）」を表す表現として覚えておくと便利。☞ Useful Expressions 10-1

例文 Japan has *the second largest* GNP among the world's free economies. (10)

2

Genji Monogatari <u>is considered to be</u> the apex of Heian court literature.

ノート be considered to be ... 「〜であると考えられている、〜であると見られている」

例文 He *is considered to be* one of the leading states-men of Japan.

3

Can you <u>give me an example</u>?

ノート 例を求めるのに便利な表現。

4

It <u>is typical of</u> the literature of this period.

ノート be typical of ... 「〜を代表する、〜を象徴する、いかにも〜らしい」前置詞 to を使う場合は、typical ではなく peculiar を使う。

例文 （×）It is typical to this period.
（○）It is *peculiar to* this period.

5

They <u>have had a very large influence on</u> postwar Japanese literature.

ノート have an influence on ... 「〜に影響を及ぼす」

Chapter
27

伝統演劇
Traditional Theater

男が女を演じる「女形」の不思議

日本の伝統的演劇には、
14世紀から盛んになった能、
17世紀から盛んになった文楽と歌舞伎があります。
文楽・歌舞伎は庶民のための演劇、
能は武士階級のものとして発展してきました。

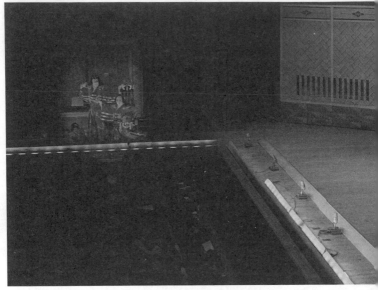

Vocabulary

〜の予備知識を持つ	☐☐	to learn . . . in advance
古典演劇	☐☐	a classical drama
最も多くの愛好者が いる	☐☐	to have the largest following
〜からとり入れる	☐☐	to borrow from . . .
集大成	☐☐	summarization
総合演劇様式	☐☐	an integrated theatrical form
演技	☐☐	acting
踊り	☐☐	dancing
音曲	☐☐	music
大仕掛けな舞台装置	☐☐	elaborate stage equipment
〜の伴奏に合わせて	☐☐	to the accompaniment of . . .
約束事	☐☐	predefined significance
省略	☐☐	omission
誇張	☐☐	exaggeration
女優	☐☐	an actress

（舞台に向かって右側を上手、左側を下手という。一般に花道は下手側にある）

27

Traditional Theater

女役を専門に演ずる男優	☐☐	a male actor who specializes in female roles
世襲で	☐☐	by heredity
回り舞台	☐☐	a revolving stage
楽劇	☐☐	a musical drama
面	☐☐	a mask
きらびやかな装束を着る	☐☐	to dress in gorgeous costumes
簡潔な動作	☐☐	a clean movement
象徴化されている	☐☐	to be symbolic
個性的な表情に乏しい	☐☐	to lack individuality of expression
喜怒哀楽	☐☐	emotions
人形劇	☐☐	a puppet theater
（人形を）動かす	☐☐	to manipulate
語り	☐☐	a chant
微妙な動作	☐☐	a subtle movement

男が女を演じる「女形」の不思議

歌舞伎・能・文楽

歌舞伎

ジョーンズ夫人：近いうちに私たち歌舞伎を見に行きたいと思っていますの。そこですこし予備知識を持っておきたいのです。いろいろと教えていただけるとありがたいんですけど。

鈴木夫人：それはよいお考えですね。私も歌舞伎のファンです。お役に立ちたいですわ。滞在中に歌舞伎を見学されると、きっと来日のよい思い出になると思いますよ。私の渡米中にも、歌舞伎のことについては、たびたびアメリカの友人から質問されたものですわ。

ジョーンズ夫人：多少なりとも日本に関心のあるアメリカ人なら、歌舞伎が日本の伝統的な演劇であることは、ほとんどの人が知っていますからね。

鈴木夫人：そうですね。ご存じのとおり、歌舞伎は日本の代表的な古典演劇です。能や文楽もやはりそうですが、現在では、歌舞伎の愛好者がいちばん多いんです。そのうえ歌舞伎には、能や文楽の要素もとり入れられているので、日本の伝統的演劇の集大成ともいわれています。

**歌舞伎の
起源**

ジョーンズ氏：歌舞伎はいつごろから始まったのですか。

鈴木夫人：起源は江戸時代の初期、つまり17世紀の初めごろからだといわれています。

**歌舞伎の
特色**

ジョーンズ氏：すると、イギリスの植民地開拓者が初めてバージニアにやってきた頃ですね。歌舞伎にはどんな特色があるのですか。

鈴木夫人：歌舞伎は演技、踊り、音曲、大仕掛けな舞台装置などからなる総合芸術です。近代演劇と

C h a p t e r 27

Mrs. Jones: We're hoping to take in a *kabuki* performance sometime soon and we'd like to learn a little about kabuki in advance. I wonder if you could teach us a few things.

Mrs. Suzuki: That's a wonderful idea. I'm a kabuki fan myself, you know. I'll be happy to help you if I can. And I'm sure that if you see a kabuki play while you're here, it'll turn out to be one of the best memories of your visit. While we were living in the U.S., my American friends often asked me questions about kabuki.

Mrs. J: That's not surprising because almost any American who knows anything at all about Japan knows that kabuki is a traditional form of Japanese theater.

Mrs. S: Yes, as you know, it's a form of classical Japanese dramatic art. So are *noh* and *bunraku*, but today kabuki has the largest following. And since kabuki borrows heavily from both of these other forms, it can well be called a summarization of traditional Japanese theatrical art.

Mr. Jones: How far back does kabuki go?

Mrs. S: To the beginning of the Edo era, which would be early in the 17th century.

Mr. J: That's about the time the first British colonist came to Virginia. What distinguishes kabuki from other kinds of theater?

Mrs. S: It's an integrated theatrical form that combines acting, dancing, music and elaborate stage equipment. Differently

は違い、リアリズムには重きを置いていませんが、独特の様式を持っています。

ジョーンズ氏：それはどんな様式ですか。

鈴木夫人：作品の多くが、三味線などによる日本固有の音曲を伴奏にし、俳優のせりふや動作にも独特な「歌舞伎的」リズムがあります。あらかじめ約束事がたくさんあります。たとえば、省略・誇張・形式化された動きなどです。

ジョーンズ夫人：女の役も男が演ずるそうですね。本当ですか。

鈴木夫人：はい、そのとおりです。歌舞伎には女優はひとりもいません。歌舞伎の長い歴史のなかで、「女形」（おやま）という女の役を専門に演ずる男優が、独自の世界をつくりあげてきました。女形の演ずる女性は、より女性らしいともいわれています。それに歌舞伎の俳優はほとんど世襲で、幼少の頃から芸を厳しく仕込まれています。

ジョーンズ夫人：それはたいへん興味深いですね。

鈴木夫人：そのほか「花道」といって、舞台に向かって観客席を貫いて設けられている俳優の通路があったり、大仕掛けな「回り舞台」などもあります。いずれも歌舞伎独特のものです。

ジョーンズ氏：歌舞伎で演じられる主題は、どんなものなんですか。

鈴木夫人：大きく分けると、むかしの貴族や武士の運命を描いたものと、庶民の生活を描いたものの2つになります。

ジョーンズ夫人：お話を伺ってますます興味がわいてきました。歌舞伎見学がいまから楽しみですわ。

ジョーンズ氏：さきほどお話のあった能とか文楽

Side notes:

27

伝統演劇

• 女形

• 花道

• 回り舞台

292

from modern drama it doesn't stress realism, but has its own peculiar formalities.

Mr. J: What kind of formalities?

Mrs. S: Most of the plays are performed to the accompaniment of typical Japanese melodies played on the *shamisen* and other Japanese instruments, and the actors follow a specific "kabuki" rhythm in their speech and movements. Many things have predefined significance — such as omissions, exaggerations and many of the actors' movements.

Mrs. J: I've heard that all roles are played by men, even those of the female characters. Is that true?

Mrs. S: Yes, it is. There are no actresses in kabuki. And over kabuki's long history, the male actors who specialize in female roles, the *oyama* as they are called, have helped create a very special atmosphere peculiar to the world of kabuki. Many say that a woman portrayed by an oyama is the most feminine of all. Also, most kabuki actors become actors by heredity and they are trained severely from a very early age.

Mrs. J: I must say, that's really interesting.

Mrs. S: Then there's the *hanamichi*, which is a walk-like extension of the stage that runs through the audience to the back of the theater, and the *mawaributai*, or revolving stage. These are both special to kabuki.

Mr. J: What are kabuki plays about?

Mrs. S: For the most part, they're either about the fortunes of the noble and warrior classes in ancient times or about the lives of the common people.

Mrs. J: The more I hear, the more interested I get. Now I'm really looking forward to seeing kabuki.

Mr. J: You mentioned noh and bunraku earlier. What are they

は、どんなものですか。

鈴木夫人：能は、14世紀ごろから盛んになりました。日本最古の演劇のひとつで、かつて武士階級が愛好しました。これも一種の楽劇です。出演者は面をかぶり、きらびやかな装束を着用します。そして謡曲という歌曲に合わせて、ゆったりとした簡潔な動作で演技します。題材の多くは、仏教思想の影響を受けています。

ジョーンズ氏：どんな面をかぶるのですか。

鈴木夫人：木製の面で種類はいろいろあります。すべて象徴化されていて個性的な表情に乏しいのです。しかし、演技者は動作や面の角度によって、喜怒哀楽を見事に表現します。文楽は人形劇の一種で、17世紀から盛んになりました。人形の背丈は1〜1.5mで、独特の節回しの浄瑠璃という語りと音曲に合わせて、それぞれの人形を3人で動かします。

ジョーンズ氏：3人で動かすのですか。どのようにするのですか。

鈴木夫人：それぞれ首と右手・左手・足の動きを分担します。人形の微妙な動作で、感情の動きなども表現します。

ジョーンズ夫人：文楽も一度拝見したいわ。

鈴木夫人：ぜひ、ご覧になってください。私ども日本人でも、文楽、歌舞伎、能などに使われている言葉を、全部わかっているわけではありません。現代の日本語とはかなり違うからです。だけど、ストーリーの流れは、言葉がわからなくても理解できます。ですから、外国の方が初めてご覧になってもかなり楽しめると思いますわ。

like?

Mrs. S: Noh first became popular in the 14th century. It's Japan's oldest theater form and in the past was popular among the warrior or *samurai* class. It's also a type of musical drama. The principal characters wear masks and dress in gorgeous costumes. The actors perform in slow, clean movements to noh-singing, or *yokyoku* as it is called. The concepts of most plays show Buddhist influences.

Mr. J: What do the masks look like?

Mrs. S: They are wooden masks and there are various kinds. All are symbolic, and they lack individuality of expression. But depending on the movements of the actor and the angle from which the mask is viewed, they are capable of expressing a wide range of emotions. Bunraku is a kind of puppet theater that has flourished since the 17th century. The puppets are a meter to a meter and a half in height and each is manipulated by three puppeteers as the story is related in a special chant called *joruri*.

Mr. J: By three puppeteers? How is that accomplished?

Mrs. S: One manipulates the head and right hand, one the left hand and one the feet. The emotions of the character represented by the puppet are expressed by its subtle movements.

Mrs. J: I'd like to see bunraku sometime too.

Mrs. S: Please do. Even we Japanese can't understand everything the actors say in bunraku, kabuki and noh because the language is quite different from modern Japanese, but the story is fairly easy to follow even if you can't understand the words. So even a foreigner seeing one of these plays for the first time will be able to enjoy it.

1

They often <u>asked me questions</u> about *kabuki*.

ノート

　ask には大きくは（1）「尋ねる」（2）「頼む」（3）「招待する」の意味がある。基本的な使い方は「（<u>人に物事を</u>）尋ねたり、頼んだり、招待したりする」と理解しておくと混乱しないですむ。「尋ねる」の意味のときは、使い慣れるまでは上の例文を繰り返して正しく覚えておくこと。

例文

（○）She *asked me a question*.

（×）She asked a question to me.

2

<u>I must say</u>, that's really interesting.

ノート

　I must say は言葉どおりに訳せば、「いわなければならない、いわざるをえない」だが、口語の感情表現の一形式で、日本語でいえば、「（ずいぶん）～ですわね」くらいに当たる。

　こうした感情表現形式は本書にも随所に出てくるが、これらを感覚的に理解して自由に使えるようになると、会話に深みが出てくる。

例文1

That is an odd question, *I must say*.

　「ずいぶん妙なお尋ねですわね」

例文2

Tell me, what do you think are the main factors?

(24)

　tell me はここでは、「ところで」くらいの感じ。もっとくだけた会話では、日本語の「ねえ」に当たることが多い。

Chapter
28

音楽と現代演劇
Music and Modern Theater

演歌は東南アジアでも人気があります

日本の歌謡曲は、
東南アジアの国々でも人気が高く、
中国公演や香港公演をする歌手もいます。
クラシックの分野では
世界的に活躍する指揮者や演奏家も増えています。

〔ジャンル別レコード・CD・カセット売上枚数〕

	シングル	LP	CD	カセット
フォーク & ロック	1,321.5万枚 (34.0%)	1,162.5 (52.0)	364.1 (44.2)	678.9 (54.3)
演歌	311.8 (8.0)	3.1 (0.1)	1.4 (0.2)	55.8 (4.5)
ポップス	2,137.3 (55.0)	585.5 (26.2)	174.1 (21.1)	321.0 (25.7)
ジャズ その他	0.2 (0.0)	37.2 (1.7)	46.6 (5.6)	18.8 (1.5)
洋楽	113.3 (2.9)	448.7 (20.1)	238.1 (28.9)	174.8 (14.0)

（1985年12月～1986年11月）

Vocabulary

〜の指揮で	☐☐	under the direction of . . .
演奏	☐☐	a performance
演奏家	☐☐	an instrumentalist
歌番組	☐☐	a popular music show
クラシック	☐☐	classical music
ポピュラー・ミュージック	☐☐	popular music
〜を日本的にまねたもの	☐☐	a Japanese imitation of . . .
バラード	☐☐	a ballad
日本人の心情	☐☐	Japanese feelings
違ったファンの層がある	☐☐	to have different appeal
年配の人たち	☐☐	older people
アマチュア歌手	☐☐	an amateur singer
プロ並みの水準	☐☐	professional standards
熱烈なファン	☐☐	a devoted fan
交響楽団	☐☐	an orchestra
満員（売り切れ）になる	☐☐	to be sellouts
人気のある歌手	☐☐	a popular singer
合唱曲	☐☐	a chorus
ベートーベンの第九交響曲	☐☐	Beethoven's Ninth
ミュージカル	☐☐	a musical
なかなかの女優ぶり	☐☐	to be quite the actress
民謡	☐☐	a local folk song
仕事の歌	☐☐	a working song
祭りの歌	☐☐	a festival song
遊びの歌	☐☐	a party song
酒宴の歌	☐☐	a drinking song
わらべ歌	☐☐	a children's song

28

Music and Modern Theater

演歌は東南アジアでも人気があります

歌謡曲・演歌・紅白歌合戦・第九交響曲・現代劇

日本の
音楽家

ジョーンズ夫人：日本に来るちょっと前、小沢征爾
指揮のボストン・シンフォニーを聴きました。た
いへん素晴らしい演奏でした。

鈴木夫人：それはよろしかったですね。このごろは、
小沢征爾指揮のオーケストラは、日本ではなかな
か聴く機会がないんですの。

ジョーンズ氏：最近は日本の音楽家で、海外で活
躍している人がたくさんいますね。

鈴木氏：確かに増えています。とくに、バイオリン、
ピアノなどの演奏家が多いようです。

歌番組

ジョーンズ夫人：きのう、歌番組のテレビを見まし
たの。日本のポピュラー音楽にも、いろいろな種
類があるようですわね。

鈴木夫人：そうなんです。クラシックや伝統的なも
のばかりではないんです。日本のポピュラー・
ミュージックにも何種類かあります。そのなかで
いちばん大衆的なものが、歌謡曲ですわ。これは、
西洋のポピュラー・ミュージックを日本的にまね
たものから始まったんです。もうひとつが演歌な
んです。これはバラードですわ。日本的な心情の
詞やメロディーと西欧の音楽が合わさったものな
んです。そのほかに西欧から入ってきたポップス
系やフォーク系の音楽もありますの。

歌謡曲

演歌

ジョーンズ夫人：ファンの年齢層はそれぞれ違うん
ですか。

鈴木夫人：かなり違いますわ。演歌のファンは年配
の人たちが多いのです。ポップス系・フォーク系
の音楽は10代の若者の間で人気があります。

C h a p t e r 28

Mrs. Jones: Just before we came to Japan we went to a concert by the Boston Symphony Orchestra under the direction of Seiji Ozawa. It was a beautiful performance.

Mrs. Suzuki: I envy you. In Japan we don't have many opportunities to hear Ozawa conducting these days.

Mr. Jones: I see quite a few Japanese musicians are active overseas now.

Mr. Suzuki: There are more than there used to be. Especially instrumentalists — such as violinists, pianists.

Mrs. J: We watched a popular music show on TV yesterday. It seems that you have a few styles of pop music.

Mrs. S: Oh, yes. Not all our music is classical and traditional. We have several types of popular music. One of the most common is *kayokyoku*. This started as a Japanese imitation of Western popular music. Another is *enka*. These are ballads. They combine lyrics and melodies that express typical Japanese feelings with Western music. There is also Western pop and folk music.

Mrs. J: Do these different types of music have different age appeal?

Mrs. S: Pretty much. The enka songs are popular among older people. The pop and folk music from overseas is most popular among teenagers.

鈴木氏：日本の演歌は、東南アジアでもファンが増えているということです。また、日本に住んでおられる外国の方の間でも、演歌ファンは多いようです。テレビでも演歌や歌謡曲の好きな外国人のアマチュア歌手が出る番組もあります。「外国人歌謡大賞」といっています。プロ並みの歌を聞かせてくれる人もいるんです。

ジョーンズ氏：日本のポップ・ミュージックもだんだん国際的になっているようですね。しかし、日本にはクラシック音楽のファンもかなりいるんでしょう。

・クラシック

鈴木夫人：ポピュラーな音楽と比べると、数は少ないですが、どこでも同じように熱烈なファンがいます。海外から有名な音楽家や交響楽団が来ますと、演奏会はたいてい満員になるようです。

・紅白歌合戦

鈴木氏：歌謡曲の分野での、その年の大きな催し物は、大みそかに放送される「紅白歌合戦」です。その年でいちばん人気があった歌手を２つのチームに分けます。紅チームは女性歌手で、白チームは男性歌手です。番組の終わりに、審査員が勝利チームを決めるんです。

ジョーンズ氏：それは、お楽しみの一晩ですね。

・第九交響曲

鈴木氏：外国の方は意外に思われるようですが、クリスマスの頃に、第九交響曲の合唱曲を歌いたいという人たちもたくさんいるんです。まったくの素人で、あらゆる職業の人たちです。市や町の団体とか同好のグループなど、たくさんのコーラスの組織があります。一年がかりで合唱の練習をするところもあるほどです。

ジョーンズ夫人：それは驚きましたわ。このまえ、歌舞伎は見学したのですが、現代演劇もあるのかしら。それとも古典だけなんですか。

Mr. S: We hear there are an increasing number of enka fans in Southeast Asia. These songs also seem to be popular among foreigners living in Japan. There's even a program on TV for amateur foreign singers who like enka and kayokyoku. It's called the *Foreigners Singing Contest*. Some of the contestants are right up to professional standards.

Mr. J: So it seems Japanese pop music is getting more international. On the other side of it though, I know there are many Japanese who like Western classical music.

Mrs. S: The following is smaller than for popular music, but like anywhere, the classical music lovers are very devoted fans. Almost all concerts by famous foreign artists and orchestras are sellouts.

Mr. S: The big event of the year in the pop music field is the *Red and White Singing Contest* broadcast on New Year's Eve. The year's most popular singers are divided into two teams: the Red Team made up of female vocalists and the White Team made up of men. At the end of the program the judges pick the winning team.

Mr. J: That sounds like a fun evening.

Mr. S: It probably seems strange to non-Japanese but there are many people who like to get together and sing the chorus from Beethoven's Ninth around Christmas. They are absolute amateurs — people from all walks of life. A lot of choruses are organized — some by cities and towns, others by groups of individuals. Some groups spend the whole year practicing.

Mrs. J: What an interesting hobby! You know we went to see *kabuki* the other day, and were wondering if there was also Japanese modern theater. Or only old classics?

現代劇	鈴木夫人：ええ、ございます。現代劇もミュージカルも、ヨーロッパの演劇やアメリカの現代劇の翻訳劇など、いろいろあります。このまえも、『風と共に去りぬ』をやっていましたし、シェークスピアの作品もかなりやりますのよ。
シェークスピア	
	ジョーンズ夫人：日本語で一度シェークスピアを見てみたいわ。私、高校のときはシェークスピアが大好きで、自分で演じたこともあるんですの。
	鈴木氏：奥様は、きっとジュリエットやオフィーリアをおやりになったんでしょう。
	ジョーンズ氏：友人の話では、家内はなかなかの女優ぶりだったようですよ。
	ジョーンズ夫人：あなた、あんまり褒めると皆さんが本気にしてしまいますわよ。
日本民謡	ジョーンズ氏：ところで、世界のどの国にも民謡はありますが、日本の民謡にはどんなものがありますか。
	鈴木氏：日本中どこに行っても、民謡はあります。なかには日本中に知れ渡っているものもたくさんあります。流行歌ほどではありませんが、民謡も根強い人気があります。テレビでも民謡番組を組んでいますし、プロの民謡歌手もいます。民謡には、仕事の歌、祭りの歌、遊びの歌、酒宴の歌、わらべ歌などいろいろな種類があります。歴史はそうとう古いのですが、現在の曲節で歌うようになったのは16～17世紀の仕事の歌が多いようです。

Mrs. S: Oh, no, we have our own modern plays and musicals — and also modern theater brought in from Europe and America and translated into Japanese. Not long ago, *Gone with the Wind* was playing, and quite a few Shakespeare's plays are performed.

Mrs. J: It'd be interesting to see something by Shakespeare done in Japanese. I was really crazy about Shakespeare when I was in high school — and did some acting myself.

Mr. S: Juliet or Ophelia, I bet.

Mr. J: According to her friends, she was quite the actress.

Mrs. J: Careful, honey. Mr. and Mrs. Suzuki might think you're serious.

Mr. J: Let's get back to music for a moment. Every country has its folk music. What's Japan's like?

Mr. S: Oh, wherever you go in Japan you'll find local folk songs. Many have become famous throughout the country. The following is not as large as for pop music, but there are a lot of devotees. There are folk song programs on TV, and many professional folk song singers. The songs have various themes. There are working songs, festival songs, party songs, drinking songs, children's songs . . . Some of them go very far back, but the types of tunes sung today come mostly from the 15th and 16th centuries.

1

We don't <u>have many opportunities to hear</u> Ozawa.

ノート　　have many opportunities <u>of hearing</u> Ozawa とい ういい方もある。

例文　　We *have little opportunity to* hear [of hearing] Ozawa.

2

<u>I see</u> quite a few Japanese musicians are active overseas now.

ノート　　この I see も Useful Expressions 27-2 で触れた 感情表現の一種。しいて日本語でいえば「〜ますね」 に当たる。

例文1　　*Don't tell me* you don't remember.
　　「まさか忘れたんじゃあるまいね」

例文2　　*You mean to say* you've never heard of George Gershwin?
　　「ジョージ・ガーシュインを知らないという<u>んで</u> <u>すか</u>」☞Useful Expressions 8-3

3

Some of the contestants <u>are right up to</u> professional standards.

ノート　　be up to ... 「〜に匹敵している、〜に近似して いる」ここでは「プロフェッショナルの水準にまさ に達している」→「プロ並み、玄人はだし」

4

Japanese pop music <u>is getting</u> more <u>international</u>.

ノート　　get＋形容詞［過去分詞］で「（ある状態に）なる」。
例文　　It *is getting warmer and warmer.*

Chapter
29

伝統芸術
Traditional Arts

形より心を重んじる茶の湯

茶の湯や生け花などに対する
外国人の興味と関心はひじょうに高いようです。
お茶を飲む、花を飾る、字を書くという
日常生活の一部を芸術にまで高めた点が、
どこか神秘的に映るのでしょう。

〔生け花のおもな花形〕

立華（りっか）

最も古い生け花様式。室町時代に生まれ江戸初期に大成した。そびえ立つ峰や野の草木が互いに調和して作りあげる大自然の情趣を表現する

生花（せいか）

江戸時代に発祥した様式。植物の自然な姿である向日性に注目し、その美しさを「天地人」という三角法で表現。生け花の大衆化をもたらす

投入花（なげいればな）

15世紀ころ、床の間以外の柱や壁にかける花として生まれ、茶室などに飾る花の様式として発展。生花と同様、植物の自然な美しさを尊重する

盛花（もりばな）

広口の花器に花を盛る形式。西欧の花や花器の影響を受け、明治末期に誕生。色彩と量感を重視する。投入花とともに広く自由花と呼ばれる

29

伝統芸術

Vocabulary

花を生ける	☐☐	to arrange flowers
実用的な	☐☐	practical
芸術的な	☐☐	artistic
何か意味がある	☐☐	to represent something
目が高い	☐☐	to have a good eye
流派	☐☐	a school
基本の枝	☐☐	basic sprays
天・地・人	☐☐	the heavens [sky], the earth and mankind
～を三角形になるように整える	☐☐	to arrange . . . in a triangle
深みがある考え方	☐☐	a philosophy
花と木	☐☐	flowers and sprigs
意味を持つ	☐☐	to take on the meaning
根もとを焼く	☐☐	to singe the cut ends
～を水の中で切る	☐☐	to cut . . . under water

〔茶道具の名称〕

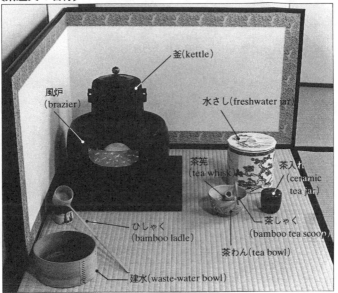

釜(kettle)

風炉
(brazier)

水さし(freshwater jar)

茶筅
(tea whisk)

茶入れ
(ceramic
tea jar)

ひしゃく
(bamboo ladle)

茶しゃく
(bamboo tea scoop)

茶わん(tea bowl)

建水(waste-water bowl)

たしなみ	☐☐	an accomplishment
前衛的な	☐☐	avant-garde
〜にとらわれない	☐☐	to put no restrictions on . . .
〜を趣味として楽しむ	☐☐	to take up . . . as one's hobby
茶をたてる	☐☐	to do the tea ceremony
作法	☐☐	etiquette
心の交流	☐☐	spiritual exchange
〜を心を込めてもて なす	☐☐	to be devoted to serving . . .
感謝の心を表す	☐☐	to express one's gratitude
お茶の粉末	☐☐	powdered leaves of tea
茶筅	☐☐	a (tea) whisk
泡が立つ	☐☐	to be frothy
仏教の影響を受ける	☐☐	to be influenced by Buddhism
大成される	☐☐	to be perfected
伝統的な礼儀作法	☐☐	traditional customs and manners

形より心を重んじる茶の湯

生け花の基本と歴史・茶の湯の作法と歴史

• 生け花

ジョーンズ夫人：きれいなお花ですね。奥様がお生けになったのですか。

鈴木夫人：ええ、お気に召してうれしいですわ。

ジョーンズ夫人：これは何の花ですの。

鈴木夫人：この背の高いほうは桃の花です。

ジョーンズ夫人：こちらの黄色のは？

鈴木夫人：これは菜の花、この花の種から食用の油がとれるんですわ。

ジョーンズ夫人：桃と食用油？　2つとも実用と芸術とを兼ねたお花ですのね。（笑い）この枝の配置や全体の形には、何か意味があるんじゃございませんかしら。

• 生け花の
基本・形

鈴木夫人：まあ、奥様はお目が高いですわ。生け花の流派はたくさんありますけれど、私の流派では、全体を天・地・人の3つの基本の枝でほぼ三角形になるように形を整えて、調和のとれた自然を表現するように教えられていますの。

ジョーンズ夫人：生け花の美しさには深みがありますのね。日本では、ずいぶんむかしからこうしてお花を生けていたんですか。

• 生け花の
歴史

鈴木夫人：生け花が芸術として盛んになったのは、16世紀ころからです。初めは、自然の花や木をそのままの姿で飾っていたんです。だんだんに全体の形に、さきほどお話ししましたように意味づけをするようになったんだと申しますわ。

ジョーンズ夫人：このお花はこんな平らな盤にどのようにして立っているのでしょう。

• 生け花の
作法

鈴木夫人：剣山という針のたくさん出た金属の台に

C h a p t e r 29

Mrs. Jones: Oh, what lovely flowers! Did you arrange them?

Mrs. Suzuki: Yes. I'm glad you like them.

Mrs. J: What kind of flowers are they?

Mrs. S: The long one is a small branch of peach flowers.

Mrs. J: And the yellow ones?

Mrs. S: Rape. The seeds of this plant are used to make a cooking oil.

Mrs. J: Peaches and cooking oil? Practical and artistic at the same time. (Laughs) I get the feeling that the arrangement is supposed to represent something.

Mrs. S: You have a good eye. Though there are many different schools of flower arrangement, the one I belong to uses three basic sprays to represent the sky, the earth and mankind. We are taught to arrange them in a triangle to express the harmony of nature.

Mrs. J: The philosophy behind it is very beautiful. Have the Japanese been arranging flowers like this for many years?

Mrs. S: Flower arrangement began as an art around the 16th century. At first they just used flowers and sprigs for decoration. Over the years though, the shape of the arrangement took on the meanings I just mentioned.

Mrs. J: How do you get the flowers to stand up in the flat dish?

Mrs. S: The tips of the stems are pressed into a *kenzan* — a

刺してあるんです。そのほかにもいろいろな手法を使いますのよ。たとえば、花を元気に保つためには、根もとを焼くとか、茎を水の中で切って気泡が入るのを防いだりするんです。

ジョーンズ氏：鈴木さんは、芸術家を奥さんにお持ちで幸せですね。

鈴木氏：いや、どうも。家内は結婚前からやっているといいますから、かなり年期が入っているわけですよ。

ジョーンズ夫人：日本女性はだれでも生け花を習うんですか。

鈴木夫人：いえ、だれでもというわけではありませんが、結婚前の女性のたしなみとしてかなりの人が習っていますよ。

流派

ジョーンズ夫人：生け花の流派はたくさんあるとおっしゃいましたわね。

鈴木夫人：3,000くらいあるといわれていますわ。私のやっておりますのは本当に伝統的な流派ですけど、形式や素材にとらわれない前衛的なものもあります。ですから、いまでは趣味としていろんなスタイルの生け花を楽しむ人が増えていますわ。

近代的
生け花

鈴木氏：何やら難しいものもありますよ。花の代わりに鉄板や石を使ったりするんです。

ジョーンズ氏：石花ですか。それは初耳ですな。

茶の湯

鈴木夫人：生け花はこのくらいにして、こんどはこちらにいらっしゃいません。こちらでお茶をおたてしますので、一服召しあがってください。

ジョーンズ夫人：うれしいわ。私、いままで正式な日本風のお茶をいただいたことございませんの。

ジョーンズ氏：何か特別な飲み方の作法があるそう

metal disk with many needles sticking out. There are a lot of other techniques we may use, too. For example, to make the flowers stay fresh longer, we sometimes singe the cut ends, and when we cut the stems, we do it under water to keep air bubbles from getting in.

Mr. Jones: It must be nice to have such an artistic wife.

Mr. Suzuki: Well, she's been at it for quite a few years — since way before we were married.

Mrs. J: Do all Japanese women learn flower arrangement?

Mrs. S: Not all, but many do. It's an accomplishment they try to master before marriage.

Mrs. J: You said there were many schools . . .

Mrs. S: I've heard there are around 3,000. My school is quite traditional. But a lot of avant-garde schools have sprung up that put almost no restrictions on materials or form. These days more and more people are taking up various styles of flower arrangement as their hobby.

Mr. S: Some are completely over my head. They use steel and stones in place of flowers.

Mr. J: Stone flowers, huh? That I've never heard of.

Mrs. S: Let's leave the flowers for a moment and come over here. This is where I do the tea ceremony. Let me make you some.

Mrs. J: How lovely! I've never had tea made in the formal way before.

Mr. J: I hear there's a special etiquette. I'm afraid we don't

ですが、私たちは知らないんですが。

形より心の
茶道

鈴木氏：そのご心配はいりません。私も同じような
　　ものですよ。茶道では、形より心を重んじていま
　　す。お茶の中心は、主人と客との間の心の交流な
　　んです。主人はひたすら心を込めて客をもてなし、
　　客はこれに感謝の心を表します。ですから、楽し
　　くお飲みいただけばそれでいいんですよ。

鈴木夫人：では奥様のほうから。どうぞまずお菓子
　　を召しあがってください。

ジョーンズ夫人：はい、ありがとうございます。

鈴木夫人：それではお茶をどうぞ。

ジョーンズ夫人：ありがとうございます。まあ、よ
　　い香りですね。このお茶は普通のお茶とは違うよ
　　うに思いますけれど。

鈴木氏：それは、抹茶といって、ごく質のよいお茶
　　を粉末にしたものです。それを、あのように茶碗
　　にとってお湯を注いで、茶筅でかき回して泡立て
　　るんです。

ジョーンズ夫人：この茶碗は普通のものよりかなり
　　大きいですわ。それに色も何か違うようですわ。

鈴木夫人：そうです。これは茶の湯用の特別のもの
　　ですの。

茶の湯の
歴史

ジョーンズ氏：茶の湯の伝統は古いんですか。

鈴木氏：茶の湯も生け花も、むかしの武家の文化と
　　習慣から発達したもので、仏教の影響を強く受け
　　ています。茶道は16世紀後半に、千利久という人
　　が大成したんです。そして、茶道は、日本の伝統
　　的な礼儀作法に強い影響を与えています。ですか
　　ら、茶道は、いまでも若い女性が教養や趣味とし
　　て習うことが多いんです。

know anything about it.

Mr. S: Nothing to worry about. I know very little myself. ⌐In
the tea ceremony, inner spirit is more important than form.
The heart of it is the spiritual exchange between the host and
the guests. The host is totally devoted to serving the guests
and the guests express their gratitude. So all you have to do
is enjoy yourself!╱

Mrs. S: Mrs. Jones, would you like to start? First, please try
the cakes.

Mrs. J: Thank you.

Mrs. S: And now the tea.

Mrs. J: Thank you. Mmmm, the aroma is lovely. This is different from ordinary tea.

Mr. S: It's *matcha*. It's made from the powdered leaves of the
very highest grade tea. My wife puts the powder in the cup,
pours boiling water over it and then whips it with a whisk until it's frothy.

Mrs. J: The cup is much larger than the usual one. And the
color is different, too.

Mrs. S: Yes, it's made especially for the tea ceremony.

Mr. J: Does the ceremony have a long tradition?

Mr. S: The tea ceremony and flower arrangement both grew
out of the culture and customs of the old *samurai* class and
have been strongly influenced by Buddhism. The tea ceremony was perfected by Rikyu Sen in the latter half of the
16th century. Its effect on traditional Japanese customs and
manners has been great. That's why it's still often studied by
young Japanese women as a way of self-improvement — and
as a pastime.

1

<u>You have a good eye</u>.

ノート

　「お目が高いですね」このほかに good をつけないで、have an eye for ... 「〜を見る目がある、〜の審美眼がある」という表現もある。

例文
He has an eye for paintings.

2

<u>That</u> I've never heard of.

ノート

　倒置の強調表現。普通の語順だと、I've never heard of that.

3

<u>I'm afraid</u> we don't know anything about it.

ノート

　I'm afraid ... は悪い知らせを伝えるときに、聞き手が不快に感じないように表現をやわらげる働きをする。No! という返事をするよりも、I'm afraid not. というとやわらかくなる。

4

Nothing <u>to worry about</u>.

ノート

　(There's) Nothing to worry about. で「ご心配はいりません」の慣用表現。

5

<u>All you have to do</u> is enjoy yourself.

ノート

　「あなたがすべきことといえば、楽しむことです」
→「あなたは楽しんでくださればいいんです」

例文
All you have to do is (to) press the button.

Chapter
30

扇子は日本の輸出品第１号です

扇子は、中国から伝わったうちわを原型にした
日本人の発明品だといわれています。
小さく折り畳む仕組みには、
日本人の発想の原点が見られる
という研究者もいます。

〔各地の代表的工芸品〕

〔青森県〕	津軽塗(漆器)		輪島塗(漆器)
〔岩手県〕	秀衡塗(漆器)		山中漆器(漆器)
	浄法寺塗(漆器)		金沢漆器(漆器)
〔宮城県〕	宮城伝統こけし(人形)	〔福井県〕	若狭塗(漆器)
〔秋田県〕	川連漆器(漆器)		越前漆器(漆器)
〔山形県〕	置賜紬(織物)	〔滋賀県〕	近江上布(織物)
〔福島県〕	大掘相馬焼(焼物)		信楽焼(焼物)
	会津塗(漆器)	〔京都府〕	西陣織(織物)
〔茨城県〕	結城紬(織物)		京友禅(織物)
〔栃木県〕	結城紬(織物)		京小紋(織物)
	益子焼(焼物)		京鹿の子絞(織物)
〔群馬県〕	伊勢崎絣(織物)		京黒紋付染(織物)
	桐生織(織物)		京繍(織物)
〔東京都〕	村山大島紬(織物)		京焼・清水焼(焼物)
	本場黄八丈(織物)		京漆器(漆器)
	多摩織(織物)		京扇子(扇子)
	東京染小紋(織物)		京うちわ(うちわ)
	東京手描き友禅(織物)	〔兵庫県〕	丹波立杭焼(焼物)
	江戸木目込人形(人形)		出石焼(焼物)
〔神奈川県〕	鎌倉彫(漆器)	〔和歌山県〕	紀州漆器(漆器)
	小田原漆器(漆器)	〔鳥取県〕	弓浜絣(織物)
〔新潟県〕	小千谷紬(織物)	〔岡山県〕	備前焼(焼物)
	小千谷縮(織物)	〔徳島県〕	阿波正藍しじら織(織物)
	塩沢紬(織物)	〔香川県〕	香川漆器(漆器)
	本塩沢(織物)	〔愛媛県〕	砥部焼(焼物)
	十日町絣(織物)	〔福岡県〕	博多織(織物)
	十日町明石ちぢみ(織物)		久留米絣(織物)
	村上木彫り堆朱(漆器)		小石原焼(焼物)
〔長野県〕	信州紬(織物)		上野焼(焼物)
	木曽漆器(漆器)		博多人形(人形)
〔山梨県〕	甲州水晶石細工(人形)	〔佐賀県〕	伊万里・有田焼(焼物)
〔愛知県〕	有松・鳴海絞(織物)	〔長崎県〕	三川内焼(焼物)
	名古屋友禅(織物)		波佐見焼(焼物)
	名古屋黒紋付染(織物)	〔宮崎県〕	本場大島紬(織物)
	赤津焼(焼物)	〔鹿児島県〕	本場大島紬(織物)
	常滑焼(焼物)	〔沖縄県〕	久米島紬(織物)
〔岐阜県〕	美濃焼(焼物)		読谷山花織(織物)
	一位一刀彫り(人形)		読谷山ミンサー(織物)
〔三重県〕	四日市万古焼(焼物)		宮古上布(織物)
	伊賀焼(焼物)		琉球絣(織物)
〔富山県〕	高岡漆器(漆器)		首里織(織物)
〔石川県〕	加賀友禅(織物)		琉球びんがた(織物)
	九谷焼(焼物)		壺屋焼(焼物)

(1984年)

Vocabulary

よいお土産になる	☐☐	to make good souvenirs
かさばる	☐☐	to take up much space
発明	☐☐	invention
折り畳みの扇子	☐☐	a folding fan
歴史文献	☐☐	a historical record
～に欠かせない	☐☐	to be indispensable in . . .
実用品	☐☐	a practical item
使われなくなる	☐☐	to go out of style
陶磁器	☐☐	ceramics
陶工	☐☐	a craftsman
磁器	☐☐	porcelain
～辺りで発展する	☐☐	to flourish around . . .
～に影響を受ける	☐☐	to be influenced by . . .
焼き物	☐☐	pottery
素地の粗い	☐☐	coarse
漆器	☐☐	lacquer ware; japan
人形	☐☐	a doll
収集	☐☐	collection
伝統がある	☐☐	to have a long history
～で重要な役割を 　果たす	☐☐	to play an important role in . . .
～を飾る	☐☐	to set up a display of . . .
(人の)将来の幸福を 　祈る	☐☐	to wish someone a happy future
強く健康に成長する	☐☐	to grow up strong and healthy
～に深く入っている	☐☐	to be closely associated with . . .

扇子は日本の輸出品第1号です

扇子・うちわ・陶磁器・漆器・人形

・**扇子**

ジョーンズ氏：先週、京都へ行ってきましたが、家内はすっかり扇子が気に入ってしまったようです。ほら、例の折り畳み式のものですよ。友人のお土産にするんだといって、10本以上も買ってきました。

鈴木氏：それはたいへんよいお土産になると思いますよ。なにしろ扇子はかさばりませんからね。日本人の発明した製品で、輸出品の第1号になったものは、何だと思いますか。

・**輸出品**

第1号

ジョーンズ氏：ふーむ、いまのヒントがなかったなら、陶磁器と答えたところですが。

鈴木氏：いや、陶磁器は日本人の発明したものではありません。ある人の説によると、扇子だというんです。もともとは、うちわが、中国や朝鮮から1,000年以上も前に日本に入ってきたわけです。歴史文献では、これを最初に折り畳みの扇子にしたのは、日本人のようです。そして、これが朝鮮、中国に逆輸出されて、ヨーロッパにまで広まったんです。つまり、輸出品第1号だというのです。

・**うちわ**

ジョーンズ氏：面白いですね。扇子は、現代でも、よく使われているんですか。

鈴木氏：歌舞伎、能、日本舞踊、そのほか古典演芸などには欠かせませんが、実用品としては、だんだん使われなくなっています。

・**陶磁器**

ジョーンズ氏：さっき、陶磁器は日本人の発明ではないとおっしゃいましたが、どこから入ってきたのですか。

鈴木氏：最初は5、6世紀ころに、中国・朝鮮から

C h a p t e r **30**

Mr. Jones: My wife became totally infatuated with Japanese fans while we were in Kyoto last week. You know, the ones that fold up. She bought more than ten of them as souvenirs for our friends back home.

Mr. Suzuki: Folding fans do make good souvenirs. For one thing they don't take up much space. Do you have any idea what Japanese invention was the first to be exported?

Mr. J: Hmmm. If it hadn't been for the hint, I'd've said ceramics.

Mr. S: No, ceramics is not a Japanese invention. No one really knows, but there's a theory that it was the folding fan. The fan itself came to Japan from China or Korea more than 1,000 years ago. From historical records though, it seems pretty certain that it was the Japanese who first invented a fan which folds. Then this was exported back to Korea and China, and eventually made its way as far as Europe — Japan's first export product.

Mr. J: Interesting. Is the folding fan used very much these days?

Mr. S: It's still indispensable in *kabuki*, *noh*, Japanese dancing and the like. But as a practical item, it's going out of style.

Mr. J: You said that the Japanese didn't invent ceramics. Where did that come from?

Mr. S: First from China and Korea in the fifth to sixth centu-

入ってきました。技術的には、17世紀に朝鮮から来た陶工の技術の影響が、きわめて大きかったようです。その時期に日本で初めて磁器ができたのです。その技術はとくに九州の伊万里を中心に発展し、伊万里の製品は広く海外にも知られました。最近の研究によると、ドイツのドレスデンの陶磁器にも伊万里の技術が影響しているようです。

ジョーンズ氏：現代ではどんな焼き物が有名なんですか。

鈴木氏：素地の粗い陶器では、志野焼、薩摩焼が2大名品です。磁器で代表的なものは、有田焼、清水焼、九谷焼などです。

漆器

ジョーンズ氏：陶磁器の話が出たので、漆器のことがふっと思い浮かびましたが、これも日本のものは優秀でしょう。なにせ漆器のことを、英語でjapan というのですから。

鈴木氏：確かにそうですね。漆の利用はそうとう古くから行われています。漆器に文様を描く方法もいろいろあります。

ジョーンズ氏：二、三よい例を教えてもらえますか。

鈴木氏：漆で文様を描いて、金属粉などをまきつける「蒔絵」。色の漆で文様を描いた「漆絵」などがあります。名産品を作っている所がほうぼうにありますが、全国的には、輪島塗が知られています。漆器もお土産にいいですよ。気に入ったものがあれば、お買い求めになってはいかがですか。

人形

ジョーンズ氏：もうひとつ、家内が好きでたまらないものが、人形なんですよ。旅行に出るたびに、人形収集をしています。京都で買った人形がたいへん気に入っているようです。

ries. Then it got a big boost from techniques introduced by Korean craftsmen in the 17th century. That's when the first porcelain was made here. Porcelain making flourished especially around Imari in Kyushu and Imari's products became internationally known. Some recent research indicates that Dresden porcelain was influenced by Imari techniques.

Mr. J: What are the more famous kinds of ceramic ware today?

Mr. S: Well, for pottery, which is made from relatively coarse materials, two big names are *shinoyaki* and *satsumayaki*. For porcelain, the typical ones are *aritayaki*, *kiyomizuyaki* and *kutaniyaki*.

Mr. J: The subject of ceramics also makes me think of lacquer ware, which I'm sure must be of very high quality here. Even the word "japan" means lacquer ware in English, you know.

Mr. S: That's right, isn't it? The Japanese have used lacquer from very early times. They developed a lot of different methods.

Mr. J: Can you give me a couple of good examples?

Mr. S: Well, there's the *makie* method of producing a pattern by sprinkling on metal powder, and the *urushie* method of making patterns in colored lacquer. There are lots of places throughout the country that are famous for their lacquer ware, but the best known is Wajima. Lacquer ware also makes a nice gift. You might buy a piece or two if you find something you like.

Mr. J: Another thing my wife adores is dolls. Every time we go on a trip she buys one or two for her collection. She picked one up in Kyoto that she thinks is out of this world.

鈴木氏：それはたいへんよかったですね。京都の人形は有名だし、伝統もあります。

ジョーンズ氏：日本の人形の伝統はそうとう古いんですか。

鈴木氏：人形を玩具として使い始めたのは、1,000年以上も前なんです。生活のなかでも人形は大切な役割を果たしています。

ジョーンズ氏：どんなふうにですか。

鈴木氏：たとえば3月3日には、雛人形を飾って、女の子の将来の幸福を祈ります。また、5月5日には、男の子が強く健康に成長することを願って、武者人形を飾ります。

ジョーンズ氏：人形が生活習慣のなかに入っているんですね。京都の人形以外に、日本滞在中に家内に何を買ったらよいといえばいいですか。

鈴木氏：日本全国には、名物の人形を生産している所が数えきれないくらいありますので、これといって勧めるのはなかなか難しいですね。だけど博多人形やこけしは、外国人にもたいへん人気がありますよ。

Mr. S: That's wonderful. Kyoto dolls are famous — and have a long tradition.

Mr. J: Do Japanese dolls have a long history, too?

Mr. S: As a kind of toy they've been around for more than 1,000 years. Dolls have always played an important role in the lives of Japanese people.

Mr. J: How is that?

Mr. S: For example, on March 3, many families set up a display of *hina* dolls as a way of wishing their daughters a happy future. Then, on May 5, families with boys display a warrior doll, hoping that it will help their sons to grow up strong and healthy.

Mr. J: I can see dolls are closely associated with customs here. Can you suggest any other type of doll my wife might buy while we are in Japan?

Mr. S: There are so many places all over the country that make famous dolls that it's hard to recommend just one or two. But I do know that Hakata and *kokeshi* dolls are quite popular among foreign visitors.

30

Traditional Crafts

1 My wife is totally infatuated with Japanese fans.

ノート infatuate はおもに、上例のように be infatuated with ... の成句で使う。「～に夢中になる、～にうつつを抜かす」やや高級な表現。

2 Do you have any idea what Japanese invention was the first to be exported?

ノート Do you have any idea ...? 「～と思いますか」
the first to be exported 「輸出された最初のもの」

例文 She was *the first to arrive.*
　　「彼女が最初に到着した人だった」

3 It's going out of style.

ノート go out of style 「時代遅れになる、すたれる」
go out of fashion だと「流行遅れになる」。

4 She picked one up in Kyoto that is out of this world.

ノート out of this [the] world は口語で、「(この世のものとは思えないくらい) とびっきり上等な、素晴らしい」の意。

例文 I think Hiroshige prints are beautiful—just *out of this world.*
　　「広重の版画はみんな美しいと思います——まったくこの世のものとは思えないくらいです」

Chapter
31

日本庭園と盆栽
Japanese Gardens and Bonsai

築山式と枯山水が日本庭園の基本様式

西洋庭園の特色は、
樹木や石を整然と幾何学的に配置した美しさにあります。
一方、築山式や枯山水に代表される日本庭園は、
自然の風情や景観を生かして、
屋内から眺めて楽しむように造られています。

〔盆栽の樹形の例〕

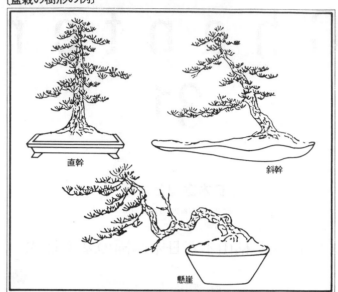

直幹

斜幹

懸崖

Vocabulary

黒松	☐☐	a black pine
樹形	☐☐	the form of a tree
木の古さ・樹齢	☐☐	the age of a tree
常緑樹	☐☐	an evergreen
落葉樹	☐☐	a deciduous tree
樹形を小さくする	☐☐	to dwarf a tree
～を応用する	☐☐	to make use of . . .
(樹形を)整える	☐☐	to trim
太根	☐☐	the main root
成長を抑える	☐☐	to restrain the tree's growth
空気の通り	☐☐	the circulation of air
水はけ	☐☐	water drainage
細根	☐☐	a fine root
手をかける	☐☐	to give a lot of care
山奥	☐☐	back in the mountains
険しい崖	☐☐	a steep cliff

〔築山式と枯山水〕

法華寺(奈良)の
築山式庭園

代表的な枯山水庭園、
龍安寺(京都)の石庭

本格的な日本庭園	□□	a first class Japanese garden
時代の流れとともに	□□	with the times
築山式	□□	the artificial hill style
枯山水	□□	the dry garden style
大海を表す	□□	to symbolize the sea
滝	□□	a waterfall
驚くような	□□	breathtaking
飾りを削りとられて	□□	to be stripped of frills and ornamentation
日本人の「美」の見方	□□	the Japanese sense of beauty
借景を活用する	□□	to blend with the surroundings
事前の申し込みをする	□□	to make reservations
日本三庭園	□□	The Three Japanese Gardens
大名屋敷	□□	a mansion of a feudal lord
造園する	□□	to landscape
反映	□□	a reflection

築山式と枯山水が日本庭園の基本様式

盆栽・築山式と枯山水・借景・日本三庭園

・盆栽

ジョーンズ氏：鈴木さん、素晴らしい盆栽をたくさんお持ちですね。

鈴木氏：気に入っていただいてよかったですよ。盆栽は私の趣味でしてね。

ジョーンズ夫人：よいご趣味ですね。あの花の咲いている木は何ですか。

鈴木氏：梅です。梅はよくプラムと訳されていますが、実際にはアプリコットのほうに近いんです。

・樹齢

ジョーンズ氏：ずいぶん古い木のようですね。樹齢は何年くらいなのですか。

鈴木氏：70〜80年だと思います。

ジョーンズ夫人：そんなに古いんですか。

鈴木氏：ええ、たとえばこの黒松ですがね。これは100年以上です。盆栽は数十年から、古いものでは数百年もたっているものもあります。盆栽の価値は、樹形のよさと木の古さにあるんです。

・盆栽の素材

ジョーンズ氏：どんな種類の木が盆栽にできるのですか。

鈴木氏：常緑樹、落葉樹、花の咲く木、実のなる木など、たくさんあります。人気のあるのは黒松です。

・盆栽の育て方と管理

ジョーンズ氏：しかしどうしたら、こんなに樹形を小さくしたり葉を細かくしたりできるのですか。

鈴木氏：盆栽の技術は、根と木の密接な関係を応用したものです。根を小さくすれば、木も小さくなります。まず木を全体の形が格好よくなるように整え、個々の枝に特別の性格を持たせます。それから、木の幹や枝の大きさとバランスをとって太

C h a p t e r 31

Mr. Jones: You certainly have a beautiful collection of *bonsai* trees, Mr. Suzuki.

Mr. Suzuki: I'm glad you like them. It's my hobby.

Mrs. Jones: A very nice one. What kind of tree is that — the one that's in bloom.

Mr. S: That's an *ume* tree. Ume is often translated as plum but it's really closer to an apricot.

Mr. J: It looks very old. How old is it?

Mr. S: Seventy or eighty years, I think.

Mrs. J: That old?

Mr. S: Yes. Now take this black pine here. It's over 100. Bonsai trees range in age anywhere from a few decades to several centuries. The worth of a bonsai is based on its form and its age.

Mr. J: What kind of trees can be made into bonsai?

Mr. S: Many kinds — various evergreens and deciduous trees, and trees that blossom and bear fruit. A favorite is the black pine.

Mr. J: But how in the world do you dwarf the trees and get them to produce such short needles or leaves?

Mr. S: The art of bonsai makes use of the close relationship between a tree's roots and its size. If you keep the roots small the tree will be small. First the tree is trimmed to give it a pleasing overall shape and the individual branches a special character. Then the main roots are cut proportionally to the

根を切って、成長を抑えていくんです。また、根を切ったときに、新しい土に木を植え替え、空気の通りや水はけをよくします。こうすると新しい細根が育ち、木の大きさに見合った小枝や小葉が成長するようになります。

ジョーンズ氏：確かにずいぶん手をかけるのですね。

●樹形

ジョーンズ夫人：あの木の形は変わっていますね。

鈴木氏：あれは懸崖といって、山奥の険しい崖などにとりついて生えている姿を表したものです。

ジョーンズ夫人：そういわれてみると、まったくそのように見えますね。

●日本庭園の特徴

鈴木夫人：ところでジョーンズさん、京都の庭園はいくつかご覧になったんでしたね。

ジョーンズ氏：ええ、本格的な日本庭園を見るのは初めてでしたので、たいへん印象的でした。日本の庭園にもいくつかタイプがあるようですね。

●築山式と枯山水

鈴木夫人：そのとおりですわ。歴史的には時代の流れとともに、様式もしだいに変化していますが、基本的なタイプは2つあります。「築山式」と「枯山水」です。

ジョーンズ氏：それぞれどんな特徴がありますか。

鈴木夫人：築山式は池によって大海を表し、土を盛り岩で山を表現します。一方、枯山水は水を使いません。白砂を敷いて大海を表現し、砂の模様によって流れや波を表します。滝は青石を立てて表現します。

ジョーンズ夫人：そうでしたわね。龍安寺の庭が枯山水でしたわね。

size of the trunks and branches of the tree — in order to restrain the tree's growth. This is repeated from time to time, and each time we replant the tree in fresh soil so as to increase the circulation of air and improve water drainage. This promotes the growth of fine roots, which in turn helps the tree grow small branches and leaves matched to its size.

Mr. J: You certainly have to give the trees a lot of care.

Mrs. J: That's an interestingly shaped tree.

Mr. S: That's supposed to represent a tree growing out of a steep cliff far back in the mountains.

Mrs. J: Now that you mention it, that's exactly what it looks like.

Mrs. Suzuki: You saw some of the famous gardens in Kyoto, didn't you?

Mr. J: Yes, we did. It was our first time to see really first class Japanese gardens, and we were very impressed. There are a number of different types, aren't there?

Mrs. S: Yes, there are. The styles have gradually changed with the times, but there are two basic types. The artificial hill style and the dry garden style — called *tsukiyama* and *karesansui*.

Mr. J: What is each like?

Mrs. S: In the artificial hill style, there is a pond symbolizing the sea, and mountains are represented by banks of earth and arrangements of rocks. In the dry garden style no water is used. The sea is symbolized by a layer of white sand that is raked to form patterns that represent the rippling movement of water. Waterfalls are represented by an arrangement of blue rocks.

Mrs. J: Yes, I remember. The garden at Ryoan Temple was in the dry garden style.

ジョーンズ氏：あの庭には驚きましたよ。いっさいの飾りを削りとって、最後に純粋な美しさを残したんですね。日本人の「美」の見方がいくらかわかったような気がします。

鈴木夫人：そうなんです。天龍寺や西芳寺の庭園は築山式です。龍安寺のほかに大徳寺大仙院で枯山水をご覧になったでしょう。

ジョーンズ夫人：はい、すてきでしたわ。

鈴木夫人：まわりの山や樹木を調和させて造園したものもありますのよ。たとえば、修学院離宮や円通寺などが有名で、いまお話しした2つの特徴をとり入れ、さらに借景も活用しています。見学には事前に申し込みが必要ですけどね。

借景

ジョーンズ夫人：ねえあなた、こんどぜひそこにも行ってみたいわね。

日本三庭園

ジョーンズ氏：ところで、日本三庭園というのがあると聞きましたが。

鈴木氏：それは水戸の偕楽園、金沢の兼六園、岡山の後楽園のことです。いずれも大名屋敷の庭園で、各地の名所になぞらえて景観をつくっています。庭園で使っている石や木も、それだけで有名なものがたくさんあります。

ジョーンズ氏：庭園や盆栽のなかにも、日本の文化そのものが反映されているんですね。

鈴木氏：そういえると思います。両方とも、自然美を愛し、それをできるだけ身近にとり込もうとした日本人の発想から生まれたものです。

Mr. J: The Ryoan Temple garden is breathtaking. It's stripped of all frills and ornamentation, leaving just pure beauty. I think I learned something about the Japanese sense of beauty from it.

Mrs. S: It is something special. The gardens at Tenryu Temple and Saiho Temple are in the artificial hill style. I suppose you also saw the dry style garden at Daitoku Temple's Daisen-in.

Mrs. J: Yes, it was magnificent.

Mrs. S: Some gardens are further landscaped to harmonize with the surrounding mountains and woods. For example, the Shugaku-in Imperial Villa and Entsu Temple have famous gardens that include the features of both of the styles I just explained — and in addition are laid out to blend with the surroundings. If you want to see either of these places though, you'll have to make reservations in advance.

Mrs. J: We'll have to see them next time, won't we, dear?

Mr. J: Just one other thing. I heard that you have something called The Three Japanese Gardens . . .

Mr. S: That refers to the Kairaku Garden in Mito, the Kenroku Garden in Kanazawa and the Koraku Garden in Okayama. They are all gardens that were originally built around the mansions of feudal lords. Each one is landscaped to represent famous scenery from a different part of Japan. Many of the trees and rocks used in the gardens have become famous in their own right.

Mr. J: Somehow I get the feeling that bonsai and gardens are a reflection of a part of Japanese culture itself.

Mr. S: I guess you could say that. At any rate, both have grown out of the Japanese love of nature and their desire to bring it as close to themselves as they can.

Useful Expressions ——— 31

1

<u>That old?</u>

ノート 　口語で that は so の意味で使われることがある。

例文 　It's about *that* high (＝so high).

2

How <u>in the world</u> do you dwarf the trees and get them to produce such short needles or leaves?

ノート 　in the world は疑問詞を強めて、「いったい」の意味を表す。

例文 　What *in the world* did you do?
　　「いったい何をしでかしたのか」

3

<u>Now that</u> you mention it, that's exactly what it <u>looks like</u>.

ノート 　now that ... 「いまはもう～であるから、～してみると」look like ... 「～に似ている、～のように見える」

例文 　*What* does she *look like*?
　　「彼女はどんなふうな人ですか」

4

<u>It</u> was our first time <u>to</u> see really first class Japanese gardens.

ノート 　It は to 以下を指す仮主語。「～するのは初めてだったんです」よく使う表現。☞Useful Expressions 32-1

例文 　*It* is our first time *to* come to the United States.

Chapter
32

日本の住宅

Japanese Houses

東京で家を建てるのはたいへんです

地価の高い大都市部では
マイホームは夢のまた夢。
数量的にはほぼ行き渡った日本の住宅ですが、
広さや住環境の整備などの面では、
まだまだ努力が必要です。

〔住宅事情の国際比較〕

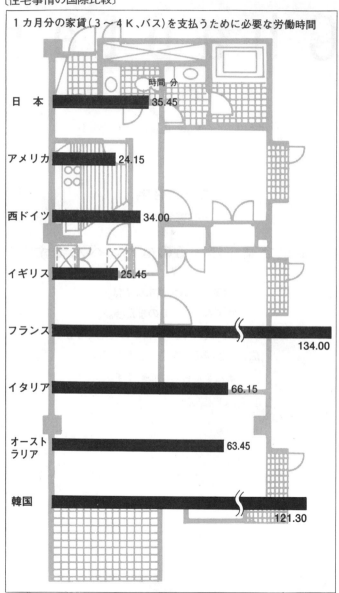

1カ月分の家賃（3〜4K、バス）を支払うために必要な労働時間

時間 分

日　本	35.45
アメリカ	24.15
西ドイツ	34.00
イギリス	25.45
フランス	134.00
イタリア	66.15
オースト ラリア	63.45
韓国	121.30

（1986年）

Vocabulary

和室	☐☐	a Japanese style room
わらの畳床	☐☐	a mat of straw
織ったいぐさ	☐☐	woven rushes
保温する	☐☐	to keep the heat in
単位	☐☐	unit
障子	☐☐	a sliding door
枠	☐☐	a lattice
採光する	☐☐	to let in light
間仕切りする	☐☐	to divide rooms
押し入れ	☐☐	a closet
板張りの床	☐☐	a wooden floor
じゅうたんを敷く	☐☐	to carpet
床の間	☐☐	a little alcove
掛け軸	☐☐	a scroll picture
置物	☐☐	a figurine; a carved ornament
木材	☐☐	wood building materials
豊富な	☐☐	plentiful
通風	☐☐	ventilation
蒸し暑い夏	☐☐	humid summer
火事	☐☐	a fire
地震	☐☐	an earthquake
鉄骨	☐☐	a steel-frame
鉄筋コンクリート	☐☐	ferroconcrete
新建材	☐☐	newly developed materials
集合住宅群	☐☐	apartment and condominium complexes
地価	☐☐	land prices
たいへんなこと	☐☐	no easy matter
(住宅が)数量的には	☐☐	as far as number of units goes
住みやすい環境	☐☐	the quality of the environment
平均床面積	☐☐	the average floor space
～に対し見劣りしない	☐☐	not to look too bad against . . .

32

Japanese Houses

東京で家を建てるのはたいへんです

畳・障子・ふすま・住宅の取得・住環境の整備

鈴木氏：ジョーンズ夫人、和室は初めてですか。

ジョーンズ夫人：はい、日本に滞在中にぜひ見たいと思っていました。これが畳ですか。

畳

鈴木氏：そうです。いかがですか。

ジョーンズ夫人：とても素晴らしいです。材料は何ですか。

鈴木氏：厚さ10cmくらいのわらで作った畳床に、いぐさを織ったシートを張ったものです。夏は涼しく、冬は保温に役立ちます。畳1枚の大きさはタテ約1.8m、ヨコ約0.9mです。1枚の畳の広さを1畳と呼び、部屋の広さをいう場合の単位に使っています。

ジョーンズ夫人：この部屋は畳が8枚ですね。

鈴木氏：はい、したがって8畳です。個人住宅のほとんどの部屋は、和室の場合4.5畳、6畳、8畳が一般的です。

ジョーンズ夫人：これは何ですか。

障子

鈴木氏：これは障子で、引き戸になっています。枠は木製で白い紙が張ってあり、閉じたときの採光も考えられています。

ジョーンズ夫人：この戸は何ですか。

ふすま

鈴木夫人：これはふすまです。この戸も左右に滑らせ、枠はやはり木製で、張ってある紙はずっと厚くなっています。ふすまは間仕切りや押し入れの扉として使います。

ジョーンズ夫人：日本の住宅の部屋はほとんど畳敷きなんですか。

C h a p t e r 32

Mr. Suzuki: Is this the first time you've been in a Japanese style room, Mrs. Jones?

Mrs. Jones: Yes. I was very anxious to see one during my visit. Is this floor what they call *tatami*?

Mr. S: Yes, how do you like it?

Mrs. J: It's very nice. What's it made of?

Mr. S: Underneath there is a mat of straw that's about ten centimeters thick and the surface is covered with a sheet of woven rushes. It's cool in the summer and helps keep the heat in during winter. Each mat is about 1.8 meters long and 90 centimeters wide. The area of one mat is called a *jo* and we use this as a unit for talking about the size of rooms.

Mrs. J: This room has eight mats, doesn't it?

Mr. S: Yes, so it's an eight-jo or eight-mat room. Most Japanese style rooms in private homes are 4.5, six or eight mats.

Mrs. J: What's this?

Mr. S: It's *shoji*, a sliding door. The frame is a wooden lattice and is covered with white paper so it'll let in light even when closed.

Mrs. J: And what kind of door is this?

Mrs. Suzuki: That's a *fusuma* door. It also slides and has a wooden frame, but the paper covering is much thicker. Fusuma doors are used for dividing rooms, and as closet doors.

Mrs. J: Do most rooms in Japanese houses have tatami floors?

和室・洋室

鈴木氏：むかしはそうでした。しかしここ30〜40年の間にさまざまな新しい生活様式が導入されました。今日では、大部分の住宅は板張りまたはじゅうたん敷きの部屋と和室をとり交ぜています。

ジョーンズ夫人：あら、これは面白いところに絵を掛けていますね。

床の間

鈴木氏：こうしたコーナーを床の間といいます。このような掛け軸の絵や花・置物などを飾る小さなスペースです。

木造住宅

ジョーンズ氏：この家も木造ですね。日本の住宅は伝統的に木造が多いと聞きましたが、それはなぜですか。

鈴木氏：ひとつには、かつては良質の木材が豊富だったからです。それに木造だと通風に優れています。また、採光もよいんです。日本の風土——とくに蒸し暑い夏に適しているからです。

ジョーンズ氏：なかなか合理的ですね。

鈴木氏：しかし最近では火事や地震のことを考慮して、新しい建築工法が開発されています。鉄骨・コンクリート・新建材などを使用して建てる住宅もかなり増えています。

ジョーンズ氏：そうですか。日本では住宅の値段がたいへん高いと聞きましたが……。

住宅の取得

鈴木氏：そうなんです。日本では小さな国土に多くの人が住んでいますので、地価がひじょうに高いんです。とくに大都市周辺では一戸建ての住宅を入手するのは、ますます難しくなっています。したがって、3階から10階建てぐらいの集合住宅群がたくさん建てられています。

ジョーンズ氏：日本の地価はどのくらいですか。

Mr. S: Years ago they did. But various new living styles have been introduced over the past 30 or 40 years. Most houses today are a mixture of rooms with wooden, carpeted and tatami floors.

Mrs. J: Oh, that's an interesting place to hang a picture.

Mr. S: This corner is what we call a *tokonoma* — a little alcove that we decorate with a scroll picture like this, and with flowers, a figurine, or a carved ornament of some kind.

Mr. Jones: This is a wooden house, isn't it? I've heard that traditionally that's the most common type. Can you tell me why that is?

Mr. S: One reason is that good wood building materials used to be plentiful. Another is that the ventilation is better in wooden houses. They also let in a lot of light. This makes them suitable for the Japanese climate — especially during our hot, humid summers.

Mr. J: Sounds reasonable.

Mr. S: Recently though, because of concern about fires and earthquakes, homes are being developed with new construction methods. A lot of other kinds of houses are being built — steel-frame and ferroconcrete houses, and other types made with newly developed materials.

Mr. J: Is that so? I heard that the price of houses here is very high.

Mr. S: Extremely high. We've got a large population on a small land area, which makes property extremely expensive. There are very few people these days who can afford to buy a house near one of the big cities. As a result, many three to ten story apartment and condominium complexes have been going up.

Mr. J: What are land prices here like?

鈴木氏：東京の中心街から、電車や車で1時間余り
　　　　離れたこの辺りを例にしましょう。たぶん1㎡当
　　　　たり20万円くらいします。

ジョーンズ氏：20万円というと1,300〜1,400ドルで
　　　　すか。それはたいへんな値段ですね。

ジョーンズ夫人：そんなにですか。でも鈴木さんの
　　　　ところは安心ですね。家をお持ちなんですもの。

鈴木氏：はい、7年前にやっと夢がかなって自分の
　　　　家を建てることができました。もっとも銀行の持
　　　　ち分のほうが多いんですけどね。(笑い)

ジョーンズ氏：アメリカでも、自分の家を買うとな
　　　　ると、それなりにたいへんですよ。日本ほどでは
　　　　ないかもしれませんがね。

● 住環境の
　充実・改善

鈴木氏：現実には、日本では住宅は、数量的にほぼ
　　　　行き渡っています。しかし問題は狭いことや住み
　　　　やすい環境が整っていないことです。これからは
　　　　もっともっとこれらを改善していく必要があるで
　　　　しょうね。しかし新築住宅の1戸当たりの平均床
　　　　面積は100㎡弱になっています。140㎡近いアメリ
　　　　カには及びませんが、西ドイツとほぼ同じです。
　　　　とにかく世界水準から見ても、どうやら見劣りし
　　　　ないところまで来ています。

Mr. S: Well, take a place an hour or so out of the center of Tokyo by train or car. You'd probably have to pay around 200,000 yen per square meter.

Mr. J: That's about 13 or 14 hundred dollars. Yes, that's expensive.

Mrs. J: As high as that? But you two don't have anything to worry about. You already have your own place.

Mr. S: Yes, seven years ago we were finally able to build our dream house. Though the bank owns a lot more of it than we do. (Laughs)

Mr. J: I can tell you that it's no easy matter to buy a home in the States either. Though maybe not so hard as in Japan.

Mr. S: Actually, Japan has enough houses as far as number of units goes. The problem is size and the quality of the environment. These are going to require a lot of improvement. On the other hand, the average floor space of new houses is just under 100 square meters. That's still considerably less than the 140 square meter figure for the U.S., but it's nearly the same as West Germany. Anyway, we've finally got to the point where we don't look too bad against world standards.

1

Is this <u>the first time you've been</u> in a Japanese style room?

ノート

Useful Expressions 31-4 の It's one's first time to ... とともによく使われる表現。

例文

This is *the first time I've seen* an American wedding.

2

I <u>was anxious to</u> see one <u>during my visit.</u>

ノート

be anxious to ... 「~することを切望する、~したがる」の意の口語的用法。during と while を混同する人がいるが、during は前置詞、while は接続詞。つまり、during＋句（名詞または代名詞）、while (＝during the time that)＋節になる。

例文

While (she was) in New York, she studied music.

3

<u>How do you like it?</u>

ノート

「(相手がどのくらい気に入っているか、嫌いかを尋ねて) ~はいかがですか」という基本的な表現。

似たいい方に How would you like ...? がある。こちらは、(1)「(勧誘して)「~ (するの) はいかがですか」(2)「(飲み物や料理の出し方や調理の仕方を尋ねて) ~はどうしましょうか」で使うことが多い。

例文 1

How do you like Los Angeles?

例文 2

How would you like (to have) steak for dinner?

例文 3

How would you like your steak — rare, medium or well-done?

Chapter
33

■

伝統的スポーツ
Traditional Japanese Sports

■

柔道の極意は「柔よく剛を制す」

■

柔道・剣道・弓道・空手などは
技を磨き、心身を鍛える伝統的な武道として
発展してきました。
とくに柔道は、
オリンピックや国際大会に各国の選手が参加する
国際的なスポーツに成長しました。

〔国籍別外国人力士入門者数の累計〕

アメリカ	○○○○○○○		○○	20人
トンガ	○○○○○○○	7人
台湾	○○○○○○	6人
ブラジル	○○○○○○	6人
韓国	○○○○	4人

西サモア	○○ 2人	アルゼンチン	○ 1人
イギリス	○ 1人	パラグアイ	○ 1人
カナダ	○ 1人		

(1987年7月)

Vocabulary

相撲	☐☐	sumo wrestling
一勝負	☐☐	a bout
土俵	☐☐	the *sumo* ring
足の裏	☐☐	the bottoms of one's feet
～から押し出される	☐☐	to be pushed out of . . .
投げ(技)	☐☐	a throw
技	☐☐	technique
～に興味をそそられる	☐☐	to get a kick out of . . .
位(くらい)	☐☐	ranks
(相撲の)場所	☐☐	a tournament
(地位が)上下する	☐☐	to go up and down
武道	☐☐	martial arts
～を重んじる	☐☐	to put emphasis on . . .
心身を鍛錬する	☐☐	to train the mind and body
(柔道の)国際試合	☐☐	an international judo tournament
「柔よく剛を制す」	☐☐	"Flexibility is stronger than stiffness."

〔オリンピック柔道無差別級メダリスト〕

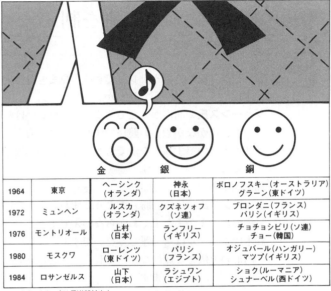

金　　　　銀　　　　銅

1964	東京	ヘーシンク (オランダ)	神永 (日本)	ボロノフスキー(オーストラリア) グラーン(東ドイツ)
1972	ミュンヘン	ルスカ (オランダ)	クズネツォフ (ソ連)	ブロンダニ(フランス) パリシ(イギリス)
1976	モントリオール	上村 (日本)	ランフリー (イギリス)	チョチョシビリ(ソ連) チョー(韓国)
1980	モスクワ	ローレンツ (東ドイツ)	パリシ (フランス)	オジュバール(ハンガリー) マツプ(イギリス)
1984	ロサンゼルス	山下 (日本)	ラシュワン (エジプト)	ショク(ルーマニア) シュナーベル(西ドイツ)

1968年(メキシコ)は柔道競技なし

倒す	□□	to defeat
(柔道の固め技で)動けないようにする	□□	to pin or immobilize
(競技を)体重別にする	□□	to set up weight classes
~の興味をそぐ	□□	to take the fun out of . . .
護身	□□	self-defense
~を有効に使う	□□	to make best use of . . .
組み合う	□□	to grapple
(手で)突く	□□	to strike
1対1の勝負	□□	one-to-one fighting
竹刀	□□	a bamboo sword
防具	□□	protective gear
面打ち	□□	a cut to the face
小手打ち	□□	a cut to the hand
胴打ち	□□	a cut to the body
咽頭部への突き	□□	a stab to the throat

柔道の極意は「柔よく剛を制す」

相撲・柔道・空手・剣道・弓道

・相撲

ジョーンズ氏：きのうテレビで相撲を見ましたよ。

鈴木氏：それでいかがでしたか。

ジョーンズ氏：面白かったですよ。時間は短いけれ
ども、なかなか激しい競技ですね。それに力士の
体も大きいですね。なかでもハワイ出身の小錦は
とても大きかったです。

鈴木氏：小錦はきのう勝ったでしょう。

ジョーンズ氏：はい、勝ったようですね。しかし相
撲のルールがまだよくわからないんですよ。

鈴木氏：ルールはそう難しくないですよ。テレビで
円形の土俵をご覧になったでしょう。あの土俵は
直径が4.55mあります。土俵のなかで、さきに足
の裏以外の部分が土につくか、土俵の外に押し出
されたほうが負けです。相撲には70種類の投げや
いろんな技があるんです。

ジョーンズ氏：ああ、なるほど。それに審判員がな
かなか独特ですね。衣装や動作が本当にエキゾ
チックな感じでしたよ。

・行司

鈴木氏：あれは行司といって、むかしながらの衣装
をつけているのです。

ジョーンズ氏：力士にはいろんな位があるそうです
ね。位はどんな仕組みになっているんですか。多
く勝つと位が上がるんですか。

鈴木氏：相撲は年に6場所行われます。各場所は15
日間行われ、ひとりひとりの力士は1日1回対戦
相手と戦います。15日間の総合成績によって次の
場所での地位が上下します。相撲には10のランク
があって、このランクのことを相撲用語では番付

C h a p t e r 33

Mr. Jones: I watched sumo wrestling on TV yesterday.

Mr. Suzuki: Oh? How'd you like it?

Mr. J: It was fascinating. The bouts were short but there was a lot of action. There were some really big guys. Konishiki, the one from Hawaii — he's enormous, isn't he?

Mr. S: Yes he is! Did he win yesterday?

Mr. J: It looked like he did. But I don't know enough about the rules to say for sure.

Mr. S: Oh, the rules aren't very difficult. You noticed the ring on TV? Well, that's 4.55 meters across. Inside the ring, the first one who touches the ground with any part of his body other than the bottoms of his feet loses. Otherwise the first one to be pushed out of the ring is the loser. There are 70 different throws and techniques.

Mr. J: Oh, I see. I got a kick out of the referee. His clothes and the way he strikes different poses and moves around — pretty exotic.

Mr. S: We call him the *gyoji*. He dresses the way they did hundreds of years ago.

Mr. J: I hear the wrestlers have different ranks. How does that work — the more wins the higher the rank?

Mr. S: Well, you see there are six tournaments a year. Each runs 15 days and each wrestler has one match a day. His rank in the next tournament will go up or down depending on how many of his 15 matches he wins. There are ten ranks or *banzuke*. The top rank is *yokozuna*. In all of sumo's history only

横綱

といいます。番付の最上位は横綱といって、過去60人ていどしか横綱になった力士はいません。

ジョーンズ氏：そのほかに、日本の伝統的スポーツというと、どんなものがありますか。

鈴木氏：柔道・剣道・弓道・空手などがあります。これらはすべて日本の伝統的な武道で、技を磨くとともに、心身の鍛錬をも重んじます。現在ではスポーツとして親しまれています。むかしは男性だけがやるものでしたが、最近は女性や外国人の愛好者も増えています。

柔道

ジョーンズ氏：柔道はオリンピックの種目にもなっているのですこし知っています。

鈴木氏：そうです。そのほかにも、毎年何回か国際大会が開かれています。

ジョーンズ氏：私の友人にも、アメリカで熱心に柔道をやっている人がいますよ。ところで「柔道」という言葉はどこから来たんですか。

鈴木氏：柔道の「柔」は、柔らかく、しなやかという意味で、「道」は道という意味です。ですから直訳すると「柔軟性のある道」というようになるでしょう。このスポーツは、「柔よく剛を制す」という基本理念から名づけられました。ですから柔道には、相手の力をうまく利用して相手を倒す技がいろいろあります。技を大別すると、相手を投げ倒す投げ技と、相手を押さえつけたり、動きを封じたりする固め技とがあります。小さい者が大きい者に勝つというのも、柔道の魅力のひとつです。けれども最近では、競技が体重別に行われるようになったので、私個人としては、やや残念な気もしています。

空手

ジョーンズ氏：空手というのも、よくアメリカで聞きますが、詳しく知らないんです。どんな競技で

about 60 wrestlers have reached yokozuna.

Mr. J: What other traditional Japanese sports are there?

Mr. S: *Judo*, *kendo*, *kyudo*, *karate* . . . They've all grown out of traditional Japanese martial arts, which put as much emphasis on training the mind and body as on technique. Today they are just sports. In the past they were for men only, but recently quite a few women are taking them up too. They are also becoming more popular outside of Japan.

Mr. J: I know a little about judo because that's an Olympic sport.

Mr. S: Right. There are also a number of international judo tournaments held every year.

Mr. J: I've got some friends in the States who are crazy about doing judo. By the way, where does the word "judo" come from?

Mr. S: "Ju" means soft and flexible and "do" means way so a direct translation would be something like "the way of flexibility." The sport is named after its working principle — that "flexibility is stronger than stiffness." Many of the judo techniques are designed to defeat the opponent by using his own strength. There are two categories of techniques: those for throwing the opponent to the floor, and those used on the floor for pinning him down or immobilizing him. One of the fascinating things about judo has always been that a little guy has a reasonably good chance of beating a big one. Some years ago though, they started setting up weight classes. That's taken some of the fun out of it for me.

Mr. J: Karate is a word you hear quite often in America, but I don't know much about it. What's it like?

すか。

鈴木氏：武器を持たずに身を守る技が基本になっているんです。つまり、体のいろいろな部分を有効に使って身を防ぎ、相手に勝つ技を決めるんです。相手をつかんではいけませんが、手の突きや足のけりをよく使います。もともとは中国で生まれたものです。空手の熟練者になりますと、かわらを十数枚とか15mmくらいの板を5枚くらいは素手で割ってしまいます。

ジョーンズ氏：いつかテレビで見たことがあります。本当にすごいですね。では剣道とか弓道とかは、どんな競技ですか。

●剣道

鈴木氏：剣道は竹刀を持って1対1の勝負をします。対戦者は防具を身につけます。基本的な技は面打ち、小手打ち、胴打ち、喉頭部の突きです。

ジョーンズ氏：日本式のフェンシングというところですか。

●弓道

鈴木氏：よくそういわれますね。弓道は日本式アーチェリーです。弓は木と竹を接合してできていて、矢は竹で作ったものです。的までの距離は、近距離の28mと遠距離の約60mに分かれています。それぞれ的の大きさが違います。

ジョーンズ氏：日本の伝統的なスポーツのなかにも、西欧と似通ったものがあることがわかりましたよ。アメリカ人もフェンシングやアーチェリーは好きですよ。

Mr. S: It's based on techniques developed for self-defense without a weapon. The point is to make best use of many different parts of the body to defeat your adversary. There's no grappling, but there's a lot of striking and kicking. It comes from China. A karate expert can break a stack of ten or more tiles, or a stack of around five 1.5 centimeter boards, with his bare hand.

Mr. J: I've seen that done on TV. It's really fantastic. And what kind of sports are kendo and kyudo?

Mr. S: Kendo is one-to-one fighting using bamboo swords. The participants wear rather elaborate protective gear. The fundamental touches are cuts to the face, hands and body and stabs to the throat.

Mr. J: I guess you'd call it Japanese fencing.

Mr. S: It's sometimes called that. Kyudo is Japanese archery. The bow is a combination of bamboo and other woods, and the arrows are made of bamboo. The target is set either at 28 meters or about 60 meters and the size is different depending on the distance.

Mr. J: Well, I see that some of your traditional sports have something in common with those in the West. We also like fencing and archery.

1

I <u>watched</u> sumo wrestling <u>on TV</u> yesterday.

ノート

watch は「じっと見る、動作・状態・変化などしばらく目で追って観察する」という意味。テレビ、スポーツを見るのに使う。

see は「意識的に見ようとはしないのに、自然に目に入ってくる」場合の「見る」だが、映画のときは watch でなく、see を使う。

例文

We *saw* a movie.

2

I got a <u>kick out of</u> the referee.

ノート

get a kick [one's kicks] out of [from] ... は「〜でひじょうな快感 [喜び] を覚える、ぞくぞくする」の意味の口語表現。この表現は、こっけいなものを見たり聞いたりして「楽しかった」ときにもよく使う。

例文

How did you spend last night? — I saw a comedy. I really *got a kick out of* it.

3

I <u>hear</u> the wrestlers have different ranks.

ノート

「〜だそうだ」のいい方は、口語では、I hear「(人の話 [うわさ] では) 〜だそうだ」のほかに、They say／People say などが使われる。I understand も使われるが、ややフォーマルな感じ。It's said that ... は、改まったいい方で、スピーチや文章で使われることが多い。

例文

They say the climate and customs of a place change the people.　　　　　　　　　　(2)

Chapter
34

習慣と生活様式
Customs and Beliefs

４と９はなぜ不吉な数字なんですか

私たちは外国で
カルチャーショックを受けることがあります。
日本に来た外国人も同様です。
日本の習慣や行動様式を、
折にふれてわかりやすく説明することは
相互理解のためにとても大切なことです。

〔日本の習慣と生活様式のいろいろ〕

お酒を温めて飲む

はちまきをしめる

はしを使い、食器を
手に持って食事をする

おじぎをする
正座する

Vocabulary

左側通行する	☐☐	to drive on the left-hand side
運転席	☐☐	the driver's seat
反対側	☐☐	the opposite side
ひやひやするような	☐☐	nervous
（運転が）うまい	☐☐	skillful
チップ	☐☐	a tip
チップをやる	☐☐	to tip
気をもむ	☐☐	to worry
とまどう	☐☐	to get flustered
末尾に〜がつく	☐☐	to end in . . .
不吉な数字	☐☐	an unlucky number
〜を意味する言葉と 　同じ発音を持つ	☐☐	to have the same sound as the word for . . .
背番号	☐☐	a uniform number
〜を気にしない	☐☐	to think nothing of . . .
〜を目立たせる	☐☐	to make . . . stand out

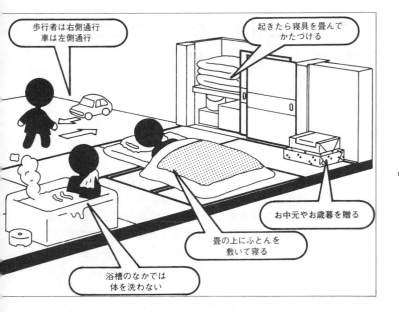

日本式の旅館	☐☐	a Japanese style inn
(旅館の)従業員	☐☐	the help
正座する	☐☐	to get down on one's knees
床に手をつける	☐☐	to touch one's palms to the floor
湯船に(湯が)たっぷりある	☐☐	a (bath) tub is filled right to the top
ゆっくりつかる	☐☐	to take a long soak
(体を)温める	☐☐	to warm oneself
(体が)温まる	☐☐	to warm up
入浴する	☐☐	to bathe
はし	☐☐	chopsticks
茶碗を持つ	☐☐	to hold a rice bowl
食器を手で持つ	☐☐	to hold a dish in one's hand
酒を温める	☐☐	to warm *sake*

4と9はなぜ不吉な数字なんですか

不吉な数字・おじぎ・風呂・日本料理

鈴木夫人：日本にいらっしゃる間、アメリカ人と日本人の習慣や生活様式の違いについて、何かお感じになったことがありますか。奥様は日本にいらしたのが初めてですので、私とくに興味がありますの。

ジョーンズ夫人：それはもう、いろいろありますわ。

鈴木夫人：たとえば、どんなことですか。

- **車は**
- **左側通行**

ジョーンズ夫人：まず車が左側通行のことです。車の運転席の位置も、アメリカとは正反対ですね。それに幅の狭い道が多くて、ひやひやします。だけど日本の皆さんの運転のうまいのには感心しています。

鈴木夫人：道幅が狭いのは、たしかに問題なんですの。日本は車の数が急速に増えているのに、道幅はむかしのままで、狭いところが多いですからね。

- **チップ**

ジョーンズ夫人：それから、日本ではチップがいらないことですね。

鈴木夫人：そうですね。ですから私などは、チップを渡すことに慣れていないんですよ。外国に行ったときに、だれにいくらチップを渡したらよいか、いつも気をもんだり、とまどったりします。

ジョーンズ夫人：チップをいちいち気にしなくてもいいというのは、素晴らしいですわ。日本式のほうがいいですよ。

ジョーンズ氏：以前から疑問に思っていたことがあるんです。どこのホテルに泊まっても、部屋番号の末尾に4と9のつく部屋がないですね。

ジョーンズ夫人：そうそう、あれはどうしてですか。

C h a p t e r 34

Mrs. Suzuki: During your stay in Japan have you noticed any differences between American and Japanese customs? I'm especially interested because I know this is your first visit here.

Mrs. Jones: Oh, many things.

Mrs. S: For example?

Mrs. J: Well, you drive on the left-hand side of the road. The driver's seat is also on the opposite side. The roads are often so narrow that it makes me nervous. But I'm impressed by how skillful your drivers are.

Mrs. S: The narrow roads are a problem. The number of cars has increased very rapidly but many of the streets and roads are still as narrow as ever.

Mrs. J: Another thing is that there's no tipping in Japan.

Mrs. S: That's right. I'm not used to giving tips. When I go overseas, I'm always worried about who and how much to tip — and always get flustered.

Mrs. J: Not having to worry about tipping is nice. I like the Japanese system.

Mr. Jones: There's something I've been wondering about for some time. None of the hotels here have room numbers ending in four or nine.

Mrs. J: Why is that?

不吉な数字　鈴木氏：日本では、4と9を不吉な数字として嫌う人が多いんです。その理由は、4は「し」とも読み、これは死を意味する言葉と発音が同じだからです。また9は「く」と読み、苦しみを意味する言葉と発音が同じだからです。

ジョーンズ夫人：アメリカのホテルで13を使わないのと同じようなものですね。

鈴木氏：はい、そうです。日本のホテルも13は使っていないと思います。プロ野球の選手も、背番号に4や9のつく数字を使っている人は、ひじょうに少ないんですよ。しかし日本のプロ野球には、外国から来ている選手もかなりいるんで、彼らは49番なんていう番号もぜんぜん気にしないようなんです。こういう選手は本当に目立ちますよ。

ジョーンズ氏：アメリカにも日本にも、不吉な数字があるということですね。

お辞儀　ジョーンズ夫人：この間日光見物に行ったとき、日本式の旅館に泊まったんです。旅館の従業員の人たちが座って手をついてお辞儀をしていました。

鈴木夫人：ああ、あれは畳の部屋でする伝統的なおじぎです。あれは日本の行儀作法の基本です。

風呂　鈴木氏：日本式のお風呂にもお入りになりましたか。

ジョーンズ氏：ええ、初めてでした。浴槽にお湯がたっぷりあって、なかなか気持ちがよかったですよ。日本の家庭にあるお風呂も、ああいうスタイルですか。

鈴木氏：もっと狭いですが、形は同じです。日本人は入浴するとき、浴槽につかってゆっくりと温まるのが好きなんです。浴槽は、なかの湯を加熱して適当な温度に保てるようになっています。浴槽の湯は家族全員が交代で入浴し終わるまで抜きま

Mr. Suzuki: Four and nine are unlucky numbers in Japan. The Japanese word for four is *shi*, which has the same sound as the word for death. Nine is *ku* and that's also the word for suffering.

Mrs. J: That's like the American hotels not using 13.

Mr. S: Yes, and I think you'll find that Japanese hotels don't use 13 either. There are also very few professional baseball players in Japan that have uniform numbers including four or nine. But there are quite a few foreign players on Japanese teams, and they seem to think nothing of wearing a number like 49. It really makes them stand out.

Mr. J: It seems like there are unlucky numbers in both our countries.

Mrs. J: On our trip to Nikko, we stayed at a Japanese style inn. When the help bowed to us, they got down on their knees and touched their palms to the floor.

Mrs. S: That's the bow traditionally used in tatami rooms. It's a standard part of Japanese etiquette.

Mr. S: Did you take a Japanese style bath?

Mr. J: Yes, for the first time. It was a deep tub filled right to the top. Very relaxing. Are the baths in ordinary homes the same style?

Mr. S: Well, smaller, but the same type. Japanese like to take a long soak in the bath and warm themselves thoroughly. The bath tub is made so that the water can be heated in the tub to keep it at just the right temperature. The whole family takes turns bathing and we don't drain the tub until everyone

せん。湯が減った分は水を追加します。

ジョーンズ氏：だから浴槽のなかでは、石鹸を使わ
ないのですね。

鈴木氏：そうです。ほとんどの欧米の国々の入浴法
とは違って、体は浴槽の外で洗い流します。

● **日本料理**　ジョーンズ夫人：その旅館で日本料理をいただいた
んです。もちろん私にはすべて珍しいことばかり
でした。おはしを使って食べる料理もさることな
がら、食器や料理の盛りつけがとてもきれいでし
● **茶碗**　　　た。それにご飯を入れた茶碗は、手に持って食べ
るんですね。あれに最初はとまどいました。

鈴木氏：そういえば、日本以外には、ご飯を食べる
アジアの国々でも、食器を手で持ち上げて食べる
国はあまりないようですね。

● **日本酒**　　ジョーンズ氏：そうですか。それから、温めて飲む
酒というのも、珍しいですね。日本酒は私も家内
もたいへん気に入りました。

鈴木氏：そうですね。温めた酒を飲むと、寒い夜で
も体がすぐに温まります。だから風邪をひいたと
きは、温かい酒を少々飲んで早く寝てしまうのが、
いちばんの良薬だと、私はいつもいっているんで
すよ。

is finished. When the level goes down too far, we add more water.

Mr. J: And that's why you don't use soap in the tub?

Mr. S: Correct. Differently from the way people bathe in most Western countries, we wash and rinse ourselves outside the tub.

Mrs. J: We had a Japanese meal at the inn. It was all new for me, of course. The food, using chopsticks. . . But the dishes and the way the food was arranged were both simply beautiful. And you eat the rice while holding the rice bowl in your hand, don't you. That took me some time to get used to.

Mr. S: Come to think of it, aside from Japan there are probably not many countries where people hold the dish in their hand while they eat from it, even among the rice-eating countries in Asia.

Mr. J: Is that right? And the way you warm your *sake* is also unique. My wife and I both love it.

Mr. S: Yes, one of the quickest ways to warm up on a cold night is to drink some hot sake. And for a cold, I always say the best cure of all is to drink a little hot sake and go straight to bed.

34

Customs and Beliefs

1

I'm impressed by how skillful your drivers are.

ノート

be impressed by [with] ... 「～に感動する、～に感銘を受ける」by の代わりに with も使う。とくに副詞（句）で限定されていない限り「好ましい印象」の意味に用いられるのが普通。

例文

Most foreigners seem to *be impressed by* them.

(37)

2

I'm not used to giving tips.

ノート

「～に慣れる」の be used to のあとには名詞、代名詞、動名詞 (ing) が続く。used to do「かつて～した」と混同しないように。

例文

She *isn't used to* walking long distances.

3

They seem to think nothing of wearing a number like 49.

ノート

think nothing of ... 「～を何とも思わない、心にとがめない」of のあとには動名詞がくることが多い。

例文

He seems to *think nothing of* working all night.

4

Come to think of it, there are probably not many countries where people hold the dish in their hand.

ノート

Come to think of it＝Now (that) I come to think of it「考えてみると」

例文

Come to think of it, she was absent yesterday, too.

Chapter
35

着物
Kimono

着物にもいろんな種類があります

最近では
特別な場合にしか着ることのない着物ですが、
世界で最も美しい民族衣装の
ひとつとして、外国人からも
注目されています。

〔女性用着物のおもな名称〕

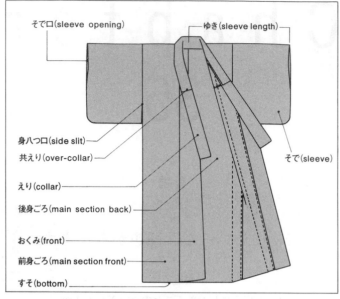

そで口(sleeve opening) ゆき(sleeve length)

身八つ口(side slit)
共えり(over-collar)
えり(collar)
後身ごろ(main section back)
おくみ(front)
前身ごろ(main section front)
すそ(bottom)
そで(sleeve)

Vocabulary

成人の日	☐☐	Coming-of-Age Day
お祝いの式典	☐☐	a congratulating ceremony
晴れ着	☐☐	the best kimono
そで	☐☐	sleeves
布地	☐☐	fabric
結び目	☐☐	a knot
装飾	☐☐	an ornament
ふだん着	☐☐	everyday dress
大学の卒業式	☐☐	a university graduation ceremony
結婚式	☐☐	a wedding
お花の会	☐☐	a flower arrangement exhibition
お葬式	☐☐	a funeral
正装	☐☐	formal attire
披露宴	☐☐	a wedding reception
金糸や銀糸で刺繍した	☐☐	to be embroidered with gold and silver threads

〔着物（絹物）の着用回数と機会〕

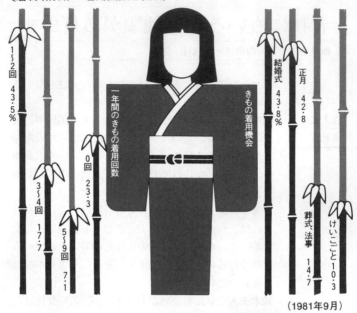

一年間のきもの着用回数

きもの着用機会

1～2回 43.5%

3～4回 17.7

5～9回 7.1

0回 23.3

結婚式 43.8%

正月 42.8

葬式、法事 14.7

けいこごと 10.3

（1981年9月）

民族衣装	□□	national costume; garments of the people
お褒めにあずかって光栄です	□□	I'm flattered to hear that.
（雰囲気を）かもし出す	□□	to create
着付け師	□□	a kimono fitter
専門家に着せてもらう	□□	to have a fitter dress one
（色合いが）地味な	□□	conservative
羽織	□□	a half-coat called *haori*
はかま	□□	a divided skirt called *hakama*
浴衣	□□	a kimono-like cotton robe
染めた模様	□□	a dyed pattern
お盆	□□	a Buddhist festival period called *bon*
先祖の霊	□□	the spirits of ancestors
（霊が）休まる	□□	to rest in peace
民謡に合わせて踊る	□□	to dance to folk music

着物にもいろんな種類があります

振りそで・帯・内掛け・着付け・浴衣

ジョーンズ夫人：きょうは着物を着た女性をたくさん見かけますね。どうしてですか。

・
成人式の
晴れ着

鈴木夫人：きょうは成人の日なんです。国民の祝日のひとつで、この1年間に満20歳になった人たちをお祝いする日です。地域ごとにお祝いの式典があります。女性は晴れ着を着て式典に出席したあと、思い思いに街を歩いているんです。

ジョーンズ夫人：アメリカでも着物を着た日本女性には、パーティーなどでときどきお会いしましたが、こんなにたくさんの人たちが着物を着ているのを見るのは初めてですわ。それにしても本当にきれいだわ。

鈴木夫人：私にも経験がありますが、若い女性はだれでも成人式に晴れ着を着るのを楽しみにしているんです。若い女性にとって青春時代のひとつの夢なんです。

ジョーンズ夫人：そうでしょうね。ところで着物は、そでがずいぶん長いんですね。

・
振りそで

鈴木夫人：あれは振りそでといって、結婚前の女性は、あのように長いそでの着物を着るのです。

ジョーンズ夫人：結婚した女性の着物のそでの形は、あれとは違うんですか。

・
未婚者と既
婚者の着物

鈴木夫人：はい、もっと短いんです。女性の着物は、着る人が未婚者か既婚者かによって、あるいはどういう場に着ていくかによって、布地・模様・色合い・仕立て方などが違います。

ジョーンズ夫人：まあ、そうなんですの。着物にもいろいろ種類があるんですね。それからあの背中

Chapter 35

Mrs. Jones: There are a lot of girls wearing *kimonos* today, aren't there? Any special reason?

Mrs. Suzuki: Today is Coming-of-Age Day, a national holiday for congratulating everyone who became 20 years old during the past year. Each community holds a ceremony. The girls go in their best kimonos and afterward they go out for a stroll around town.

Mrs. J: In America I've met Japanese women dressed in kimonos at parties a few times. But this is the first time I've seen so many kimonos at one time. They certainly are beautiful.

Mrs. S: Every young girl looks forward to going to the coming-of-age ceremony in her best kimono. I know I did. It's a dream that every girl has.

Mrs. J: It's only natural. But the sleeves of the kimono hang down very far, don't they?

Mrs. S: That's the *furisode* style. Unmarried women wear kimonos with long sleeves like that.

Mrs. J: Married women have different style sleeves?

Mrs. S: Yes, they're shorter. Depending on whether a woman is married or not, and on what the occasion is, the kimono she wears will be different — in the kind of fabric, the pattern, the color, the style . . .

Mrs. J: Really? So there are various kinds of kimono then. The piece at the back — that's really very pretty.

のところの結び目、とてもすてきですね。

帯

鈴木夫人：あれは帯を結んだ大きな結び目なんです。帯は着物を体に固定するために使いますが、背中のところに独特の仕方で結び目を作ります。これが着物を着たときの、アクセントと装飾にもなります。うしろから見たときにいっそう美しく見えるわけです。

着物を着る とき

ジョーンズ夫人：日本の女性はどんなときに着物を着るのですか。

鈴木夫人：むかしはふだん着でしたが、洋服が普及しましたので、現在では、お正月・成人式・大学の卒業式・結婚式・お茶やお花の会、お葬式などがおもな機会になりました。年配者のなかには、日常、着物を愛用している人もいます。

ジョーンズ夫人：結婚式の着物はどんな種類のものですか。

打ち掛け

鈴木夫人：結婚式や披露宴の列席者も、正装として着物を着て行くのが一般的です。ですが、着物のなかで最も豪華なのは、結婚式に花嫁が着る打ち掛けです。これは絹の布地に、金・銀の箔を織り込んだ金糸・銀糸で刺繍されています。いちばん多い模様は花や鳥などです。打ち掛けを着るときには、髪形も伝統的な日本髪にします。

ジョーンズ夫人：それはきれいでしょうね。私は着物は、世界でも最も美しい民族衣装のひとつだと思いますよ。

鈴木夫人：お褒めにあずかって光栄ですわ。着物の美しさは、もちろん染色や模様の美しさにもよりますが、そのこと以上に、着物を着ることによっ

Mrs. S: That's actually a large knot tied in the *obi*. The obi is the sash that holds the kimono in place and it's knotted in a special way at the back. The knotted part is an ornament in its own right. It adds to the beauty of the kimono when viewed from behind.

Mrs. J: When do women wear kimonos?

Mrs S: The kimono used to be everyday dress. But now that Western style clothing has become so commonplace, the main occasions for wearing them are the beginning of the New Year, the coming-of-age ceremony, university graduation ceremonies, weddings, tea ceremonies, flower arrangement exhibitions, funerals and other such occasions. But some elderly women still like to wear a kimono almost every day.

Mrs. J: What kind of kimono is worn at weddings?

Mrs. S: The kimono is very popular as formal attire for a woman attending a wedding or wedding reception. But by far the most gorgeous of all is *uchikake* kimono worn by the bride. It's made of silk and embroidered with gold and silver threads. The most common patterns are of flowers and birds. When a bride wears an uchikake, she also has her hair done up in the traditional Japanese style.

Mrs. J: Gorgeous, I'm certain. I believe that the kimono is one of the most beautiful garments of any people anywhere in the world.

Mrs. S: As a Japanese, I'm flattered to hear that. We say though that while the beauty of a kimono depends a lot on its color and pattern, it comes even more from the elegant and

てかもし出される優雅な雰囲気によるといわれて
います。

ジョーンズ夫人：それは素晴らしいことですね。と
　　ころで着物は簡単に着られるのですか。

着付け

鈴木夫人：いいえ、これがかなりむずかしいんです。
　　洋服は着る人の体型に合わせて作られています
　　が、着物は着付けによって体に合わせていくんで
　　す。それで着方が難しいんです。現代の女性の大
　　部分は、日常は洋服を着るのに慣れてしまってい
　　ますので、自分ひとりで着物を着ることができな
　　くなっています。ですからとくに正装するときは、
　　専門の着付け師に依頼しなければいけないんで
　　す。たいていは美容院でしてもらいます。

ジョーンズ夫人：鈴木夫人はいかがですか。

鈴木夫人：私もあまり自信がありません。正装する
　　ときには着付けの専門家にお願いしますわ。

男性の着物

ジョーンズ夫人：男性も着物を着るんですか。

鈴木夫人：ええ、でもそんなに多くありません。結
　　婚式・お正月などの正装として着るんです。それ
　　に室内着として着るていどです。

ジョーンズ夫人：男性の着物にはどんな特色がある
　　んですか。

鈴木夫人：男性の着物は青色か茶色系の地味な色合
　　いで、正装には着物の上からはかまをはき、羽織
　　を重ねて着ます。

ジョーンズ夫人：ご主人は着物をお召しになります
　　か。

鈴木夫人：いいえ、ほとんど着ません。夏にお風呂
　　のあと、ときどき浴衣を着ることがありますけれ
　　ど。浴衣は木綿地に簡単な模様を染め抜いた着物
　　の形のくつろぎ着なんです。

浴衣

ジョーンズ夫人：ああ、それならこのまえ、京都の

refined atmosphere created by the way it is worn.

Mrs. J: Isn't that wonderful? But is it easy to put one on properly?

Mrs. S: No, it's pretty hard. Western dresses are tailored to fit the wearer but the kimono is adjusted to the person's body as it is being put on. And it's not easy to do. Most women today are so used to wearing Western style clothing that they are unable to put on a kimono correctly. When they wear a kimono for a formal occasion, they have to get the help of a professional kimono fitter. Usually at a beauty salon.

Mrs. J: And how about you, Mrs. Suzuki?

Mrs. S: I'm not so good at it. On special occasions, I have a fitter dress me.

Mrs. J: Do men wear kimonos, too?

Mrs. S: Some, but not many — as formal wear for weddings, and during the New Year holidays. And sometimes for relaxing at home.

Mrs. J: What are men's kimonos like?

Mrs. S: They're fairly conservative — dark blue or brown. The formal type consists of a half-coat called a *haori* and a divided skirt called a *hakama*.

Mrs. J: Does your husband ever wear one?

Mrs. S: Almost never. Though in the summer he sometimes puts on a *yukata* after having a bath. A yukata is a kimono-like cotton robe with a simple dyed pattern. It's for relaxing in.

Mrs. J: Oh, yes! I wore one of those at a hotel when we were

ホテルで私も着ましたわ。

鈴木夫人：あら、そうですか。そうそう、ここでお話ししておきましょう。浴衣を着る機会がもうひとつあるんです。日本には真夏に、祖先の霊を慰める仏教上の行事で、盆というものがあります。その期間中、町や村で盆踊り大会を開きます。そのとき皆で浴衣を着て、民謡に合わせて踊りを楽しむんです。浴衣はそれほど高価なものではありませんので、ご主人とおそろいでお土産に買っていかれてはいかがですか。

食事中のエチケット

外国人と食事をするさいに、
①スープは音をたてて飲まないこと
②机の上に両ひじをつかないこと
③食べ物を口に入れたまま話をしないこと
④ガチャガチャ食器の音をたてないこと
⑤人前でゲップをしないこと
⑥談笑しながら食事をすること
などが、基本的エチケットである。

しかしもうひとつ、ぜひ気をつけたいのがたばこである。食後の一服は、周囲の了解さえ得られれば構わないが、食事中の喫煙は、ぜったいに慎まなければならない。たばこに関しては、日本人は ルーズな行動をとりやすいので気をつけたい。

食事中のみならず、周囲に人がいる場所でたばこを吸いたいときには、日本人同士でも同じことだが、外国人に対してはかならず、

"Do you mind if I smoke?" とか、

"May I smoke here?"

in Kyoto.

Mrs. S: Did you really? There's another time we wear yukatas
I should mention. In the middle of summer we have a
Buddhist festival period called *bon*. It's a time for praying
that the spirits of our ancestors will rest in peace. During
bon, most towns and villages hold outdoor dances, and
everyone comes in a yukata to dance to folk music. Yukatas
are not very expensive. You and your husband might consider buying some to take back as souvenirs.

35

Kimono

などと断ってからにすること。

　ちなみに、こう相手から聞かれたとき、吸って構わな
ければ、

　　"No, I don't mind." とか、

　　"Yes, please."

と答えればよいが、吸わないでほしいときの表現は、

　　"I'd rather you don't, if you don't mind."

　　"It might be better if you don't."

　　"I'd appreciate it if you don't."

などである。

　ついでながら、初対面の人を食事に誘うときに、相手
の食習慣（宗教上や食事療法上の制約など）が不明確な
場合には、あらかじめ、たとえば、

　　"Excuse me, but is there anything you can't eat?"

と尋ねておくとよい。

　また、初対面の人に向かって、食事中の話題に「ご家
族は何人ですか」とか、「お子さんはいらっしゃいますか」
とか、個人的なことをあまり突っ込んで聞かないこと。
とくにプライバシーを尊重する欧米人に対しては、この
種の話題は、親しくなるまで避けておいたほうが賢明で
ある。

1

ノート

Today is a national holiday for <u>congratulating</u> everyone who became 20 years old.

congratulating に引っかけて、「おめでとう」についてひと言。結婚式の場合、従来からCongratulations. は努力して成功した人に贈る言葉だから、花嫁に対しては使ってはならないとされていた。いまでも年輩のアメリカ人にはこの考えを守っている人たちもいる。だが現実には結婚する女性に対してもCongratulations. を使うことが圧倒的に多い。

これは、女性の自立、男女平等の考えの影響もあって、価値観が変わってきたからだと見られている。

Congratulations. のほかに、花嫁に対しては、Best wishes. 丁寧には I wish you every happiness. ／I hope you'll be very happy. などのいい方がある。

2

ノート

Every young girl <u>looks forward to going</u> to the ceremony in her best kimono.

look forward to ... 「～を楽しみにして［首を長くして］待つ」to のあとには to go to the ceremony のように to 不定詞は用いないことに注意。

3

Some elderly women still like to <u>wear</u> a kimono.

4

ノート

They are unable to <u>put on</u> a kimono correctly.

wear は「身につけている」という状態を表すのに対し、put on は「身につける」という動作を表す。

Chapter
36

日本料理

Japanese Cuisine

日本料理は季節感を大切にします

日本料理の神髄は、
旬の素材の持ち味を生かし、
器の色彩や形と料理を調和させ、
季節感を盛り込むことです。
美しく盛りつけて並べられた日本料理は、
まさに芸術と呼ぶにふさわしいものです。

日本料理	フランス料理
●先付け 鯛肝時雨煮 菊菜ひたし干し子 子芋白煮	●オードブル フォアグラ　マスカット添
●椀 清汁仕立 はも 松茸 人参 三つ葉 ユズ ●造り 明石鯛 伊勢エビ いか ●はし休め むかごの飯蒸し ●焼き物 かますの幽庵焼き ●煮物 かぶと穴子の炊き合わせ ●止め椀 清汁仕立 椎茸 カマボコ ●御飯 新生姜のごはん 季節の香のもの	●スープ コンソメ　うずら卵と野菜入り ●魚料理 平目の蒸焼　マスタード風味 ●肉料理 特撰牛フィレ肉のステーキ 　アンティーヴ添 ●サラダ 季節のサラダ ●パン フランスパン
●水菓子 柚子シャーベット	●デザート 栗のムース 　バニラアイスクリーム添 コーヒー 小菓子

Vocabulary •————————————————————

（酒が）強い	☐☐	strong
アルコール含有量は ～％である	☐☐	to contain . . . percent alcohol
タイ	☐☐	a sea bream
煮付ける	☐☐	to boil (with soy and sugar)
配置する	☐☐	to arrange
～の持ち味	☐☐	the natural flavor of . . .
季節の素材	☐☐	seasonal materials
季節感	☐☐	a feeling of the season; a sense of the season
独特の香り	☐☐	the distinctive aroma
刺身	☐☐	sliced raw fish
伊勢エビ	☐☐	a lobster
イカ	☐☐	a squid
味つけをする	☐☐	to season
醤油	☐☐	soy
酢	☐☐	vinegar
旨味を出す	☐☐	to bring out the full flavor
カツオ節	☐☐	dried bonito flakes
昆布	☐☐	tangle—a kind of seaweed
ゴテゴテ味をつける	☐☐	to season very heavily
焼き物	☐☐	a broiled fish
カマス	☐☐	a barracuda
生ウニ	☐☐	a sea urchin
カブ	☐☐	a turnip
穴子	☐☐	a conger eel
すまし汁	☐☐	light soup
かまぼこ	☐☐	fish sausage
香の物	☐☐	pickles
緑茶	☐☐	green tea
本場ものの茶	☐☐	tea from one of the famous tea-growing districts

36

Japanese Cuisine

日本料理は季節感を大切にします

日本酒・日本料理と季節感・日本茶

・日本酒

鈴木氏：きょうはジョーンズさんも奥さんも、日本
酒を召しあがってはいかがですか。

ジョーンズ夫人：ぜひいただきますわ。

ジョーンズ氏：私は酒には目がありませんので。

鈴木氏：私もですよ。

ジョーンズ氏：米から造ることは聞いていますが、
日本中どこでも造っているんですか。

鈴木氏：そうなんです。各地にその土地土地の酒が
あります。こうした違った種類を味わうのが、酒
好きにはたまらない楽しみになっています。旅行
のたびに地方の酒をかならず試す人もたくさんお
ります。よい水の出る所とよい米のとれる所に名
酒があるといわれています。このお酒は兵庫県の
灘のもので、むかしから全国的に知られたお酒の
ひとつです。

ジョーンズ夫人：お酒ってどのくらい強いのです
か。

鈴木氏：アルコール含有量は15〜16％です。

鈴木夫人：さあ、お料理をお召しあがりください。

ジョーンズ夫人：まあ、きれい。これは何ですか。

・先付け

鈴木夫人：このお料理は「先付け」といいます。前
菜に当たるものですわ。タイの肝の煮付けと菊菜
のひたし、それに芋を煮たものですわ。

ジョーンズ氏：料理の配置が美しいですね。

**・日本料理の
特色**

鈴木氏：日本の料理は季節の素材の持ち味を生か
し、器の色彩と料理を調和させます。それに季節
感を出すことを大切にしているんです。盛りつけ
方もたいへん重要です。

C h a p t e r 36

Mr. Suzuki: We'd like you to have some *sake* with us this evening.

Mrs. Jones: I'd love to.

Mr. Jones: I love sake.

Mr. S: So do I.

Mr. J: I know it's made from rice. Is it produced in all parts of Japan?

Mr. S: Yes, each district has its own local sake. Sake connoisseurs take delight in testing all the different kinds. Many people make it a point to try the local sake wherever they travel. The best sakes come from areas that have good water and good rice. This sake is from Nada in Hyogo prefecture and has long been famous throughout Japan.

Mrs. J: How strong is sake?

Mr. S: It contains 15 to 16 percent alcohol.

Mrs. Suzuki: Come, let's eat.

Mrs. J: Oh, how pretty. What is this?

Mrs. S: Hors d'oeuvres, what we call *sakizuke*. There's liver of sea bream boiled with soy and sugar, boiled chrysanthemum leaves flavored with soy and vinegar, and boiled potatoes.

Mr. J: The dishes are very artfully arranged.

Mrs. S: Japanese cooking stresses the natural flavors of seasonal materials, and there should be harmony between the color of the food and the dish it's served in. An important point is to create a feeling of the season. A lot of care is

ジョーンズ氏：何か決まった盛りつけのパターンが
　　　　　　あるんですか。左右対称とか、何とか。

鈴木夫人：丸い料理は角形の器に盛り、逆に四角い
　　　　　料理は丸形の器に盛るのが基本になっています。

汁椀

ジョーンズ夫人：こんどはスープのようですね。

鈴木夫人：そうです。ハモと松茸、人参、三つ葉の
　　　　　汁椀です。一種独特の香りは、ユズという果物の
　　　　　皮の小片が椀のなかに入っているからです。

ジョーンズ夫人：皆、いまの季節にとれるものです
　　　　　　　ね。こうして季節感を出しているんですね。

造り

鈴木氏：そこが大切なところなんです。さあ、造り
　　　　です。ご存じの刺し身です。きょうはタイ、伊勢エ
　　　　ビ、イカを盛り合せたものです。

ジョーンズ氏：たいへんおいしいですね。

はし休め

鈴木夫人：つぎは「はし休め」といいまして、口直
　　　　　しのあっさりした料理です。山芋とご飯を蒸して、
　　　　　カニの甲羅に盛ったものです。山芋は合衆国にあ
　　　　　るサツマ芋ではありません。

味つけ

ジョーンズ夫人：日本の料理の味つけにはどんなも
　　　　　　　のを使うんでしょうか。

鈴木夫人：塩、醤油、酢、砂糖のほかに、旨味を出
　　　　　すために、カツオ節、昆布、シイタケなどを使い
　　　　　ます。一般的には、あまりゴテゴテした味つけは
　　　　　しません。

ジョーンズ氏：日本酒と日本料理の味がたいへんよ
　　　　　　　く合いますね。

鈴木氏：ジョーンズさんは料理にかけてはそうとう
　　　　な通なんですね。

ジョーンズ氏：いや、それほどでもないんですよ。

taken in arranging the food to match the dish.

Mr. J: In some particular pattern? Symmetrically, or what?

Mrs. S: The basic rule is to serve round foods in square or rectangular dishes and to serve square-shaped foods in round dishes.

Mrs. J: It looks like we are having soup next.

Mrs. S: Yes, it contains pike conger, *matsutake* mushroom, carrot and stone parsley. The distinctive aroma comes from a small sliver of citron peel in each bowl.

Mrs. J: I take it that these are all things that are in season now. Is this what you mean by creating a sense of season?

Mr. S: It's an important part of it. And now for the sliced raw fish — which by now I think you know as *sashimi*. Today we have sea bream, lobster and squid.

Mr. J: Mmmmm, delicious.

Mrs. S: Next we have what we call the *hashiyasume* dish, a kind of mid-course mouth refresher somewhat on the bland side. Today we are having steamed yam and rice served in crab shells. The yam is not the sweet potato yam you have in America.

Mrs. J: Could you tell me a little about how you season your food?

Mrs. S: We use salt, soy, vinegar and sugar. To bring out the full flavor, we also use dried bonito flakes, tangle — a kind of seaweed — and *shiitake* mushrooms. Generally we don't season very heavily.

Mr. J: Sake and Japanese food go very well together.

Mr. S: You seem to be quite an epicure.

Mr. J: Hardly, but I do like to try the local food wherever I go.

各地の料理を食べ比べるのは好きですがね。

焼き物

鈴木夫人：さあ、これが焼き物ですわ。

ジョーンズ夫人：まあ、これは松葉を敷き詰めたんですね。

鈴木夫人：そうですわ。これはカマスを焼いたものです。上に乗っているのは生ウニです。

ジョーンズ夫人：本当に見事な飾りつけですこと。食べるのが惜しいようですね。

鈴木夫人：食べるために出てきたんです。どうぞ遠慮なさらずに。つぎにまいりますのは、カブと穴子の炊き合わせです。

炊き合わせ

ジョーンズ氏：なかなかおいしいですな。

汁物

鈴木夫人：さあ、メニューのしめくくりは汁物です。すまし汁にシイタケ、かまぼこなどを入れたものです。ご飯もどうぞ。

ジョーンズ氏：ご飯は食事中にとり、食事の終わりにとるものではないと、思っていましたよ。

鈴木夫人：お酒が出ているときは出ないんです。お酒が出るときは、ご飯は、たいてい汁物と香の物と一緒に終わりに出します。

香の物

ジョーンズ夫人：これが香の物ですか。

鈴木夫人：ええ、お気に召していただけるといいんですが。西欧のピクルスとはぜんぜん違いますの。

日本茶

ジョーンズ氏：日本に来て、緑茶が気に入りましたよ。帰国するときには、本場のよいものを買っていくつもりです。

鈴木氏：お茶は宇治、静岡、狭山などがいちばんよく知られています。

ジョーンズ夫人：きょうのお料理はまったく素晴らしかったですわ。本当にありがとうございました。

鈴木夫人：お気に召してうれしいですわ。

Mrs. S: Ahh, here comes the broiled fish.

Mrs. J: Look. It's on a bed of pine needles.

Mrs. S: Yes. That's broiled barracuda. The paste on top is made from sea urchin.

Mrs. J: It's such a work of art, it really seems a shame to eat it.

Mrs. S: But that's what it's for. Go right ahead. Coming up next will be a boiled turnip and conger eel dish.

Mr. J: Excellent.

Mrs. S: And the last item on the menu is a light soup. It's a clear broth with shiitake mushrooms and a slice of fish sausage added to it. Please have some rice, too.

Mr. J: I always thought that you ate rice during the meal not at the end.

Mrs. S: Not when sake is served. Then we have rice at the end of the meal, usually with a soup and pickles.

Mrs. J: These are the pickles?

Mrs. S: Yes, I hope you like them. They are quite different from Western-style pickles.

Mr. J: I've come to like green tea while we've been in Japan. I'd like to buy some before we leave but I want to get something good from one of the famous tea-growing districts.

Mr. S: Uji, Shizuoka and Sayama are three of the best known.

Mrs. J: It was truly a splendid meal. Thank you very much.

Mrs. S: We are happy you liked it.

1

I know sake <u>is made from</u> rice.

ノート　　製品が材料の姿をとどめていない場合は be made from . . . と from を使い、材料の面影をとどめているときには be made of . . . と of を使うのが原則。しかし材料などに対する考え方は人によって違うので、この原則によらない場合もある。

例文　　The samples *are made of* wax.　　　　　　　(37)

2

<u>I take it that</u> these are all things that <u>are in season</u> now.

ノート　　「思う」という場合、「解釈する」という意味の「思う」には take it (from . . .) that . . . をよく使う。

be in season は「(果物・魚などが)出盛りである、旬である」「(商売など) 最盛期である」の意。

例文 1　　*I take it that* you don't like it.

例文 2　　Oysters *are now in season*.

3

Sake and Japanese food <u>go</u> very well <u>together</u>.

ノート　　go together は一緒に行く意味から、「つり合う、調和する」。食べ物のとり合わせが合うという場合はぴったりの表現。

例文　　Bacon and potatoes *go well together*.

4

I've <u>come to like</u> green tea while we've been in Japan.

ノート　　come to do 「～するようになる」☞Useful Expressions 38-4

Chapter
37

一

食生活
Japanese Diet

バラエティー豊かな日本人の食卓

米、野菜、大豆などを主材料とする日本食は、
蛋白質、脂肪、炭水化物のバランスが
ほぼ理想的であるといわれています。
最近では、低カロリー食として、
外国人からも注目されるようになりました。

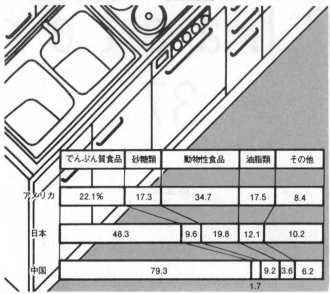

〔3カ国国民の食品群別カロリー供給構成〕

	でんぷん質食品	砂糖類	動物性食品	油脂類	その他
アメリカ	22.1%	17.3	34.7	17.5	8.4
日本	48.3	9.6	19.8	12.1	10.2
中国	79.3	1.7	9.2	3.6	6.2

（1979年〜1981年の平均）

Vocabulary •

実質的な	☐☐	down-to-earth
〜に心がこもっている	☐☐	loving care goes into . . .
主食と副食	☐☐	the main dish and other dishes
汁	☐☐	soup
注目される	☐☐	to attract attention
低カロリー食	☐☐	foods with low-calorie content
蛋白質	☐☐	protein
脂肪	☐☐	fat
炭水化物	☐☐	carbohydrate
伝統的家庭料理	☐☐	the traditional style of home cooking
野菜	☐☐	vegetables
大豆	☐☐	soybeans
味噌	☐☐	bean paste
醤油	☐☐	soy sauce
調味	☐☐	seasoning
栄養価が高い	☐☐	nutritious

37

食生活

〔各国の肉と魚の消費比較（ひとり1日当たり）〕

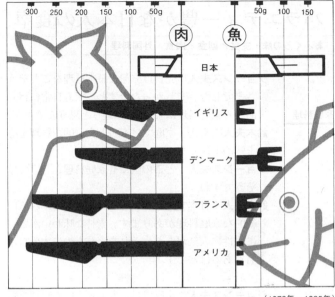

（1979年〜1985年）

イノシシ	☐☐	a wild boar
パン	☐☐	bread
学校給食	☐☐	school lunch
乳製品	☐☐	dairy products
インスタント食品	☐☐	instant foods
簡単な食品	☐☐	convenience foods
増える	☐☐	to become widespread
カレーライス	☐☐	"curry rice"（日本でできた英語）
ハンバーグステーキ	☐☐	hamburger steak
外国の料理	☐☐	foreign recipes
フランス料理	☐☐	French cuisine
一流店	☐☐	a top-rate place
本物の	☐☐	authentic
安くて手軽な料理	☐☐	a reasonably priced and simple dish
ファストフードの店	☐☐	a fast food place

バラエティー豊かな日本人の食卓

おふくろの味・主食と副食・肉食・外国料理

- **家庭料理**

ジョーンズ夫人：先日は立派な日本料理をごちそうさまでした。楽しかったですわ。でも日常に召しあがる家庭料理は、あれとは違うと思うんですが。

鈴木夫人：ええ、家庭ではもっと実質的な料理を心を込めて作りますね。

ジョーンズ夫人：どこの国でも家庭料理というのはそうですね。

鈴木夫人：日本では「おふくろの味」と呼ばれる伝統的な家庭料理があります。素朴な味わいがとくに男性に人気があり、それを売りものにする料理店もあるほどです。

ジョーンズ夫人：家庭では、普通どういう料理を召しあがっているんですか。

- **日本食の特徴**

鈴木夫人：日本人の食生活には伝統的な主食と副食という考え方があります。米が主食で、野菜や魚・肉などが副食です。日本食の基本形は、ご飯とおかずに汁と漬物を添えたものです。

ジョーンズ夫人：低カロリー食として日本食のよさが最近アメリカでも注目され、たとえば豆腐などを食べる人が増えてきました。

鈴木夫人：伝統的な日本食は蛋白質、脂肪、炭水化物のバランスがほぼ理想的だといわれています。現代の日本人にも、米、野菜、大豆を主材料として、味噌、醤油で調味する伝統的日本料理が見直されてきました。

C　h　a　p　t　e　r 37

Mrs. Jones: We very much enjoyed the splendid Japanese dinner that you treated us to the other evening. I would imagine though that everyday home cooking is different.

Mrs. Suzuki: Yes, home cooking is more down-to-earth and more loving care goes into it.

Mrs. J: I guess you could say that about the home cooking all over the world.

Mrs. S: In Japan we talk about "Mother's Cooking" as if it were an independent tradition in home cooking. It refers to rather simple dishes and is especially popular among men. There are even restaurants that claim to specialize in Mother's Cooking.

Mrs. J: What kind of dishes do you usually eat at home?

Mrs. S: Traditionally, Japanese think of a meal as having two parts — the main dish and the other dishes. The main dish is rice, and the other dishes are vegetables, fish and meat. The basic pattern of a Japanese meal is rice, one or two other dishes, soup and pickles.

Mrs. J: Japanese foods have recently been attracting attention in America for their low-calorie content. For example, more people are eating *tofu* these days.

Mrs. S: They say that the traditional Japanese meal has nearly an ideal balance of protein, fat and carbohydrate. Modern Japanese are themselves rediscovering the traditional style of home cooking which uses rice, vegetables and soybeans as the main materials and bean paste and soy sauce for seasoning.

・肉食

ジョーンズ夫人：肉食が普及したのはそんなに古い
　　　　　　　　ことではないそうですね。

鈴木夫人：肉食はそうとう古くから行われてきまし
　　　　　　たが、仏教の影響によって食べなくなりました。
　　　　　　それが明治になってから復活したのです。

ジョーンズ夫人：仏教の禁令は厳しく守られていた
　　　　　　　　んですか。

鈴木夫人：そうでもありません。獣肉は栄養価が高
　　　　　　いことが知られていて、病気のときや寒いときに
　　　　　　食べました。またイノシシを「山鯨」と呼んで禁
　　　　　　止をうまく逃れて食べていました。

ジョーンズ夫人：アメリカでいちばんよく知られて
　　　　　　　　いる日本料理はすき焼きです。あれも明治以降普
　　　　　　　　及したんでしょう？

・食生活の
**　変化**

鈴木夫人：そうです。パンを食べるようになったの
　　　　　　も明治以降です。とくに第二次大戦後、学校給食
　　　　　　で出されるようになってパン食が普及しました。
　　　　　　また経済が成長し、人々が裕福になるとともに肉
　　　　　　類、乳製品などもたくさん食べるようになりまし
　　　　　　た。最近ではさまざまなインスタント食品も好ま
　　　　　　れるようになり、日本人の食生活はむかしに比べ
　　　　　　るとずいぶん多様化しました。

ジョーンズ夫人：アメリカでもテレビディナーなど
　　　　　　　　の調理の簡単な食品がひじょうに増えています。

鈴木夫人：以前は、ある特定の場所とか一年のある
　　　　　　時期にしか手に入らない食物もたくさんありまし
　　　　　　た。最近では技術が発達し、いつでも、どこでも、
　　　　　　いろんな野菜が手に入るようになりました。

・家庭での
**　外国料理**

ジョーンズ夫人：旬や新鮮さを大切にするという日
　　　　　　　　本料理の特色も影響を受けますね。日本の家庭で
　　　　　　　　食べる外国料理にはどんなものがありますか。

鈴木夫人：戦前から、西洋風や中華風の食べ物が家

Mrs. J: I hear that eating meat is relatively new.

Mrs. S: People ate meat in ancient times but gave it up after Buddhism was introduced. It wasn't until about 100 years ago, during the Meiji period, that it became popular again.

Mrs. J: Was the Buddhist ban strictly followed?

Mrs. S: Not completely. People knew that animal meat was nutritious and ate it to recover from sickness and during cold weather. Also, in some places people ate wild boar, getting around the ban by calling it "mountain whale."

Mrs. J: One of the most famous Japanese meat dishes in America is *sukiyaki*. That also became popular from the Meiji period, didn't it?

Mrs. S: Yes, it did. The eating of bread also started from the Meiji period. It's become an everyday food since the end of the Second World War, when it started to be served as part of the school lunches. As the economy has improved and people have become better off, the Japanese have started eating more and more dairy products and meat. Instant foods have also caught on. People today eat a much greater variety of foods than before.

Mrs. J: Convenience foods have become very widespread in America, too. TV dinners and things like that.

Mrs. S: In the past there were a lot of things that were available only in certain areas or at certain times of the year. But there are lots of new methods now and in most places you can get many vegetables almost anytime.

Mrs. J: That's going to have an effect on the traditional Japanese ideas of using fresh, seasonal produce. What kind of non-Japanese cooking do the Japanese do at home?

Mrs. S: Oh, from before the war many housewives made West-

37

Japanese Diet

庭料理のなかにありました。「カレーライス」というインド風のカレー料理はずっと以前から好まれていました。戦後はハンバーグステーキやイタリアのパスタ料理、韓国系の焼き肉などもたいへんポピュラーになり、とくに子供たちに好まれています。

• レストラン

ジョーンズ夫人：とくに近年は、外国の食品や料理が家庭にいろいろと取り入れられているのでしょうね。外国の料理といえば、日本には世界各国の料理のレストランがありますね。とくに東京などの大都会には。

鈴木夫人：はい。たとえば、フランス料理店はたくさんありまして、私どもは西洋料理といえばフランス料理のことを思い浮かべるくらいですの。ですけれど、店数としては中華料理店のほうが多いんです。こういうレストランには、上は本格的なフランス料理、中華料理を出すお店から、下はずっと安くて手軽な料理を出すお店までいろいろありますわ。そのほかに韓国、イタリア、インド、ロシア、ドイツ、スペイン、メキシコや北欧、東南アジアなどいろんなレストランがあります。

ジョーンズ夫人：ほんとにそうですね。世界中の料理が食べられるといってよいくらいですね。

鈴木夫人：それから、アメリカのマクドナルドやケンタッキーフライドチキンなどのファストフードの店や、ファミリーレストランのチェーン店もたくさんお見かけになると思います。

• 食品サンプル

ジョーンズ夫人：レストランの店頭にある見本は実物そっくりですね。初めは本物だと思いました。

鈴木夫人：いえ、あれはろう細工なんです。たいていの外国の方は珍しがられるようですが、なかにはお土産に買って帰られる方もあるそうですよ。

ern and Chinese style dishes at home, and an Indian-style dish we call "curry rice" has also been popular for many years. Since the end of the war, dishes like hamburger steak, Italian pasta, and Korean barbecued beef have become very popular. They are real favorites with the children.

Mrs. J: I get the feeling that you are using both more foreign foods and more foreign recipes in your home cooking, especially in recent years. Restaurants, too, seem to be specializing in almost every kind of foreign cooking. Especially in Tokyo and the other large cities.

Mrs. S: Yes, there are lots of French restaurants, for example. We Japanese tend to think of French cuisine as representing all Western-style cooking. But we have even more Chinese restaurants. These restaurants range from top-rate places that serve authentic French or Chinese dishes to more reasonably priced places that serve simpler fare. You will also find many other kinds of restaurants — Korean, Italian, Indian, Russian, German, Spanish, Mexican, Scandinavian, Southeast Asian . . .

Mrs. J: Yes, that's true. I guess you could have just about any kind of food in the world.

Mrs. S: You'll also see quite a few American fast food places like McDonald's and Kentucky Fried Chicken, and also family chain restaurants.

Mrs. J: The samples out in front of the restaurants here look exactly like the real thing. I thought they were at first.

Mrs. S: No, they are made of wax. Most foreigners seem to be impressed by them and I've heard that some buy them to take home as novelties.

37

Japanese Diet

Useful Expressions —————— 37

1
Home cooking is more <u>down-to-earth</u>.

ノート

   down-to-earth「現実的な、実際的な」おもにアメリカで使われている。

2
Japanese foods have <u>recently</u> been <u>attracting attention</u> in America.

ノート

「最近」の意味の recently と lately の使い分けは、否定文・疑問文には lately と説明されてきた。しかし最近は、「時間上の1点を指している場合」は recently、「継続状態と見るとき」は lately を使うという見方が正確だとされている。したがって、

例文1

（○）I *recently* read a book by F.K.　　　　(38)
（×）I *lately* read a book by F.K.

例文2

Imported foods have been *attracting attention* in Japan.

3
Instant foods have also <u>caught on</u>.

ノート

   catch on「人気を博する」

例文

This style will *catch on* next year.
　　　「このスタイルは来年はやるでしょう」

4
These restaurants <u>range from</u> top-rate places <u>to</u> more reasonably priced places.

ノート

   range from A to B「A から B までにわたる、A から B まである」

例文

The students *range* in age *from* 14 *to* 18.
＝The students' ages *range between* 14 *and* 18.

Chapter
38

日本人の特質
Characteristics of the Japanese

自己主張が苦手な日本人

世界各国の人たちは、
その国の文化や伝統などを背景として、
それぞれ異なった特質を持っています。
外国人とのコミュニケーションを円滑に進めるには、
この特質をお互いが認識し合う必要があります。

Q：給料は従来どおりで週休４日になったら余った時間は？

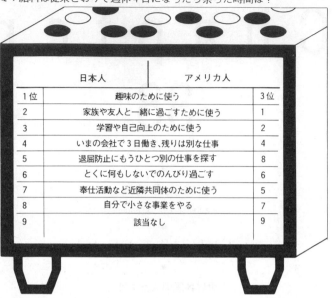

	日本人	アメリカ人
1位	趣味のために使う	3位
2	家族や友人と一緒に過ごすために使う	1
3	学習や自己向上のために使う	2
4	いまの会社で３日働き、残りは別な仕事	4
5	退屈防止にもうひとつ別の仕事を探す	8
6	とくに何もしないでのんびり過ごす	6
7	奉仕活動など近隣共同体のために使う	5
8	自分で小さな事業をやる	7
9	該当なし	9

（1980年１月）

Vocabulary

すごく礼儀正しい	☐☐	to be extremely polite (and well-mannered)
序列の意識	☐☐	a sense of rank
社会的地位	☐☐	social status
公的な場で	☐☐	in public
個人的な会話では	☐☐	in private conversation
許し難い侮辱	☐☐	an unforgivable offense
無礼	☐☐	rudeness
敬語	☐☐	the honorific style of speech
集団主義	☐☐	groupism
自己主張が苦手である	☐☐	to be poor at asserting oneself
他人の感情を考える	☐☐	to consider the other person's feelings
独立心がある	☐☐	to be independent
責任をとる	☐☐	to take responsibility
創造力を発揮する	☐☐	to develop one's imagination and creativity

Q：仕事をするうえでたいせつなのは？

	日本人	アメリカ人
1位	よい同僚	2位
2	よい給料	1
3	失業のおそれのなさ	4
4	好ましい勤務時間	6
5	心理的圧迫感のなさ	11
6	他者との出会い、接触	8
7	好ましい休暇制度	12
8	何かを成し遂げることのできる仕事	3
9	社会に役立つ仕事	10
10	独創性を発揮できる仕事	7
11	世間から尊敬されている仕事	9
12	昇進の機会	5

（1980年1月）

38

Characteristics of the Japanese

個性を発揮する	☐☐	to develop one's personality
論理的に考える	☐☐	to think logically
批判する	☐☐	to criticize
「イエス・ノー」をはっきりさせる	☐☐	to give clear-cut yes or no answers
等質の社会	☐☐	a homogeneous society
傾向	☐☐	a tendency
摩擦を避ける	☐☐	to avoid conflicts
甘えのある	☐☐	reliant and overly-familiar
社会学者	☐☐	a sociologist
態度をとる	☐☐	to take an attitude
征服する	☐☐	to conquer
自然に屈伏する	☐☐	to bow to nature
～と調和を保つ	☐☐	to maintain a harmonious balance with . . .

自己主張が苦手な日本人

序列意識・敬語・集団主義・自然への対応

ジョーンズ氏：このまえ、友人の日本の大学教授の研究室を訪ねたところ、学生が何人か訪ねてきました。学生はとても礼儀がきちんとしていましたよ。部屋に出入りするときも、先生に対してたいへん丁寧にお辞儀をしていました。

序列意識

鈴木氏：よいところに目をつけられましたね。日本では、年齢とか社会的地位などの基準によって、序列を意識するんです。行動の仕方も、相手が目上の人か目下かによって違ってきます。先生には、友人などと比べるとずっと深いお辞儀をします。

ジョーンズ氏：合衆国ですと、公的な場で教授を呼ぶときは違いますが、個人的な会話では、教授も学生もまったくくだけた話し方をすることが多いんです。ファーストネームで教授を呼ぶ学生さえいます。日本では、どうですか。

鈴木氏：日本で、学生が先生にそんなことをしたら、たいへんなことになります。とても考えられません。先生は失礼だと、たぶん怒りだすでしょうね。上下の関係を重視しますので、言葉も先生に対しては敬語を使います。これは社会に出てからも同じです。上司や目上の人には敬語を使います。ビ

敬語

ジネスのうえでも、敬語を適切に使えない人は、日本ではビジネスができないでしょうね。セールスマンが友人に話すような言葉遣いでは客はぜったい買ってくれません。

C h a p t e r 38

Mr. Jones: I visited a Japanese professor friend of mine at his office the other day and a number of his students came in while I was there. They were all extremely polite and well-mannered. They bowed deeply to the professor when they came in and again when they left.

Mr. Suzuki: What you saw is quite typical. Japanese have a strong sense of rank based on age and social status. They behave differently depending on whether the person they are talking to is of higher or lower rank than themselves. A student will bow more deeply to his professor than to his friends.

Mr. J: In America we would address a professor rather formally in public, but in private conversation professors and students will often use quite informal speech. A student might even call his professor by his first name. How about in Japan?

Mr. S: In Japan it would be an unforgivable offense. Unthinkable. Any student who tried would probably receive a very severe upbraiding for his rudeness. When talking to their teachers, students have to use a special style of language that includes many honorific words and expressions. It's the same later on when they get jobs. All members of an organization use the honorific style of speech with anyone of higher rank. The honorific style is also used in doing business with customers. A person who can't use it properly simply can't do business in Japan. No customer would buy anything from a salesman who spoke to him in the same way as he would speak to a friend.

ジョーンズ氏：その点、英語はつくづくありがたいと思いますよ。私が日本語で微妙な意味合いの違いをつけられるようになるなんて、とても考えられませんね。

鈴木氏：言葉はその国の文化そのものとしっかり結びついています。外国で育った人が敬語までマスターするのは、たいへんでしょうね。また、日本人は一般に他人とかけ離れた行動をとるのを避ける傾向があります。他人がどう思うか気にしたり、影響を受けたりします。

・集団主義

ジョーンズ氏：集団主義だといわれるのも、そんな点にあるのではないでしょうか。

・日本人の
自己主張

鈴木氏：それに関係があると思いますね。ですから、日本人は自己主張が苦手なんです。相手の気持ちや立場を察して、それらを考えながら発言したり、行動したりする傾向も強いんです。

・アメリカの
教育

ジョーンズ氏：これは欧米人とはずいぶん違いますね。アメリカでは、子供に、独立心、責任感、創造力、独創性、個性を持つように教えています。これは、ひじょうに小さいときから始まります。また論理的に考えたり、自分の意見や意思を自由に発言できるように訓練しています。

鈴木氏：そのようですね。私も子供がアメリカの小学校へ通っていましたので、何回か授業を見学したことがありますから、知っています。日本とだいぶ違っていますね。日本人は「イエス・ノー」がはっきりしないと外国人からよく非難されます。日本という国は基本的には同質単一民族からできていますし、摩擦を避けようという傾向が伝統的にあるんです。これはまた他人に対する甘えにもつながることがあるんです。

Mr. J: Give me good old English! I don't think I could ever learn to make the subtle distinctions you need in Japanese.

Mr. S: It's so tied in with the whole culture. It's difficult to master for someone who grew up in another country. Also, most Japanese tend to avoid doing anything that sets them off from others. They worry about what others think and change their behavior accordingly.

Mr. J: That's probably one of the reasons why people talk about Japanese groupism.

Mr. S: It's a factor. It's also why Japanese are poor at asserting themselves. We tend to speak and act only after considering the other person's feelings and point of view.

Mr. J: You can't say that about most Westerners. In America, we try to teach our children to be independent, take individual responsibility, develop their imaginations and creativity, develop their personalities . . . This starts from a very young age, from babyhood practically. We also try to train them to think logically, and to learn how to express their thoughts and opinions.

Mr. S: Yes, I know because my children went to an American primary school for a while and I had a chance to look in on their classes a few times. It was a lot different than in Japan. Foreigners often criticize us Japanese for not giving clear-cut yes or no answers. This is probably connected to our being basically a homogeneous society and our traditional tendency to try to avoid conflicts. So is the tendency of a Japanese to become reliant and overly-familiar as he gets to know you better.

ジョーンズ氏：このあいだアメリカの女性社会学者のフローレンス・クラックホーンの本を読んでいたら、面白いことが出ていましたよ。

鈴木氏：それはどういうことです。

自然への対応

ジョーンズ氏：人間と自然とのかかわり方に対する態度が国民によって違うんだそうですよ。

鈴木氏：アメリカ人はどう対応するんですか。

ジョーンズ氏：アメリカ人は「自然は人間に征服される」べきものであると考えているんです。

鈴木氏：確かにその指摘は当たっていると思いますね。そのほかの国民はどうなんですか。

ジョーンズ氏：メキシコの農民は「人間は自然に屈服すべきものだ」と考え、日本人は「人間は自然と調和を保つべきものだ」と考えているそうです。

鈴木氏：確かに日本についてのその考え方は本当ですね。そのことは、たとえば日本の建築や庭園を見てもわかります。日本人は、自然のものをその自然のままの形で生かしていこうとします。

日本語と英語の狭間で⓫

豊かな国際感覚を養う

　長い間外国人との交流に乏しく、急激に国際社会に仲間入りをした日本人が、発想や行動面で一般的に陥りやすい傾向は、

①単一民族のため、世界の文化の多様性に気づかず、自分たちの発想や行動様式が世界中どこにでも通用するかのように、無意識のうちに錯覚しがちなこと

②異文化意識が希薄な反面、日本文化や日本語は特殊なので、外国人には理解できないと最初から決め込んでしまう人が多いこと

Mr. J: I recently read a book by Florence Kluckhohn, the American sociologist. She makes an interesting observation.

Mr. S: What's that?

Mr. J: She says that different societies take different attitudes toward the relationship between man and nature.

Mr. S: What's the American attitude?

Mr. J: The Americans see nature as something to be conquered.

Mr. S: I guess I can go along with that. What about other countries?

Mr. J: She says the attitude of Mexican peasants is that man should bow to nature, and the attitude of the Japanese is that man should maintain a harmonious balance with nature.

Mr. S: The part about Japan is certainly true. You can see that in our buildings and gardens, for example. We try to use natural things in their natural form.

Column

③自分の属する集団内ではきわめて仲間意識が強いが、他集団（とくに外国人）に対してはひじょうに排他的なこと

④自己主張が苦手で、日本人同士の場合と同様に外国人に対しても、あいまいな態度をとりやすいこと

⑤外国人に対してコンプレックスや優越感を持ちやすく、とくに経済的尺度や価値観で外国を評価する傾向が強いこと

などである。

　こうしたことから脱却して豊かな国際感覚を養うことが、日本人の国際化にとってとくに重要な課題であろう。

1

Japanese <u>have a strong sense of</u> rank based on age and social status.

ノート

have a strong sense of ... 「〜を強く意識する」
なお、日本語になっている「センス」は英語では
sense よりも taste に当たる。

例文1

He doesn't *have a strong sense of* being a specialist. (40)

例文2

She has good *taste* in dresses.
「彼女は服装のセンスがよい」

2

The honorific style is used <u>in doing business with</u> customers.

ノート

in doing business with customers は when you do business with customers. の意。

例文

We *do business with* the XYZ Company.

3

Japanese <u>are poor at asserting themselves</u>.

ノート

be poor at ... 「〜が下手である、〜が苦手である」反対は be good at ... ☞ Useful Expressions 24-4

assert oneself は「自説[自分の権利]を主張する、自己主張する」の意。

例文

Mike *is poor at* mathematics.

4

He becomes overly-familiar as he <u>gets to know</u> you better.

ノート

get to know と come to know はともに「知り合いになる」意味だが、come to know のほうがややかしこまった場合に使うことが多い。

Chapter
39

■

日本人の労働観
Attitude Toward Work

■

日本人はなぜよく働くのですか

■

「働き過ぎの日本人」
いまや外国人の間で定説になっています。
これが批判的な発言につながるようになったのは、
経済大国日本の行動が、
外国に大きな影響を及ぼすようになったからです。

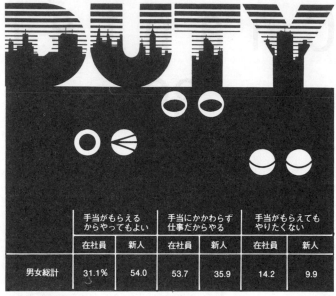

〔残業についての意識調査〕
Q：残業についてどう思いますか。

	手当がもらえるからやってもよい		手当にかかわらず仕事だからやる		手当がもらえてもやりたくない	
	在社員	新人	在社員	新人	在社員	新人
男女総計	31.1%	54.0	53.7	35.9	14.2	9.9

（1987年）

Vocabulary ●

丸の内ビジネス街	□□	the Marunouchi business district
明かりがついている	□□	the lights are on
休日出勤する	□□	to work on one's day off
～を顔負けさせる	□□	to put . . . to shame
家に仕事を持ち込む	□□	to bring work home with one
経営トップ	□□	top management people
エリート社員	□□	the company elite
稲作農業者	□□	a rice farmer
耕作地が小規模である	□□	the amount of farm land is limited
家畜を使う	□□	to use animals
人力で	□□	by humans
労力を惜しむ	□□	not to work hard
収穫が増える	□□	to get good harvests
収穫が減る	□□	to get poor harvests
～の手入れをよくする	□□	to take good care of . . .
2毛作	□□	two crops a year

Q：デートの約束があったとき残業を命じられたら？

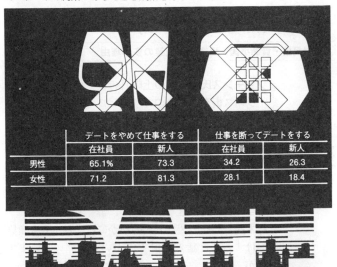

	デートをやめて仕事をする		仕事を断ってデートをする	
	在社員	新人	在社員	新人
男性	65.1%	73.3	34.2	26.3
女性	71.2	81.3	28.1	18.4

（1987年）

３毛作	□□	three crops a year
小作料	□□	a farm rent
資源	□□	natural resources
日本人の職業観	□□	the way most Japanese think about their jobs
社会に貢献する	□□	to make a contribution to society
社会的地位が上がる	□□	to advance socially
収入が上がる	□□	to increase one's income
日本国民一般の気風	□□	a trait of the Japanese people in general
就業時間以上に働く	□□	to work overtime
所定時間内に	□□	within regular hours
～の割増賃金を払う	□□	to pay someone a higher rate for . . .
納期	□□	a delivery date
私的な事情	□□	personal affairs
集団志向	□□	group mentality

日本人はなぜよく働くのですか

農耕民族・資源小国・職業観・残業の多い理由

休日出勤

ジョーンズ氏：先週の土曜日の夜、車で丸の内のビジネス街を通ったのです。ビルの窓に、明かりのついているところが多いんですね。あの辺りの企業は、土曜日は休日だと思うのですが、とするとずいぶん休日出勤している人がいるのですね。

鈴木氏：実際、休日出勤している人は多いんですよ。

ジョーンズ氏：日本人は確かによく働きますよ。

鈴木氏：でもアメリカ人のなかには、日本人も顔負けするほど猛烈に働く人がいると聞いていますが。

ジョーンズ氏：アメリカ人のなかにも、確かに朝早くから夜遅くまで働き、また家にまで仕事を持ち込んで働いている人もいます。だけど、それはごく一部の経営トップとか、エリート社員です。日本人のようにごく普通のビジネスマンの多くが、長時間働いているわけではありませんよ。

長い労働時間

鈴木氏：確かにそうです。平均的には、日本人のほうがアメリカ人より、仕事で働いている時間は長いですね。

ジョーンズ氏：それにしても鈴木さん、日本人はなぜよく働くんでしょうかね。世界中で有名ですよ。

稲作農業と収穫

鈴木氏：そうですねえ。いくつかの理由が考えられます。まず日本人は2,000年以上、水田で稲作をする農業を続けてきました。日本は、山地が多く土地が狭いので、稲作も小規模耕作です。家畜を使うことも制約があり、人力に頼るところが大きかったんです。しかも、日本の気候では、成り行

C　h　a　p　t　e　r　**39**

Mr. Jones: I was riding through the Marunouchi business district in a car last Saturday evening and I noticed that the lights were on in many of the windows. I don't think Saturday is a working day for the companies with offices in that area. So there must be a lot of people working on their day off.

Mr. Suzuki: Many people do work on their days off.

Mr. J: You Japanese certainly do work a lot.

Mr. S: True, but I've heard that in America there are people who would put most Japanese to shame by the way they work.

Mr. J: Oh, sure. Some Americans work from early morning till late at night — and then they bring more work home with them. But these are only a small percentage of the total — top management people, the company elite . . . But it's not like in Japan where even the ordinary office worker works long hours.

Mr. S: Yes, that's true. On the average, we Japanese spend more time working at our jobs than you Americans.

Mr. J: But why? Why do the Japanese work so hard? They've become famous for it throughout the world.

Mr. S: Well, there are a number of reasons. One is that the Japanese people have been paddy-field rice farmers for more than 2,000 years. The country is mountainous and the amount of farm land is limited so the individual farmers had only very small plots. This made it difficult to use animals and most of the work had to be done by humans. Also, since

きまかせにしておいては米は育ちません。労力を惜しむと収穫は減り、手入れをよくすればそれだけ収穫が増えるんです。その点、あまり手入れをしなくても、2毛作、3毛作のできる東南アジアなどの稲作とはずいぶん違います。

ジョーンズ氏：なるほど。

鈴木氏：それに封建時代には、農民は高い土地の税金や小作料を支払わなければならなかったのです。これらは物品で支払われたので、農民たちは狭い土地のなかで、すこしでも多くの収穫をあげないと生活していけなかったのです。それでよく働く習慣がついたと思います。状況は日本が経済大国になった現在でも、むかしと変わっていません。人口が多いのに土地は狭く資源が乏しいからです。生きていくためには働くほかないんです。

ジョーンズ氏：アメリカの西部に入植した開拓民も、ずいぶん苦労しました。もっとも状況は違っていたでしょうが。

鈴木氏：私も存じています。フロンティアとしてのアメリカ農民の苦労のことは。それに日本では、儒教の影響で、働くこと自体に価値を認める倫理観が農民ばかりでなく一般の人々の間でも強かったのです。

ジョーンズ氏：その考え方はプロテスタンティズムによく似ていますね。

鈴木氏：この点は、多くの日本人が現在でも持っている職業観に結びついていると思います。自らの職業を通じて社会に貢献していこうと考えているのです。

ジョーンズ氏：なるほど。

鈴木氏：さらにもうひとつ重要なことがあります。それは1867年の明治維新後、それまであった厳格

・資源小国

・職業観

・階級制度の
撤廃

rice doesn't grow naturally in the Japanese climate, those who didn't work hard got poor harvests and those who took good care of their rice got good ones. This is quite different from places like Southeast Asia where they can raise two or three crops a year, and don't have to work very hard to do it.

Mr. J: I can understand that.

Mr. S: Also, in feudal times the farmers had to pay high land taxes or farm rent. These were paid in kind and the farmers had to do everything they could to increase their harvests just to be sure they'd have enough left for themselves to eat. I think the custom of working hard also grew out of this. Basically the situation is not much different even now that Japan has become a major economic power. We have a large population but little land and few natural resources. The only way we can keep our heads above water is to work.

Mr. J: The pioneers who settled the American West didn't have it very easy either. Though the situation was different.

Mr. S: I know. The American frontier farmers also had a lot of hardships. In Japan, another thing was that because of the influence of Confucianism, the belief that work itself had an ethical value became strong not only among the farmers but among the people in general.

Mr. J: That's quite similar to the thinking of Protestantism.

Mr. S: Mmmm. And I think it's closely related to the way most Japanese think about their jobs today. They see themselves as making a contribution to society through their work.

Mr. J: Hmmm.

Mr. S: There is another important factor. The Meiji Restoration in 1867 did away with the old rigid social orders. From

な階級制度が撤廃されたことです。それからは、だれもが能力と努力次第で、高い社会的地位や多くの収入を得ることができる仕組みになりました。そのために、努力して働くという気風が国民一般に広まったわけです。

ジョーンズ氏：それで日本人がどのようにして働き者になったのか、よくわかりました。それにしても、休日までも出勤して、夜遅くまで働くというのは、働き過ぎではありませんか。

鈴木氏：日本のビジネスマンが皆、好んで就業時間以上に働いているわけではありません。企業側も割増賃金を支払わなければなりませんので、なるべく所定時間内に能率的に仕事を終えることを望んでいます。労働組合側も労働時間が過大になることには反対しています。

残業・休日出勤が多い理由

ジョーンズ氏：それにしても、どうして残業や休日出勤をする人が多いのですか。

鈴木氏：緊急な仕事があるときや、納期が迫っているときなどに、各企業の従業員が比較的抵抗なく残業したり、休日出勤したりするのは事実です。その場合に、私的な事情は少なくともあるていど抑えることも多いと思います。これは日本企業の長期雇用慣行から出てきたもので、従業員たちは「自分たちの会社」という意識を強く持っています。また日本人の特性である集団志向もあります。職場に難しい問題あるいは緊急な課題が起こったときには、全員が協力して早期に解決しようと努力するからです。

then on, the system became one in which anyone who had the ability and was willing to make the effort could advance socially and increase his income. Because of this, the custom of hard work became a trait of the Japanese people in general.

Mr. J: I now can see how the Japanese became such a hard-working people. But still, don't you think it's overdoing it a bit to work until the middle of the night on your day off?

Mr. S: I can assure you that not all employees of Japanese companies enjoy working overtime. And their companies would prefer it if they would finish their work efficiently within regular hours — because they have to pay them a higher rate for overtime work. The labor unions are also opposed to long work days.

Mr. J: Why then are there so many people working overtime and coming to work on non-working days?

Mr. S: They do this when there's urgent work to be done, when there is pressure to meet a delivery date — at these times the Japanese employee probably won't object very much to working overtime and coming in on his day off. More often than not, he'll sacrifice his personal affairs, at least to some extent. This comes from the long-term employment policy of Japanese companies, which gives the employees a sense of the company being "their company." There is also the group mentality that we Japanese have. When a difficult problem or something requiring immediate attention comes up at work, we all cooperate to find an early solution.

1

They would <u>put</u> most Japanese <u>to shame</u> by the way they work.

ノート

　put ... to shame「～に恥をかかせる、～の面目をつぶす、顔負けのことをする」

例文

Her work *puts* the masters *to shame*.
　「彼女の作品は玄人はだしだ」

2

They've <u>become famous for</u> it throughout the world.

ノート

　become famous for ... は「～で有名になる」という場合の基本的な表現。「有名である」の表現では、be famous for ... ／ be well-known for ... ／ be notorious for ... などがある。famous と well-known はよいことばかりでなく、不評・悪評のときも使う。notorious は一般には不評・悪評の注意を喚起するときに使う。

3

The only way we can <u>keep our heads above water</u> is to work.

ノート

　keep one's head above water は「おぼれないでいる」の意から「借金[失敗]せずにいる、なんとか生き延びる[持ちこたえる]」の意味。

4

<u>More often than not</u>, he'll sacrifice his personal affairs.

ノート

　more often than not は「しばしば（very often）、（ほぼ）2 回に 1 度以上は（in more than half the cases）」の意味。

Chapter 40

自己紹介と相手の呼び方
How Japanese Introduce Themselves and Address Others

自己紹介が社名から始まるのはなぜ？

ふだんなにげなく行っている自己紹介の仕方も
外国人から見れば、不思議なことのひとつです。
日本人は、なぜ会社名や所属部門から
自己紹介を始めるのかと聞かれたら、
どう答えればよいでしょう。

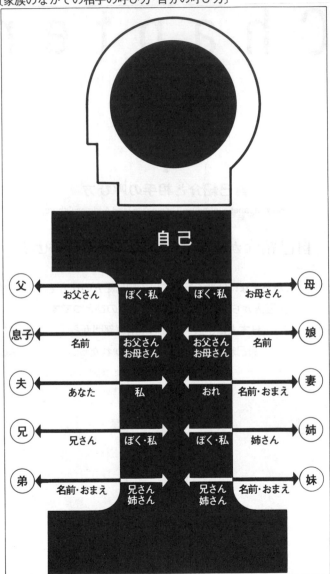

Vocabulary •————————————————

２カ国語で印刷して ある名刺	☐☐	a bilingual business card
準備がいい	☐☐	to be well prepared
（名刺を）やりとりする	☐☐	to exchange (cards)
肩書	☐☐	a job title
ビジネス習慣	☐☐	a business practice
～に入ってくる	☐☐	to be imported to . . . ; to find one's way into . . .
逆輸入	☐☐	reimporting
仕事については何も いわない	☐☐	not to say anything about one's work
～とつながりがある	☐☐	to connect with . . .
～となって表れる	☐☐	to show up as . . .
～の一員であるという 意識	☐☐	the sense of being a member of . . .
所属する部門	☐☐	the division one belongs to; one's division
職務経験	☐☐	job experiences
特定の職位を補充する	☐☐	to fill specific positions
将来発揮される潜在 能力	☐☐	latent potential to be developed
適性	☐☐	aptitude
専門家であるという 意識	☐☐	the sense of being a specialist
目上の人	☐☐	higher ranking people; persons of higher rank
目下の人	☐☐	lower ranking people; persons of low- er rank
人の名前を呼ぶ	☐☐	to call someone by his name
失礼に当たる	☐☐	to be rude
「実名敬避」	☐☐	"Respect through Avoidance of Real Name"
～をもっと広い範囲に 使う	☐☐	to carry . . . further

自己紹介が社名から始まるのはなぜ？

• 名刺

ジョーンズ氏：鈴木さん、私の名刺、2カ国語で刷ってあるんですが、お見せしましたっけ。

鈴木氏：おや、なかなか準備がよろしいですね。お名前はちゃんとカタカナで入っていますね。

ジョーンズ氏：このまえ来たとき、こんど来るときは、名刺を作ってこようと思っていたんです。名刺をやりとりする日本の習慣は、本当に便利ですね。そのときファーストネームや正確な肩書なんかを聞きとれなくても心配いりませんし、あとから電話もかけやすいですね。

鈴木氏：そうなんです。いただいた名刺を入れた箱はとても大事ですよ。これがないと仕事がスムーズにできないんです。

ジョーンズ氏：最近は日本のビジネス習慣がアメリカにも輸入されて、いまでは、私たちアメリカのビジネスマンでも名刺を使う人が増えています。ビジネスマンは、日本に行くのなら名刺を用意したほうがいいとアドバイスをしている記事を見たこともあります。

鈴木氏：元来名刺はドイツやフランスで使い始めて日本に来たものなんですが、いまや日本から逆輸入とは面白い現象ですね。

ジョーンズ氏：面白いといえば鈴木さん、私にはまえから不思議に思っていることがあるんです。日本のビジネスマンは自己紹介するとき、自分の仕事については何もいわずに、まず会社の名前をいいますね。私たちアメリカ人だったら「私はファイナンス担当です」とか、「メカニカルエンジニ

**• 会社名での
自己紹介**

C h a p t e r 40

Mr. Jones: Have I ever shown you my bilingual business card?

Mr. Suzuki: I see you came well prepared this trip and even had your name written in *katakana*.

Mr. J: I decided the last time I was here that I'd get some cards made up for my next visit. I find the practice of exchanging cards in Japan very convenient. You don't have to worry if you don't catch the other guy's first name or title. That makes it easy to phone him later if you have to.

Mr. S: I agree. And it's important to have a card file. I wouldn't be able to go about my business smoothly without one.

Mr. J: You know some Japanese business practices have been finding their way into the States recently. There are more business people using cards these days, and I've seen articles advising American business people to have cards made before they visit Japan.

Mr. S: The business card originally came from France and Germany. Now Western countries are reimporting it from Japan. Interesting, isn't it?

Mr. J: There's something else I've found interesting, and a little puzzling. Whenever a Japanese working for a company introduces himself, he always includes the name of his company, though he probably won't say anything about his work. Americans will more often say what they do. Like "I'm in finance" or "I'm a mechanical engineer."

アです」というふうに職種を紹介する場合のほう
が多いんですが。

・
集団意識

鈴木氏：なるほどねえ。私は、この習慣の背景には、
いつかお話しした集団意識という日本人の特性が
あると思うんです。

ジョーンズ氏：ああ、あのお話は覚えていますよ。
でも、それとまず会社の名前をいうのとは、どう
いうつながりがあるんですか。

鈴木氏：その集団意識が、ビジネスの社会でも、あ
る特定の企業の一員であるという強い意識になっ
て表れるんです。日本のビジネスマンが会ったと
きには、お互いに相手がどんな能力や資質を持っ
ているかということよりも、相手がどの集団、つ
まりどの会社のメンバーかということをまず知り
たがるのです。

・
所属部門の
紹介

ジョーンズ氏：なるほど。それから、自分の職種よ
りも所属する部門を紹介するのはなぜですか。

鈴木氏：これは、日本の会社員が採用されたときの
状況やその後の職場経験からそうするんです。

ジョーンズ氏：といいますと。

鈴木氏：日本の会社は、一般に特定の職位を補充す
るために人を採用するんではないんです。将来発
揮される潜在能力を見て採用するんです。採用し
てからも、とくにホワイトカラーについては、適
性・昇進・事業状況などによって、経験のない職
場に変わることもごく普通です。だから、ある特
定の仕事の専門家であるという意識が薄いんで
す。ですから、お互いどんな仕事をしているのか
を紹介するには、現在の所属部門をいうのが、い
ちばんわかりやすいということなんです。

・
職種意識

40

自己紹介と相手の呼び方

Mr. S: Hmmm. That's another aspect of the Japanese groupism we talked about the other day.

Mr. J: Yes, I remember talking about that. But how does it
connect with the way the Japanese person always gives his
company name first?

Mr. S: In the business world, this groupism shows up as a
strong sense of being a member of a particular company.
When they meet each other, Japanese business people are
not so interested in the other fellow's character or ability as
they are in what group he belongs to, that is, what company
he belongs to.

Mr. J: Ok, but then why does he continue by giving the name
of his division rather than the type of job he does?

Mr. S: That comes from the way Japanese companies employ
people and the way they treat them after they join the
company.

Mr. J: What do you mean?

Mr. S: Japanese companies generally don't hire people to fill
specific positions. Rather they look for people with latent
potential they can develop. After a person has been employed, especially if he is a white-collar worker, it's very likely that he will be frequently transferred to new jobs in which
he has no experience — depending on his aptitude, the level
he's promoted to, and changes in the company's business.
He therefore doesn't have a strong sense of being a specialist
in a particular kind of work. So the easiest way for two
Japanese business people to let each other know what kind
of work they do is for them to mention the departments they

ジョーンズ氏：それからもうひとつ面白いと思った
　　　　　ことは、日本の会社では自分より目下の人を呼ぶ
　　　　　ときは名前で呼ぶけれど、目上の人を呼ぶときは
　　　　　「部長」とか「常務」とかと呼ぶんだそうですね。
　　　　　なぜ名前を呼ばないんですか。

鈴木氏：日本ではむかしからの習慣で、自分より年
　　　　　齢・地位の高い人の名前を口にするのは失礼に当
　　　　　たると考えられているからです。「実名敬避」と
　　　　　いって、中国にもむかしからあった習慣です。

実名敬避

**教師の　　ジョーンズ氏：それでは学校の教室で生徒は先生を
呼び方**　　　　　　どう呼ぶんですか。

鈴木氏：「先生」と呼ぶんです。あなた方のように、
　　　　　生徒が先生を「ジョーンズさん」なんて呼びませ
　　　　　ん。家庭でも同じです。

**家庭内での　ジョーンズ氏：え、家のなかでもですか。
呼び方**

鈴木氏：ええ、兄や姉を下の子が呼ぶときは、「お
　　　　　兄さん」「お姉さん」と呼ぶんです。

ジョーンズ氏：すると上の子が下の子を呼ぶとき
　　　　　は、「弟さん」「妹さん」と呼ぶんですか。

鈴木氏：そうは呼びません。下の子を呼ぶときは、
　　　　　名前で呼ぶんです。

ジョーンズ氏：ははあ、「実名敬避」の原則は家庭
　　　　　のなかでもちゃんと生きている、というわけです
　　　　　ね。

work in.

Mr. J: There's another thing that caught my attention. I hear that at work, higher ranking people call lower ranking ones by their names but the lower ranking ones call their superiors by their titles — like "General Manager" or "Director." Why don't they use names in both directions?

Mr. S: It's just an old Japanese custom. It's considered rude to call a person who is older or of higher status than yourself by his name. We call this "Respect through Avoidance of Real Name." The Chinese have the same custom and it's very old there, too.

Mr. J: Then how do students address their teacher in the classroom?

Mr. S: As "Teacher." Japanese students never call their teacher "Mr. Jones" the way students do in America. It's the same in the home, too.

Mr. J: In the home?

Mr. S: Yes, the younger children call the older ones "Elder Brother" or "Elder Sister."

Mr. J: Do the older ones call the younger ones "Younger Brother" and "Younger Sister?"

Mr. S: No, the younger children are called by name.

Mr. J: Meaning that the principle of "Respect through Avoidance of Real Name" also applies in the home, huh?

1

That <u>makes it easy to phone</u> him later.

ノート　　文法的には it は to 以下を指す仮目的語。むしろ「そうすると、あとから～するのが楽になるんです」という幅広く使える型なので、このまま覚えて使い慣れておきたい表現。

例文　　This *made it difficult to* use animals.　　　　(39)

2

I wouldn't be able to <u>go about</u> my business smoothly <u>without</u> one.

ノート　　not [never] . . . without . . . 「～しないで～することはない、～すればかならず～する」の文型。
　　go about . . . は「せっせと（仕事など）をする、（仕事など）にとりかかる」

例文1　　They *never* meet *without* quarreling.
　　「彼らは会えばかならずケンカする」

例文2　　*Go about* your business!
　　「自分の仕事をしなさい［余計な世話をやくな］」

3

How does it <u>connect with</u> the way the Japanese person always gives his company name first?

ノート　　connect with . . . 「～と関係がある、つながる」
　　the way のあとには that が省略されている。

4

There's <u>another thing</u> that <u>caught my atten-tion</u>.

ノート　　another (＝an＋other) thing「もうひとつのこと」
　　catch one's attention「注意を引く、関心を引く」
　　この表現もいろいろ変化させて活用できる。

SOURCES

イラスト　データ出典一覧

●章番号	●ページ	●出典
第1章	p.14	国際連合『国連統計年鑑1983／84』1987年　原書房刊：日本の数値は北方領土を含む
第2章	p.24	1986年3月、自治省調べ
	p.25	東京天文台『理科年表』1987年　丸善刊：気温、降水量は1951年から1980年までの平均
第3章	p.34	写真(左・右)江坂輝彌氏提供
第4章	p.44	写真　和田ヒロシ撮影、世界文化フォト
第5章	p.56	写真(上)長崎市立博物館所蔵(中)渡部まなぶ撮影、世界文化フォト(下)東京国立博物館所蔵
第6章	p.66	写真　共同通信社
第7章	p.76	宮内庁『宮内庁要覧　昭和61年版』
第10章	p.106	経済企画庁『国民経済計算年報』1987年：数値は1970年度までは沖縄を含まない。億以下は切り捨て
	p.107	経済企画庁『海外経済動向指標』1987年
第11章	p.116	総務庁統計局『国勢調査』日本統計協会刊
	p.117	ILO 『労働統計年鑑1985』、総務庁統計局『労働力調査1985』1986年3月　日本統計協会刊：対象は15歳以上。第三次産業は分類不能含む。軍隊および失業者は除く
第12章	p.126	警察庁『警察白書1986』1987年：イギリスはイングランドとウェールズ。犯罪率は人口10万人当たりの犯罪件数(認知されたものに限る)
	p.127	総理府広報室『月刊世論調査』1985年9月号　大蔵省印刷局刊
第13章	p.136	日本生産性本部『生産性モデル総合賃金調査報告書　昭和62年版』1986年11月
	p.137	参考例
第14章	p.148	労働省『労働組合基礎調査』1986年：2つ以上の主要団体に重複加盟している組合は、それぞれの主要団体に重複集計してあるので、組合員数の計とその主要団体別内訳の合計とは一致しない
	p.149	同上：推定組織率は、組合員数を総務庁統計局『労働力調査』の雇用労働者数で割って算出
第16章	p.168	日本＝労働省『毎月勤労統計調査』／アメリカ＝労働省 *Handbook of Labor Statistics*／EC＝EC統計局 *Labour Costs*：日本と諸外国との比較を可能にするために以下のような方法で週当たり実労働時間を求めた①日本は規模5人以上の数値を推計②アメリカは労働費用調査により支払労働時間を実労働時間に換算した。規模は全規模③西ドイツ、フランスについては、EC統計局資料によ

		る年間労働時間を52（週）で除した。規模はそれぞれ10人以上
	p.169	経済企画庁『物価リポート'87』1987年7月：1時間当たりの各国の平均賃金を100として、東京で100円で買えるものが、世界主要都市ではいくらで買えるかの比較。たとえば、東京で100円する食パンはニューヨークでは62円で買える
第17章	p.178	日本科学技術連盟『品質月刊テキスト』153号
第18章	p.188	法務省調査部『出入国管理統計年報』大蔵省印刷局刊：出国者数は観光を目的として日本から出国した日本人の数、入国者数は同様の目的で外国から日本に入国した外国人の数
	p.189	余暇開発センター『レジャー白書'86』1987年4月：外食＝日常的なものを除く／バー・スナック・パブ＝飲み屋を含む／動物園・植物園＝水族館、博物館を含む／トランプ・オセロ＝カルタ、花札などを含む／ピクニックなど＝ハイキング、野外散歩を含む／映画＝テレビを除く／音楽鑑賞＝レコード、テープ、FMなど
第19章	p.200	国連および各国資料による
	p.201	国際連合 Demographic Statistics Yearbook 1984：日本は国勢調査と推計人口、イギリスは同国統計摘要年鑑による。インドの70歳以上の年齢構成は不明
第20章	p.210	日本＝日本新聞協会『日本新聞年鑑1986』／中国＝ラジオプレス『中国年鑑 1985』／その他＝Editor and Publisher Company, Editor and Publisher International Yearbook 1986：読売・朝日・毎日の数値は1985年11月月間平均。日経・サンケイは1987年7月の数値。アメリカは1985年9月30日現在、他は不明。数値はすべて朝刊のもの
	p.211	『ユネスコ文化統計年鑑1985』：アメリカは1981年、日本は1982年の数値。1書名を1点とする。定期刊行物はすべて除く
第21章	p.221	文部省『教育指標の国際比較1985』1987年3月：各国の高等教育機関第1学年への進学者数の該当年齢人口に対する比率を算出。日本の進学者数は、大学学部、短期大学本科の第1学年入学者数および高等専門学校4学年在学者数の合計。アメリカの数値は推計値
第22章	p.232	日本＝厚生統計協会『国民衛生の動向 昭和61年版』1986年8月／アメリカ＝U.S.Department of Health and Human Services 資料：アメリカの数値はハワイ、アラスカを含む全州の平均値。婚姻数は、州により推計または結婚許可証発行件数の値を採用した。離婚数は離婚請求件数を含む
	p.233	総理府婦人問題担当室『婦人問題に関する国際比較調査』1982年
第23章	p.242	運輸省『運輸統計季報』
	p.243	日本電信電話（株）資料
第24章	p.252	国際連合 International Trade Statistics Yearbook 1984
第26章	p.274	国立国会図書館所蔵『日本関係欧文図書目録 昭和23年－50年』1977年 紀伊國屋書店刊：国立国会図書館所蔵のものに限る。1945年以降に外国の出版社から発行された

		図書（重版・再版は含まない）。日本国内の出版社発行のものは除いた
第27章	p.288-89	写真　吉田千秋撮影
第28章	p.298	オリジナルコンフィデンス 昭和61年度ベストセラー資料
第29章	p.308	森村知加氏協力
第30章	p.318	伝統的工芸産業振興協会『全国伝統的工芸品総覧 昭和60年度版』1980年：通産大臣指定伝統的工芸品のうち、焼き物・漆器・織物・人形・うちわ・扇子のいずれかに入るものに限った
第31章	p.329	写真（左）森田敏隆撮影、世界文化フォト（右）吉田則之撮影、世界文化フォト
第32章	p.338	IMF『労働時間の購買力 —— 国際比較 1986』：3～4K、バス付きの部屋 1カ月の家賃を払うのに、その国の平均時間給では何時間働かなければならないか、の数値。データは鉄鋼産業の場合
第33章	p.348	ベースボールマガジン社協力：1987年名古屋場所までの外国人力士入門者数。廃業者を含む
第35章	p.369	日本絹業協会『現代女性1,500人に聞く「きもの」に関する意識と実態調査レポート』1981年9月
第36章	p.380	畑耕一郎、山本泰昭『日本料理入門』1985年 鎌倉書房刊
第37章	p.390	農林水産省『食料需給表』昭和61年12月、FAO資料
	p.391	同上：肉には鳥類・鯨肉を含み、魚には鯨肉を含まず
第38章	p.400	余暇開発センター『日米欧価値観調査・7カ国データブック』1980年1月
	p.401	同上
第39章	p.410	日本経済青年協議会『働くことの意識調査報告』1982年：入社3‐5年目の社員対象
	p.411	同上

KeyWords

日本を語るためのキーワード インデックス

キーワード インデックス

432

Index

本文中に中見出しとしてとりあげられている
項目とその収載ページは、太字で示されています

キーワード インデックス

434

か行

キーワード インデックス

た行

キーワード インデックス

あとがき

　本書の出版にさきがけて、新日本製鐵㈱能力開発部から『日本──その姿と心』を、まず社内版として昭和53年に発刊した当初から、同書に見合う会話形式による書物の作成は、私たち関係スタッフの念願であった。さらに、昭和57年に同書が市販（学生社刊）されるに至り、読者や愛用者のなかからも、同書に類する会話編の刊行を期待する声が、しばしば寄せられていた。

　こうした気運がしだいに盛り上がりつつあったさなかに、㈱アルクの平本社長から、この本の出版についてご相談があり、これを機会に、私たちのかねてからの念願が実現する運びとなった。

　私たちは、さっそくプロジェクトチームを編成し、『日本──その姿と心』に記載されている186項目の内容を、さらにポイントを絞って40項目に再編成して、昭和60年の秋から執筆・編集にとりかかった。

　各項目について、限られた紙面のなかにできるだ
けたくさんの情報を盛り込むことを第一に心掛け、
適切な場面の設定、自然な会話の流れ、平明な英語
表現、外国人が理解しやすい説明の仕方などに、と
くに配慮したつもりである。また、本書によって英
会話の応用力の強化が図れるように、各項目ごとに、
会話内容に関連したイラスト、関連語句、会話に役
立つ基本表現を掲げた。

　本書の企画・執筆・編集の各段階で、まえがきに
記載されている方々には、一方ならぬご尽力、数多
くの貴重なご指導・ご示唆をいただいた。これらの
方々の積極的なご協力と、私たちスタッフとの密接
なチームワークによって、本書の発刊を実現できた
ことについて、重ねて心から感謝したい。

　　昭和62年10月

　　　　　　　　　　　　青砥　安男

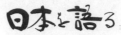

Talking about Japan

●

1987年10月16日発行　定価1,600円

●

著者──株式会社　日鉄ヒューマンデベロプメント

〒102　東京都千代田区飯田橋 4 - 6 - 9

©1987　Nippon Steel Human Resources Development Co., Ltd.

●

発行者──平本照麿

発行所──株式会社　アルク

〒168　東京都杉並区永福 2-54-12

電話　03-323-1101（大代表）

振替　東京9-131316

印刷──株式会社　ギャルド

●

乱丁・落丁本はお取り替えいたします。

●

Printed in Japan

ISBN4-900105-31-7　C0036

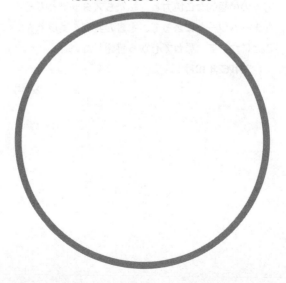